Frederick Ashton's Ballets:

Style, Performance, Choreography

Frederick Ashton's Ballets:
Style, Performance, Choreography

Geraldine Morris

Dance Books

For Pearse and Jeanne

Frontispiece photograph by Zoë Dominic

First published 2012 by Dance Books Ltd.,
Southwold House, Isington Road, Binsted, Hampshire, GU34 4PH

ISBN: 978-1-85273-159-5
A CIP catalogue record for this title is available from the British Library

Printed in Great Britain by Latimer Trend & Co. Ltd., Plymouth

Contents

Introduction   1

Chapter 1   4
The Problem of Style and Discerning the Movement

Chapter 2   37
The Foundations of Ashton's Style:
Training and Dance Influences

Chapter 3   77
Unconventional Dances:
Ashton's Style in Ballets with Words

Chapter 4   126
Non-narrative Ballets:
1950s Decorum and the Swinging 60s

Chapter 5   173
Narrative Dances:
An Abundance of Real Dancing

Conclusion: Where Now for Ashton Style?   217
Bibliography   219
Index   231

Acknowledgements

I have spent a number of years writing and researching this book and I could not have undertaken it without the help of many people. Frederick Ashton's work has dominated my thoughts for the last twenty years and it has given me immense pleasure throughout that time, so I must first thank him and his dances for keeping me busy, pleasurably, for so long.

Over the years, I have rummaged through a number of archives and the material has been invaluable. Francesca Franchi at the Royal Opera House Archive provided endless reviews and photographs many of which are quoted in this book. Jane Pritchard at the Theatre Museum was also immensely helpful and always available for discussion. The New York Public Library has a wealth of material, not only film but also some invaluable recordings of interviews and I spent many happy hours searching there. Annotated books from Ashton's library, housed at the Royal Ballet School, gave me insights into some of his works, in particular the narrative material. Although just experiencing the wealth of the collection gave me a greater appreciation of the extensive research he undertook before embarking on a new ballet.

Many individuals have helped and encouraged me and my thanks goes to all those in the Dance Department at Roehampton University. In particular to Stephanie Jordan who has guided me throughout the years. Her own research is formidable and her work on Ashton has been immensely valuable to the writing of this book. Bonnie Rowell and Toby Bennett read parts of the manuscript in earlier drafts and I am very grateful for their comments and suggestions. Andrée Grau, Larraine Nicholas and Anna Pakes have all given me great support as has Henrietta Bannerman: this was vital to the completion of this book. Earlier, Helen Thomas was an honest and rigorous critic, yet her comments were very beneficial, particularly when I worked with her on my thesis, from which some of the material in this book has been drawn. Theresa Buckland too was extremely helpful in reading Chapter II and without her I would not have discovered Chris Jones, whose suggestions and edits have helped to make the book coherent and focused, and my heartfelt thanks goes to Chris too. Both Tony Dyson and Anthony Russell Roberts were very encouraging and I hope that my exploration of Ashton's work will have repaid their interest.

But I could not have done any of this without the input of my family. Andrew and Diana both tirelessly read and corrected all my errant commas, semi-colons and colons and made some really useful suggestions. They were my benchmarks, the knowledgeable outsiders whose opinions were immensely important. My thanks goes too to Carla Morris who was immensely helpful in redoing Ann Padmore's drawings.

My photographs have come from several archives: the Victoria and Albert Museum, the Royal Opera House Archives and *The Dancing Times*. Jonathan Gray (editor of *Dancing Times*) was very cooperative in sourcing old photographs from early editions of the magazine and these have proved to be an excellent resource. Thanks too to David Leonard of Dance Books who has waited patiently for several years for this book to be completed. He has always been encouraging, even after reading a slightly raw earlier draft.

Some of the research and writing of this book was funded by Roehampton University. Both sessions of research leave were crucial in providing me with unbroken time to work on the book.

Frederick Ashton's Ballets:
Style, Performance, Choreography

Introduction

> I only like ballets which give an opportunity for real dancing, and after all that is what the whole thing is about. A re-statement of one's own personal idiom of the classical ballet is all I ask to be able to achieve.[1]

It was typical of Frederick Ashton to put dance at the centre of his works. Whilst he used the *danse d'école* as a basis for his choreography, his comment clearly shows that he was alert to the difference between it and choreographed movement. Translating that difference into his personal idiom is at the heart of his choreography. But how do we separate the two, what can and cannot be considered style and how much can the style change and still be recognisable as that of Ashton?[2] In the following chapters I investigate these questions. I explore the movement sources and consider the diverse strands which contribute to the movement, the choreography and the meanings. We must not forget though that the works had multiple creators, so there is no single element which is just the work of Ashton alone. Yet it is Ashton who draws the elements together and makes specific, identifiable choices, so I will continue to refer to the dances as Ashton ballets. My aim in writing this book is to promote greater understanding of both dance movement style and choreographic style, so that the book is not only interesting and useful for performers but also for dance academics and committed dance audiences.

The book is divided into five chapters. In Chapter I I tackle the notion of style and then move on to discuss dance analysis. Although Ashton used the *danse d'école* as a basis for his dance movement, it is unhelpful to see the movement as a series of ballet steps, so I discuss an alternative way of identifying and investigating the movement. Because the dancers' bodies and their training contribute to the style, Chapter II focuses on training during the early part of the twentieth century and the discussion provides a context and background for examining the work. The following three chapters deal with six ballets, *A Wedding Bouquet* (1937), *Illuminations* (1950), *Birthday Offering* (1956), *Jazz Calendar* (1968), *Daphnis and Chloe* (1951) and *A Month in the Country* (1976). These have been chosen for specific reasons, which I consider in due course.

Both Ashton the public choreographer and Ashton the private man have been the subject of two substantial volumes. There is also a small paperback collection of reviews and a volume of papers from a conference devoted solely to Ashton. All of these are significant and provide background material for this book. David Vaughan's first and very important exploration of Ashton's choreography in *Frederick Ashton and His Ballets* (1977/99) is seminal to any study of Ashton and amply covers his work. Julie Kavanagh's *Secret Muses: The Life of Frederick Ashton* (1996) is invaluable for its insight into the man himself. For me, Ashton was an awe-inspiring, if slightly frightening Director when I was a member of the Royal Ballet and Kavanagh's book fully demonstrates Ashton's very human qualities. Alastair Macaulay's excellent and poetic response to his dances in *Some Views and Reviews of Ashton's Choreography* (1987) is a personal and often enlightening account of some of the choreography. And finally, the papers from the Ashton conference *Following Sir Fred's Steps: Ashton's Legacy* (1994) are a diverse collection, including academic essays, reports of coaching and the memories of dancers who worked with Ashton from the 1930s onwards. Each book or collection was a response to different needs, periods and readers.

Vaughan's book, written while Ashton was still alive, traces and tracks the sources for his works including those he made for ballet companies, the commercial theatre and film. It demanded substantial detective work, since Ashton could not always remember significant details about many of his earlier works. The book identifies aspects of Ashton's choreographic style and frequently quotes from contemporary reviews. But because of its comprehensive nature, it does not give an in depth analysis of any single work or of the movement style. The work is scholarly but, because it was written just before the growth in analytic methodologies for dance, it could not make use of the research which emerged at the end of the 1970s and early 1980s. Nor did Vaughan have access to the range of video/DVD material available today. This allows extensive analysis and has provided a major source for my research. Vaughan's aim was to 'write a biography of Ashton *through* his work' to 'cast some light on his way of working'.[3] Conversely, Kavanagh's is an account of the private person but because Ashton believed that choreography was his life and that he 'pour[ed] into it all [his] love, [his] frustrations, and sometimes autobiographical details' many of her insights illuminate the gentle, yet elegant qualities that Ashton brought to his work.[4] It is an important account and guided me away from viewing the works as mere objects. They are living, changing performances, albeit with an extensive range of identifiable and constant features.

Ashton has now been dead for more than twenty years and it is time to consider how his work both can and should continue. To survive, past works need to respond to the changing world and this is particularly difficult in dance: both aesthetic values and dancers' bodies alter and sources for reviving past works are limited. Dance scores are not the same as play texts or musical scores, though they are a fundamental source for reconstructing or reviving the work. An equally acceptable practice is to hand on the choreography from dancer to dancer. But many of the dancers who first performed the dances are now dead and memory is, in any event, not always accurate. So how can movement, which was made during an earlier era and was embodied by dancers with a very different training, be revived or even reconstructed, whilst keeping faith with the spirit of the work? This is a question that has not yet been addressed and in this book I attempt to push the research a little by offering a way of approaching the problem. My suggestions will inevitably be challenged and contested but I hope they will add to the debate which centres on choreographic style and its survival. And while I recognise that the term 'style' is contentious I, nevertheless, find it useful in this context and address the concept in Chapter I.

The dancers Ashton worked with are integral to any discussion of his style. As with many other choreographers, the dancers who embodied his work and acted both as inspiration and contributors are a part of the work's style.[5] And although they cannot act as role models for today's dancers, traces of their personal performance style remain embedded in the works.[6] For instance, such details as the focus of the movement or how the choreography draws attention to different aspects of the dancing body depend on the dancer with whom the dance was made. After all, if he had not used a particular dancer, he would probably have chosen different movements. Dancers and their personal contribution are frequently excluded from analysis of dances, mainly because of the difficulty in identifying their movement styles. But I suggest that, particularly in ballet, the specific training forms a fundamental aspect of their personal dancing style. As with dance performance, training and the interpretation of the *danse d'école* changes and earlier training methods have stylistic features which do not survive. This subject has hardly been addressed, at least in writing, yet understanding the relationship between a dancer's training, training aesthetics and values and choreographic style is fundamental if the integrity of the choreographed movement is to be preserved. The dancer's ability to embrace a choreographic style which is alien to her way of moving depends to a large extent on having this kind of knowledge. In the following pages, I hope to contribute to that understanding in order to help future dancers access Ashton's dances and, by using a similar model, perhaps other twentieth century choreography as well.

Chapter 1

The Problem of Style and Discerning the Movement

The following chapter sets out my methodological approach. In it I tease out problems of identity and style in dance, drawing on a range of theoretical approaches which include philosophical accounts of style and intention and dance analysis. Style, I suggest, can be discerned from identifying recurring patterns, themes and leitmotifs which occur in both the movements and the choreography. As far as ballet movement is concerned, it is also the specific way in which the choreographer approaches the *danse d'école* that is significant. What she chooses to focus on is central to her style. My contention is that, in the case of Ashton, style is derived from several elements, principally the dancers and training of the era and his own aesthetic values and influences. It is his particular use of the *danse d'école*, informed by those elements which makes his choreography different from the work of another choreographer and from the *danse d'école*.

Identifying style is important, particularly in ballet, because it is one of the only ways in which choreography can be distinguished from the *danse d'école*. For a choreographer's dances to survive and not become interchangeable with ballet's codified movement we need to understand movement and choreographic style. This has become even more imperative recently because training tends now to be more homogenised. Soviet training, particularly that codified by Agrippina Vaganova, is inclined to dominate the majority of training systems. In Eastern countries, Japan, China and Korea,[7] it is this training which has been adopted and many of its tenets feed the training of the Royal Ballet School, English National Ballet and the Central School of Ballet.[8] It is also widely used in the United States.[9] While it can be an excellent training system, it has a major flaw – absolutism – because it focuses on teaching each codified movement separately and, according to Soviet pedagogues, there is only one correct way of executing a ballet step. Consequently, dancers become preoccupied with this notion. The system ignores the presence of other training styles and, equally, of choreographers' interpretations of the balletic code. Because of this attitude to the codified movement choreographic style can be lost. The 'correct' version of the codified steps becomes the most important element in the dances and choreographed ballet movement is subjected to contemporary notions of the *danse d'école*.

In what follows I start with a discussion of this problem and of the effects of the Soviet system in particular on the prevailing ballet aesthetic, before moving on to consider the notion of style and my approach to it. Discerning the dance movement is also important, particularly in ballet. As a profession, we tend to think in terms of steps; to avoid this, I use another method of examining the movement, that of the East European analyst and pedagogue Rudolf Laban.[10] This is explained in a later section. The final parts of the chapter deal with sources and the ballets I have chosen for discussion.

A Problematic Relationship: Technical Training and Choreographic Style

Quite apart from dogmatic training systems, the inability to recognise the difference between the choreographed and codified step is also caused by the way in which the profession discusses and writes about ballet. When pedagogues, dancers and others in the profession write about it, they almost invariably do so in terms of the *danse d'école*, the sets of movements embodied in the balletic code, which they believe to be constant. Debates, articles and text books centre on how the *danse d'école* should be performed technically but consideration of the choreography is generally omitted from the discussion; here the ballet profession is silent, less focused, and it has to be concluded that this might be because the *danse d'école* is perceived to be of greater significance. It is hardly surprising then that some teachers and dancers believe that the aim in performance is solely to achieve technically perfect steps when dancing choreography.

To complicate matters, the profession describes each ballet term as a step, though in fact the term covers more than a single movement. It is usefully explained by Valerie Preston-Dunlop as a repeatable unit of movement that has actions, spatial dimensions and rhythmic elements.[11] Steps have names such as the *glissade* or *pas de chat* which describe the basic leg actions, so the other spatial and rhythmic elements are generally omitted from descriptions of the terms in ballet dictionaries. This may be because these other elements are considered to be similar across different systems. Yet it is often just these other elements which choreographers alter to suit their choreography and aesthetic and this is rarely acknowledged. Because the technical term is used to discuss ballet movement, it is assumed that when choreographers derive their movement from the ballet code that the two are synonymous. Consequently, choreographed movement is suppressed and subjected to both technical values and the prevailing technical aesthetic of the era.[12]

That Ashton used the *danse d'école* as a basis for his choreography is not an issue, that he used a particular version of it, namely that of the pedagogue Enrico Cecchetti, is more important. Because the values of that system fed his dances, they are part of the style. In his choreography this was filtered through dancers, trained in diverse styles, not always according to the tenets of Cecchetti, so the dancers had to adapt to embrace the principles of that system. Because it was contemporaneous with their training and so was based on a similar aesthetic, this was not a major problem. The multiplicity of training styles available during the 1920s and 1930s created a different body and way of moving from today's dancers and seems to have made dancers more capable of embracing a variety of choreographic styles. Despite the international mixture of today's ballet companies, including the Royal Ballet, the dancers are more uniform in style because, as I noted above, training today has become more standardised and attitudes to the ballet code are more inflexible, allowing for less individuality. While it allows them to dance contemporary choreography, it seems to inhibit them from understanding and embodying styles of the past.

That training changes is not in itself significant and is probably necessary, but problems arise when skills acquired through earlier training styles are simply not available to today's dancers, particularly if required to perform ballets of an earlier period. The *renversé* is a good example of a lost skill; few today can manage the deep sideways bends, arch of the back and momentum derived from the upper body, which this very Ashtonian movement demands.[13] During this challenging upper body movement, the working leg sweeps round from in front of the body to an off-balance *arabesque*, eventually turning the body back to an upright front-facing positon. As Richard Glasstone has pointed out, the desire of today's dancers, both male and female, to raise their legs above shoulder height restricts the movement range of the upper body.[14] When performing this movement, today's dancers tend to omit the sweeping leg movement, performing instead a high kick to the side and a quick upright turn. This changes the quality and appearance of the movement.

In earlier articles,[15] I discuss the problems that are encountered through not recognising, or not acknowledging, the link, and possible disjunction, between training and choreography and I am not alone in believing that it has been the importation of the Soviet ballet system which has led to these problems.[16] This system seems to have a different aesthetic from those of earlier pedagogues both in Russia and elsewhere and places emphasis more on achieving technical perfection than on understanding style. Vera Kostrovitskaya, the Soviet pedagogue, argues that at the famed Vaganova School much has been done to perfect the teaching method 'as a process for mastering the technique of dance'.[17] She claims that Vaganova's method allows the dancer to master the 'whole complex of dance movements and, consequently, permits the development of technique and a *high artistic quality of execution*' (my italics). By this she means the ability of the body to express every emotion and to perform all the movements 'expressively, intelligently and unmechanically'.[18] Her attitude leaves little room for choreography and her contention that this approach develops artistry is also problematic. I have argued elsewhere (2008), that Kostrovitskaya focuses on developing the aesthetic values rather than the artistic features of ballet and that this approach does not allow for distinctions to be made between ballet as an art and the aesthetic sports such as gymnastics and ice dancing. I am not suggesting that physical ability is unnecessary, but that part of the problem is caused by misunderstanding the role of training and its relationship to choreographed dance movement. That the Mariinsky Ballet (earlier Kirov) finds it problematic to conceive of movement which does not conform to their accepted classroom code is evident from a remark by ballet master Yuri Fateyev:

> The people who taught us for the Balanchine ballets tried to teach us the American steps... some teachers, who rehearsed with the dancers after Francia (Russell) [had gone], tried a little bit to correct the steps for the Russian style.[19]

The Russians' dogmatic attitude to training prevents them from understanding that choreographers use the codified movement differently. As a result, they find it difficult to accept choreographic style, let alone one with which they are unfamiliar.

Dancer and teacher Paul Boos encountered similar difficulties to Fateyev when coaching dancers from different companies in Balanchine's style during the 1990s. He claimed that because systems, such as those of Vaganova and Bournonville, are so ingrained in the dancers, it was difficult to convince them to adopt a different style of moving.[20] Critic Robert Gottlieb in 2004 found that dancers from the Kirov still had a long way to go in understanding the Balanchine style, probably because they had Russianised it.[21] Accepting that the dancers had an accomplished technical facility, he pointed out, nevertheless, that the training seemed to prevent them from embracing other styles. In other companies and for other choreographers, similar problems are evident.[22]

The degree of certainty and a belief that there is no other correct way of performing balletic dances pervade Kostrovitskaya's book. In its foreword, the editor, Natalia Roslavleva, claims that the system is a methodological guide and provides an 'infallible way of teaching and performing the entire "alphabet" of classical dance'(16). If that is the case, then clearly the approach is problematic because the method involves teaching each step as a separate entity and to regular music counts. Musically, the book has little information beyond suggesting the use of 2/2, 2/4 or 3/4 time signatures and, without giving precise details of phrasing and tempi, these instructions are of limited use. By the same token, only the leg, arm and head movements are prescribed, omitting much essential information, such as dynamic variation and the relationship of one step to another when the context is altered.

For instance, how a linking step is performed varies when joined with different bigger steps and this is not acknowledged. Equally, the emphasis appears to be on achieving 'correct' positions as opposed to being in motion and there is no understanding that the ballet terminology is actually a qualitative description of how to move, rather than a description of which body parts are moving.[23] As a system for training in classical dance, this approach certainly produces dancers with spectacular technical abilities but the skills taught are less useful for performing choreography in general and earlier dances in particular.

It seems that the published literature from many ballet pedagogues is stuck in the cosy domain of certainties: certain that the *danse d'école* is unchanging, certain that there are objective methods of training and certain that the aim is to produce dancers who can perform the steps accurately. Both Stephen Mears's article in *Dancing Times* and the letters it generated testify to this position.[24] In the twenty-first century's fragmented world, this is an odd place to be and is out of step with theoretical thinking in the other arts.

This then is the central predicament; how can dancers perform multiple styles when their training is antithetical to style? Not only does this affect the appearance of the choreography, it also affects the meaning of the dance. Dance scholar and pedagogue, Chris Challis, suggests that a conflict of meaning occurs when performers misinterpret a dance work.[25] Using the work of modern dance choreographer Paul Taylor as an example, she notes that when ballet companies perform his works, they omit fundamental stylistic details. As a result, the expressive potentiality of the work is lost. In other words, elements such as contraction and spiral as well as a sense of weight and undercurve are misunderstood by ballet dancers. Moreover, not only do they find the movement difficult to achieve, their musicality is also at odds with Taylor's. Challis notes that today's ballet dancers are taught to move in evenly metered phrases, emphasising specific positions en route, while Taylor's choreography uses cross-phrasing across several phrases of music. She argues that, as a consequence, the dance can no longer be described as a Taylor work.

Postmodern scholars may argue that this is of no importance but when the movement of all ballet choreographers is reduced to contemporary versions of the *danse d'école*, then what is danced can no longer be described as an Ashton or Balanchine dance. Quite apart from the question of identity, this leads to homogeneity and monotony in performances. Thus dancers and dance directors need to be conscious of the difference between the requirements of the *danse d'école* and those of choreographed movement. Training, at its worst, can have an insidious hold on the body, at its best, it can be liberating. Maybe now is the time to recognise that this is a problem. Pedagogues and rehearsal directors should try to encourage students to learn about and become interested in past choreographic styles, at least if we are keen to retain those works in our repertoires.

Models of Dance Analysis

Analysis is a vital component to understanding dance for audiences and dancers alike. It is a way of rediscovering what is already there, of finding relevance in what might seem to be old-fashioned and of increasing understanding and appreciation. Various models of dance analysis have been devised since the late 1970s, differing in approach and mood. None alone is adequate for helping future performers to deal with the concept of choreographed style nor for identifying style itself, though each has something to offer.

The seminal book on dance analysis by Janet Adshead et al. (1988) is a useful starting point for both dancers and audiences. She argues that style can be gleaned from looking at the perceptible properties of the dance: the movement, dynamic, spatial elements, structuring devices, use of dancers, costumes, stage environment etc. Interpreting these elements depends on the point of view of the reader and on the many contexts of both reader and work.[26] It depends too on the purpose of the research, which in my case is to provide the dancers with enough information to allow them to make informed choices in performance. Adshead's approach is thus useful, though insufficient for my research because it ignores context.

In her later research as Adshead-Lansdale (2007), she proposes an intertextual model which creates an interwoven framework of multiple interpretations.[27] While this can be extremely useful for dealing with postmodern work and perhaps some earlier ballets, it is not suitable for my purposes because it is too open ended. Although I accept her basic premise that dance works have no fixed meanings and by analogy, a fluid style, I cannot agree that the meaning is limited only by the text itself; other factors are also significant in discerning meaning. Context is just as important to the way we derive significance and so the delimiting factors are the choreographer's complete corpus and intentions.

Adshead-Lansdale (2007) addresses readers' interpretations but her point can also be applied to performers' interpretations. She argues that although a work can have many different interpretations, interpretations are not limitless. Quoting Umberto Eco, she states that the work needs a model reader, who should not only have 'competence in the sense of knowledge of the performance text's conventions and codes, but who also has circumstantial competence, understands the rules of inference and so on.'[28] Yet Eco does not give the writer/choreographer any agency, meaning is decided between the reader and the text; so the maker's intention is not relevant. This is not help-ful for examining style in ballet, since the maker's intention is of significance; otherwise there would be no boundaries and dancers could perform all works as they chose. Like the model reader, the dancer too should have knowledge of the performance text's conventions and codes. Adshead's earlier, formalist model allows us to dissect the choreography but it does not go far enough, as she herself has acknowledged.

Analyst and scholar Bonnie Rowell (2007) discusses the problems of Adshead's methods (1988 and 1999) and those of Susan Foster (1986), another respected scholar. [29] Rowell's concerns are threefold: these models take account only of perceptible features and disregard the choreographer's intention, they ignore the work's context, which can lead to interpretative anarchy and they embrace the postmodern notion that meaning resides only in the perception of the viewer. How the choreographer intends us to view the dance is, she argues, highly significant. For example, if we interpret the dance purely from its perceptible features, we can be in danger of misunder-standing it and even trivialising the dance. This is particularly so in the case of Ashton. We could, for instance, view the film *Tales of Beatrix Potter* (1970) as a dance about furry animals but this would do Ashton a disservice. His other works show him to be a serious choreographer concerned with explor-ing dance and frequently using it to investigate and delve into human emotion. So, perceiving *Beatrix Potter* solely as entertainment for youngsters is to misunderstand it. We need to be aware that in the duet for Pigling Bland and Black Berkshire Pig the quotations from *The Sleeping Beauty*, *Giselle*, and some of Ashton's own works, are not accidental, neither are they mere pas-tiche. He used parody in several of his other works too and by quoting from a traditional work, he presents the dance material in a comical manner. In *Beatrix Potter*, the two piglets perform a section of a duet from Act III of *The Sleeping Beauty*, a work that is considered to be the height of ballet classicism. Piglets performing ballet cannot fail to make us smile but there is also a serious intention. Ashton uses both ballet's classics and his own work, albeit playfully, to draw our attention to the fact that he was not 'gaga' at age sixty-six and was aware of the ironies of a 'serious', though ageing, choreographer making a work in which the main characters are furry animals. [30] To under-stand this, however, we need to know much more about Ashton's work. Rowell alerts us to this: to prevent serious misunderstanding of a work, we need knowledge of the choreographer's intention and also to have a contex-tual framework within which to view the dance.

In developing the controversial notion of choreographic intention, Rowell draws on Stanley Cavell's discussion of art works as meaning-bearing ob-jects. Cavell (1969) offers the view that art works are intentional objects and, as a result, embody the makers' ideas, evident in the work, though not their private thoughts, since these are neither relevant nor accessible.[31] Central to Cavell's discussion is a rebuttal of the opinions proffered in the 1954 article, '*The Intentional Fallacy*', by W.K. Wimsatt and Monroe Beardsley who argue that because intentions are outside the work, they are not relevant to an understanding of the work; criticism should focus only on the work itself.[32] This Cavell contests, commenting that intention is part of the work because 'everything that is there is something a man has done' and, consequently, it is intrinsic to the art work and thus part of the meaning.[33] Examining a work involves not only considering the work itself but also looking at all the contextual elements. These are not outside the work but part of it.

Intention, according to Cavell, also acknowledges the physicality of the art work and its link with the art maker's ideas. Works are made in a particular material, which only becomes a medium because of its use in the artwork. For instance, the materials wood and stone would not be media '*in the absence of the art of sculpture*'.[34] By the same token, in ballet, classroom movement remains a collection of training exercises and would continue to be so *in the absence of the art of choreography*.[35] Choreographers use the expressive possibilities of the training exercises as their medium but because training systems are stylistically different, they will have diverse characteristic possibilities. This also means that dancers' bodies, which, largely, are moulded by the system in which they are trained, will also have different expressive possibilities. It follows then that choreographers choose a specific dancer trained in a particular style because that dancer's training and bodily movement can embody their ideas. Accordingly, the medium involves not only the particular kind of movement, dynamic and spatial elements from which the choreographer chooses, but also the dancers' bodily training.

It is clear from Cavell's arguments, that in order to appreciate the piglet duet in *Beatrix Potter*, and, as will become evident, aspects of *A Wedding Bouquet*, we need knowledge of Ashton's other works so that we do not misread them. Understanding choreographic style then depends on accessing both the context and physicality of the dance. Equally, both the dancer and the viewer need this kind of knowledge. Without it, the dancer will not be able to perform what the choreographer intended and the observer could misread the dance.

Rowell states that there are limitations in discussing the meaning of a dance, and she rejects the notion that all explanations are equally valid. Her argument counteracts postmodern theories, which position the viewer as the sole arbiter of meaning, and allows the role of the choreographer to be acknowledged. By the same token, she demonstrates that there are limits to understanding an art work; these are restricted by the choreographer's intention. It is the responsibility of both the viewer and, in dance, the dancer not to misinterpret the maker's intentions.

Another dance analyst, Sarah Whatley (2007), adds to the debate, though she is mainly concerned with the dancer and her role in performing the choreography. Whatley asks whether it is possible to distinguish between choreographic and performance style. Her investigation centres on the extent to which the dancers influence the choreographer's style and vice versa although the dance movement style rather than that of the choreography is the main focus of her analysis. Whatley analyses two versions of modern dance choreographer Siobhan Davies's *Winboro Cotton Mill Blues* which was originally made for Rambert Dance Company in 1992 and subsequently transferred to her own company, Siobhan Davies Dance Company, in 1998. Because Whatley investigates two versions of a dance on differently trained bodies, she takes into account Davies's changing choreographic method and approach to movement, which were motivated by the different ways in which the two sets of dancers embody the choreography. Not surprisingly, the performance style of the dancers has an effect on the ways in which observers view the dance and thus influences how the dance is analysed.

Whatley notes that for *Winboro Cotton Mill Blues*, Davies gave her dancers choreographic tasks and then built the choreography around the material made by the dancers. As a result, the dancers' own movement style, derived in part from their training, is a significant feature of the dance's style; consequently, both the performance of the movement and aspects of its content change from one version to the other. Despite finding differences between the two versions of the dance Whatley maintains that they are still 'unmistakable' as Davies's choreography.[36]

Having explored the dynamic range of the dancers from the two companies, Whatley notes that Davies's own dancers' style makes the work recognisable as that of Davies's post 1988 choreographic style. This becomes apparent when she discusses some of Davies's other works which share similar characteristics. Whatley argues that the constituent features of the dance and the ways in which they combine to form recurring patterns and themes can be seen as style and these recur across a number of works.[37] In other words, to establish choreographic style, it is imperative to consider the full range of work. Clearly aspects of the dances change when different dancers are involved and when their training style is not the same as that of the dancers on whom the work was first choreographed, the performance style of the dance is altered. In Davies's case this was intentional but in the work of an earlier choreographer, this may be less acceptable.

Whatley's model has similarities with that of Adshead (1988) in that it focuses on the dance's perceptible properties. Because she is concerned with style and in particular dancers' performance style, she goes beyond that approach. While there may be no definitive way of deciding whether a dance's properties exist beyond the dancer, Whatley still considers the dance itself as the primary object of analysis and the role of the dancer of major significance in any consideration of style. Her impression of Davies's work is that there is a unifying effect created by dancers familiar with Davies's style, although some individual dancers have specific movement qualities on which a choreographer draws and these recur across dances.[38] This is very much the case with Ashton who involved his dancers in the working process and used their talents and proclivities to inform his dance movement. Whatley's solution to the problem of performance style is to see it as either that of the individual performer or as something embodied collectively by a group performing in the same work. This is somewhat akin to the notion of a training style which imparts a collective way of handling codified movements.

For my analysis of Ashton's style, both dance movement and choreographic, I draw on all of these methodologies. The formalist approach of the 1988 Adshead model is a starting point but other aspects such as the choreographer's intention and the choreographic context also form part of my investigation. And because Ashton's dancers also contributed to the works, I explore their training styles, since it is generally the training that shapes their approach to movement.

Models of Style Analysis

The notion of style in dance is a problem. Dances comprise multiple, diverse strands, each of which is susceptible to style, for example, dance movement style, choreographic style, musical style and the style of the scenery and costumes. Some works are further complicated by the use of words and in several of Ashton's works, words are important. Ashton used the words to inform his choice of dance movement and imagery and so they are part of his style, both movement and choreography (see Chapter III). In this book, I distinguish between the two strands: dance movement style and choreographic style, as the movement style in Ashton is complex enough to be treated independently and his choreographic style embraces much more than the movement.

In my research into Ashton's dance movement, I devised a methodology which acknowledges that style, while having an element of fluidity, is also a recurring feature and in ballet, incorporates the choreographer's specific approach to the ballet code. In 1926, when Ashton made his first dance, diverse training systems were in place but he was most influenced by that of Enrico Cecchetti, as interpreted by Marie Rambert with whom Ashton trained. To untangle this web of interconnectedness, I sought ideas from philosophy but primarily from those who have written about style in dance.

Although there is sometimes confusion between the identity and the ontology (how it exists) of the dance work, much of the discussion on style in dance deals with the problem of identity. The question of ontology is complex and needs a much fuller discussion than is possible here and my main concern is with identity. Adina Armelagos and Mary Sirridge (1977 and 1978) use style to identify a dance. In contrast to most other writers, they interpret style as comprising two parts: general style by which they mean choreographic style and dancers' style. The former consists of an inventory of positions and sequences combined with movement flow and the latter is derived from a training style and articulates and generates the choreographer's dance movement (general style). General style can be either invented by the choreographer or derived from a pre-existing inventory of steps. Yet, even when steps are borrowed from a codified body of movement, choreographers treat them in a characteristic and distinctive manner. Armelagos and Sirridge's notion of style is limited but highly significant. It illuminates the problem of style and at the same time recognises that it is a multi-layered concept. It is important that they acknowledge the presence and contribution of the dancer. Following their lead, I explore Ashton's style in a similar way, but with more than the two layers they offer.

Graham McFee (1992) is one of the few writers in philosophy to address dance and in particular the problem of style. Central to his argument is the notion that art is an intentional activity. While accepting that style can be considered in different ways, McFee focuses on individual style; the artist's use of material in a specific way. Using Richard Wollheim's work as a basis for his discussion, McFee argues that in order for a dance work to be considered as art, it needs to be decipherable. By this he means that the work is created within artistic concepts. In other words, the work's maker has intentionally employed or rejected the canons and resources of the art form in which she is working. Decipherability is a necessary condition of the art work otherwise it would be impossible to distinguish the work of an artist from that of, for example, a child.[39] His point is that the work of children cannot be analysed because it is neither intentional nor consciously made against a background of tradition and so not made within artistic concepts.

On that basis, style exists within an artistic tradition and can, in dance, be accessed by reference to the choreographer's use or rejection of the codes and conventions of, in Ashton's case, ballet. To do otherwise risks misinterpreting the work. For instance, put simply, Adshead-Lansdale locates her analysis of Lloyd Newson's *Strange Fish* (1992) in the genre of physical theatre and postmodernism, so knowledge of the conventions associated with both is central to a discussion of his work. By the same token, Ashton was working between 1926 and 1986, so clearly comes from a different dance background and tradition. For his work to be decipherable, knowledge of

Ashton's own dance background, training and influences, such as the dancers and choreographers he admired and the stage dance of the era, have to be the starting point for discussing style in his dances. Anna Pavlova, Tamara Karsavina, Isadora Duncan and Bronislava Nijinska were all individuals from whom he drew inspiration and his style needs to be considered in relation to their respective dance movement and choreography. Ashton's sense of the body and its appearance was derived from an aesthetic coloured by the dance he had seen and taken part in during the 1920s and 1930s. Companies such as the Ballets Russes and Ballets Russes de Monte Carlo dominated the period and photographs reveal how unlike today's dancers were those earlier performers. But they were the contemporary ideals and inspirational to Ashton.

McFee takes the view that making sense of a work involves not only understanding the dance tradition from which the choreographer comes but also the historical era and geographical location in which s/he worked. Central to McFee's approach is the notion of choreographic intention and to have access to this (and that of others involved in the work), we need to examine the possibilities available to the choreographer at that time. In other words, as Rowell also argues, drawing on elements of the choreographer's background and dance culture can be perceived as part of and not extrinsic to the dances.

Using the notion of decipherability locates style in a network of artistic concepts and allows for a range of different outcomes. As I noted earlier, the choice of concepts is dependent on what outcome the dance writer is hoping to achieve and in this book, amongst other things, I am exploring the recurring features of Ashton's dances. I am not aiming to present what Victor Burgin describes as a 'master narrative',[40] more precisely, I hope to pose questions not usually asked by the ballet community in order to present a different way of thinking about Ashton's dances and the medium in which he worked. As Cavell notes, a medium only becomes a medium because of the presence of choreography. McFee takes up the point observing that a medium is not simply the material in which the choreographer works but

> is a set of characteristic possibilities, the applied range of handling and result which grows from the practice of art within that medium...the expressive potentials of the technique arise in just this way; [specific ballet] techniques typically involve not just a way of handling movement in dance, but also a way of understanding movement.[41]

McFee here mentions technique, which he interprets in a general sense, as in Graham technique or ballet technique etc., arguably meaning genre, but I use it more specifically to denote not ballet per se but the range of training systems prevalent during the early part of the twentieth century. The expressive potentials or, as McFee puts it, characteristic possibilities, of each system will vary according to the values implicit in the system; for instance, earlier twentieth century training focused on speed and motion, whereas that of today is more concerned with shape and position.

On a note of caution, however, it is clear that not every aspect of the contemporary training aesthetic is part of the choreographer's stylistic features. While the works may have been shaped according to the conventions of the era, this does not mean that all features were used as part of the style. Some aspects, which may have been part of the dance, and may have appeared permanent, have changed. For instance, the use of the lower leg in steps like the *retiré* and the *pirouette* is now quite different. Video material from the 1950s demonstrates that the working foot is placed below the knee and across the supporting leg. This was a 'correct' application of the code at that time. Now the foot is placed higher and on the side of the leg. Whether this detail is significant or not could depend on the function of the step in the choreography. I take the view that where the *pirouette* is a dominant motif, this lower position may be needed and may be part of the style. For instance in cases where the performer is required to spin, the lower height of the working leg allows this. Where the turn is not a major motif, and thus not part of the style, it is probably acceptable to use the leg in accordance with the current aesthetic.

Thus far, my methodology is taken from an extensive range of sources: for the analysis I use Adshead's 1988 model supported by Rowell's broader notion of context. From Whatley and Armelagos and Sirridge is taken the concept of two styles, that of the dancer and that of the choreographer. My overarching concept of style derives from McFee and allows for choreographic intention and decipherability to be its defining feature. As far as Ashton is concerned, this means being aware of the ways in which his dance background, the training styles, dance icons and contemporary dance culture create both the dance movement and choreographic style of his dances.

Discerning the Dance Movement

According to Adshead-Lansdale, both the terms and the systems which give rise to analysing dance movement are culturally and historically encoded.[42] This is also true of the instructions for performing the *danse d'école*. Formulated from the theatre dances of the early 1800s by the Italian dancer, pedagogue and choreographer Carlo Blasis (1797-1878), the instructions were constructed for contemporary technical and expressive purposes and based on notions of classicism − a classicism based on eighteenth century ideals of line and proportion.[43] So the dancer is advised that the body should always be held in a perpendicular stance, unless performing *arabesques*, and that the arms and legs should work in opposition to each other. Blasis recommends that aspiring dancers should observe and study paintings (by this he means those of the Italian Renaissance) and model their bodily positions on the shapes seen in them.

Blasis's manual outlines both a training system and system for analysing the body, in that it divides the body into different areas (feet, legs, arms, hands and head) but no instructions are given for the dynamic of the movement, although in some cases this can be derived from the name of the step. The system is essentially presented pictorially, with positions as the most important aspect. It is not a dictionary of ballet and lists only the following ballet steps: *entrechat, rond de jambe* and *pirouette*. This may be because many of the remaining steps came from social dance, such as the *chaconne* and *bourrée*, and the distinguishing features of the professional dancer of the period were in the carriage of the body and the formal positions.

As a way of analysing choreographed dance movement Blasis's manual is not altogether helpful because it gives no information about how an action occurs and nothing on music or tempi. It nonetheless contains the basic instructions for performing classical dance. Its lack of discussion of movement may well be the reason why today's dictionaries and manuals of ballet persist in omitting discussions of the 'how' of movement. Even in *The Video Dictionary of Ballet*, the information applies to where the action goes and in what part of the body it occurs but there is no sense of dynamic variation, of rhythm or of shape.[44] The descriptions, both in dictionaries and on the DVD, deal with little more than the biomechanical aspects of the movement. The potential for expressiveness is ignored.[45]

The dance teacher and pedagogue Enrico Cecchetti was taught by Giovanni Lepri, a pupil of Blasis, so the relationship between what Cecchetti was teaching and Blasis's instructions is close. And since Ashton's background was heavily influenced by Cecchetti, this approach to ballet's code was the basis of Ashton's dance movement. But simply naming the steps and step sequences that occur in his work will not highlight style. It would give no notion of the light and shade, where the emphasis in the movement lies nor where the impetus of the movement comes from. Blasis was also concerned with body type, though not girth or weight. He advises dancers that only specific body types can perform certain roles; tall bodies are principal dancers, medium are more suited to the demi-character roles and the stocky or short body to the comic and character roles. Ashton does not adhere to those rules and tended to prefer the smaller dancer, in most roles. He did not perceive his dancers as reified objects but as distinctly human; so size and shape were of less importance.[46]

Since my own background is in Ashton's choreography and the other dances performed by the Royal Ballet during the years Ashton directed the company, it is essential to be able to see the movement as opposed to the steps.

As the scholar Deirdre Sklar reminds us, the 'bodily patterns we master are then enacted outside of conscious awareness' and this means that we are oblivious to the cultural and historical images embodied in the style.[47] Because of my own familiarity with Ashton's dances and dance movement, I have chosen to use the theories of movement advanced by Rudolf Laban.[48] As Adshead-Lansdale indicates, they were devised to support the needs of Central-European expressionist dance. Laban's theories were formed during the years the Ballets Russes performed the choreography of Michel Fokine and, although Fokine's approach to ballet pre-dates Laban, there are links, albeit tenuous, between the aesthetics which inform both these approaches to dance.[49]

Fokine's aim was to transform a corset-bound, vertical way of performing ballet steps into a less restricted more free-flowing, expressive approach. As Lynn Garafola in her thoughtful account of Fokine writes, 'He aimed to heighten the expressiveness of the body by extending its lines and enhancing its plasticity and three-dimensionality'.[50] He changed the whole approach to ballet from one that emphasised position to one that was more concerned with movement. While not expressionist or even inspired by expressionist tenets, Fokine's attitude to the body was influenced by Duncan, whose free-flowing Greek-inspired dancing he had seen in St Petersburg in 1904 and later. Ashton admired Fokine's choreography and was introduced to aspects of Fokine's movement style through his own association with Nijinska, during his time in Ida Rubinstein's company, and later with Karsavina.[51] There are links too, however slight, between Laban's conception of movement and that of Ashton.

Initially, Laban requires us to consider the following questions: what is the nature of support? Which body parts are moving? Are distinctive shapes forming or are they traced through the space? Is a limb moving away from or towards the body? What is the resulting shape? From which part of the body is the movement initiated? The list is not exhaustive but as the notator Ann Hutchinson-Guest has written, the approach is to identify the inner workings of the dance so that subtle differences between movements are highlighted.[52] Laban offered a way of engaging with movement in movement terms whereas ballet manuals offer more of a linguistic system.

My analysis of Ashton's dance movement draws on two aspects of Laban's theory: Irmgard Bartenieff's Effort/Shape (1970) and Preston-Dunlop's notion of the choreutic strand (1983).[53] Both of these scholars built on and developed Laban's theories. Effort/Shape comprises two parts: Effort (quality or dynamic) which is how a movement is performed, and Shape, which deals with the dancers' modification of the form of the body in relation to the space around it. Quality in dance can be generated by nuances in effort, the ways in which the dancers address space, time, weight and flow. Laban

identified eight ways, and changes in effort occur within a range lying between two extremes: thus attitude to time lies between sudden and sustained,
flow between bound and free flow, space between direct and indirect and
weight between strong and light. Two aspects of Shape are pertinent to
Ashton's dances: the ways in which movements flow through the body, either growing or shrinking, moving away or towards, and how the movement
carves or sculpts the space.

Ashton's dances are strongly coloured by a variety of effort patterns. He
will suddenly accelerate or decrease the speed, creating surprise by the unexpected introduction of slow or fast steps or phrases of movement. The
Ballerina's first variation in *Scènes de ballet* (1948) is one example. She enters
joining the end of the fast running circle of dancers and, after a turning
jump, she stops suddenly following this with fast *bourrées courus* and again a
sudden stop. The dancer's attitude to space is also a key element of Ashton's
dances. In the *danse d'école* the movements are goal orientated; arms and legs
move directly to a firm position. In many of Ashton's dances, however, the
movements are frequently initiated from the torso and so are perceived as
indulgent, even luxurious. In a masterclass with Antoinette Sibley and
Anthony Dowell (shown on television in 1988), Ashton, demonstrating a
movement to Sibley, insists that it should be led from the shoulder, curling
inwards and moving down towards the foot. Many of the dances he made
with Dowell use contrasting elements of weight; some actions end with an
impact while others start from an impulse but then are perceived as lacking
in force. But the majority of movement sequences are more complicated and
many of these elements occur in clusters.

To address Ashton's attitude to space, particularly the space around the
body, I use Preston-Dunlop's notion of choreutic units. These she describes
as virtual lines in space caused by the dancer's attitude to effort. They are
perceived as projections when the energy is thrown out into the space, either
by the eyes, legs or arms, and as progressions, when the movements appear
to leave a trace in space. The opening of *Symphonic Variations* (1946) is an
example where the women trace oval patterns around the upper body, giving
the dancers the appearance of being in motion when in fact the action is
performed on the spot. Spatial tension occurs either between limbs or in the
space between dancers. For instance, in *The Dream* (1964) Oberon's *temps de
poisson* in reverse draws attention to the virtual line between his hands and
feet. Body design, which is not simply taking up a position, occurs when the
force of the action draws attention to a pattern of limbs. So, for example, in
Cinderella's solo dance in Act II of that ballet, as the dancer moves upstage,
the abruptness of the move from backbend to upright position makes us
notice the verticality of the body design. It also brings the whole body into
our vision as it occurs in between intricate footwork, where our eyes are

focusing on the feet and upper body motion. Ashton keeps us alert and we do not lose contact with the dancer as she moves upstage. He believed that the audience should not have to look at the back of the dancer's head, so creating a sudden movement diverts attention from the head to the whole body. Laban's conception of movement gives us a way of articulating what we are seeing. Ballet practitioners use the names of the steps for this and, as noted earlier, this is not helpful not only because they are historically and even geographically encoded but also because choreographers use the steps in their own way.

In my discussion of the dance movement, I divide it into basic units and phrases. Taking the ballet step as the basic unit, initially, I use the technical term to identify it but I also discuss Ashton's variations and changes. Of course, these apparent deviations can also be the result of a particular dancer's interpretation, but on several occasions dancers with whom Ashton worked have indicated that it was more important to get the body and the sense of the movement right than achieve a perfectly formed version of the classroom step.[54] For instance, Dowell, for whom Ashton created several roles, notes that 'Fred would sometimes choose a classical step and then ask you to invert it or turn it another way'.[55] In *Symphonic Variations*, the long drawn out *pas de bourrée* for all six dancers, in the slow penultimate section of the work, elongates what is usually a small movement. While the *danse d'école* version of the *pas de bourrée* emphasises rhythmical accents and footwork, Ashton converts it into a step which, although only performed three times, has to travel from one side of the stage to the other, diminishing its rhythmic qualities. Interestingly too, Ashton detracts from the triple accents of the step because the music has a slow legato quality and this makes the whole cluster appear smooth and sustained. That the dancers' performance is actually choppier is masked by the music.

In dance we talk about phrases and, in ballet, teach in phrases but delineating a phrase can differ across choreographers. I use Stephanie Jordan's method which takes moments of rest, contrast and repetition to separate one phrase from another.[56] She discusses the issue at length in her book *Moving Music: Dialogues with Music in Twentieth-Century Ballet* (2000) which includes a discussion of Ashton's work. While her notion of the phrase is supported by her musical analysis, the units she discusses link with Ashton's phrases. For example, the opening section of *Symphonic Variations*, in which the women's arms trace a path around the body, ending in a deep sideways bend followed by a moment of stillness, I take to be a phrase. Dances are made up of phrases, sometimes repeated and clustered into groups but the terms step and phrase are the smallest descriptions of the basic unit and cluster of steps that I use.

For the movement, Ashton draws on the *danse d'école* but breaks the rules, altering and adapting the steps.[57] Since it is not possible to deal with every changed step, I identify several which could be described as 'signature steps'; these are found in almost every one of his ballets, though changed and adapted to suit the choreography.[58] The term was also used by Michael Somes[59] to describe the group of steps which make up the 'Fred Step' (*posé en arabesque, coupé dessous*, small *développé à la seconde, pas de bourrée dessous, pas de chat*) and these I consider to be signature steps, together with the following: the *pas de bourrée*, in all its variations, *rond de jambe à terre* and the *ballonné simple*.[60] They are used in different ways, sometimes to create texture and arrest the flow of a phrase or as major steps in a phrase. In the latter case the function of the step is altered, since these signature steps are usually regarded as minor, linking steps. It is hard to think of another choreographer who manipulated the *danse d'école*, in a similar way.

Ashton was not interested in presenting the 'correct' version of the classroom code. For instance he was more concerned with the qualitative elements of the movement than with the linear shape; it is more important for dancers to retain the speed and emphasis than the correct shape or position.[61] This aspect of his style is not confined to the signature steps, others are similarly treated. Throughout his oeuvre, the signature steps are the ones most frequently repeated and for this reason, I chose them to highlight stylistic characteristics of his movement. Altered codified steps are thus a feature of his style and, as a result, different criteria are required for their performance. No longer dependent on the rules governing the performance of the *danse d'école*, they become other than classical steps.

It is not only the steps themselves that have significant stylistic traits; the way Ashton groups them into short phrases, or clusters of phrases, is also a feature; this is different too from the classroom *enchaînement*. The types of phrase fall into several categories, such as phrases which depend on elaborate rhythmic patterning and phrases in which there are no pauses between steps, the ending of one becoming the preparation for the next. Phrases which depend on presenting a multi-faceted body are also very important. Ashton required his dancers to twist, turn, curve, dive and stretch and when he instructed them to bend, he meant all of these features. So the three dimensional body is fundamental to his dance style.

As far as whole works are concerned, I deal with each on a separate basis. Some are episodic like *A Wedding Bouquet* (1937); others are structured according to the narrative, while ballets like *Jazz Calendar* (1968) are thematically constructed. For analysing the structural elements of the choreography, I use Adshead's (1988) approach, identifying motif and motif development and the use of floor space. The latter is central to Ashton's choreography.

Why Focus on these Ballets?

This is not meant to be a comprehensive overview of Ashton's works. Rather it is an exploration of how style in six diverse works can be identified as being a characteristic and consistent feature. Style not only embraces movement and choreography but is also informed by subject matter. The topics chosen by a choreographer closely affect the style since they form part of his aesthetic preferences. My aim in discussing these works is to show how, despite the diversity of the subject matter, Ashton retained a consistent style. As I see it, Ashton's works fall into three categories: hybrid works which include words, either spoken or sung; non-narrative works and narrative dances. Those discussed are: *A Wedding Bouquet* (1937) words by Gertrude Stein, music and décor, Gerald Berners, *Illuminations* (1950) words by Arthur Rimbaud, music, Benjamin Britten and décor, Cecil Beaton, *Birthday Offering* (1956) music, Alexander Glazunov, décor, André Levasseur, *Jazz Calendar* (1968) music, Richard Rodney Bennett, décor, Derek Jarman, *Daphnis and Chloe* (1951) music, Maurice Ravel, décor John Craxton, *A Month in the Country* (1976) music Frederick Chopin, décor, Julia Trevelyan Oman.

The hybrid dances, *A Wedding Bouquet* and *Illuminations*, discussed in Chapter III, form a small but significant aspect of Ashton's output and almost nothing has been written about them. Choosing a hybrid form, though regarded as avant garde, was not unknown in the 1930s. Nijinska's *Les noces* had been seen in 1923 and Rubinstein's company performed *Persephone* (1934): a work with words by André Gide. Ashton's desire to work in this form shows that he was not only forward-thinking but also ready to challenge his own choreographic style. Words impinge on the choreography and can dictate the choice of movement and motif structure.

Apart from his stage dances, which were included in revues, he choreographed some eleven hybrid pieces. As early as 1928 he made the dances for Henry Purcell's *Fairy Queen* and again for a new version in 1946. His last was for Igor Stravinsky's *Le rossignol* in 1981.[62] Seven of Ashton's hybrid works were ballets, while the others are found in operas with a strong dance thread. Little is written about the operas he directed and, apart from *Death in Venice*, there are no recordings of them available. The reviews give some idea of how they looked and demonstrate his use of the ensemble. Two of the operas were performed in 1947: *Albert Herring* (Britten 1947) and *Manon* (Massenet, 1884) and one, *Orpheus* (Gluck, 1762) in 1953. He also worked on *La traviata* (Verdi, 1852-3) with Franco Zeffirelli in 1948. Both *Albert Herring* and *Manon* were highly acclaimed, in particular for his choreography of the crowd scenes. Discussing *Manon* Charles Stuart in *The Observer* remarked on Ashton's concern with the group which resulted in a more convincing stage picture.

The fourth act gambling-hell of producer Frederick Ashton and designer James Bailey made eyes pop out of every head and almost excused a naively spontaneous round of hand-clapping as the curtain went up. Amid co-lumnar and gilded splendours, the tie-wigs and ruffs, the hoops and the fans diced, drank and generally misbehaved themselves with cunningly devised abandon. Never was corruption more nicely calculated. Like all the best theatrical riots it had been regimented to the last grimace.

The congenital tendency of your operatic chorus is to congeal in diagonal ranks, men on one side of the stage, women on the other. Mr Ashton has, in this scene, at least, ruthlessly scattered and re-patterned them and this without ruin to their singing. I hesitate to bring a charge so damning, but it looks to me as if Mr. Ashton is an innovator – and a successful one at that.[63]

A Wedding Bouquet (1937) has never been studied in depth. The composer and painter Lord Berners set to music sections of Stein's 1931 work *They Must. Be Wedded. To Their Wife*. Initially, Stein's words were dismissed as non-sense[64] but scholars have since rejected this early contempt and from the 1940s her work has been studied extensively.[65] Stein was an ideal partner for Ashton. Like her, he generally began any new work by forming a structure, making patterns out of dance shapes.[66] As the dancer Alexander Grant re-marked, Ashton loved to play Chinese Chequers because it reminded him of choreographing: 'He enjoyed the way everything got in a muddle and then resolved itself. He used to say "That's Choreography".'[67] The Stein scholar, Ulla Dydo, writes that 'for Stein, composing or meditating is the process of making patterns or shapes in words...'[68] So pattern and shape are one of the starting points for both; literal meaning, or storytelling is secondary. It is an interesting work, is an excellent example of Ashton's early style, and de-mands more in-depth attention.

Illuminations was first made for New York City Ballet in March 1950 with music by Britten (1938-9) and sets and costumes by Beaton. No substantial analysis has been undertaken of the work, yet it demonstrates an audacious aspect of Ashton's work, something with which he is rarely credited. John Percival, writing about the 1981 Royal Ballet revival, remarked that what it demonstrated about 'British Ballet's Grand Old Man is that at heart, he is still its *enfant terrible*'.[69]

The dance is ripe for re-assessment. Its choreography is innovative and its dance movement inventive and, although some British critics have not al-ways recognised it, it is clearly infused with Ashton's style. It was made for New York City Ballet with dancers trained in quite a different style from those with whom he usually worked. Consequently, he could not rely on them to feed the choreography as he did with his customary dancers. But my analysis (see Chapter III) shows this did not hugely affect his style. Despite the dancers, Ashton's trademarks are evident. It links with *A Wedding Bouquet* in that both works use the written words as a starting point and both have fragmentary choreography but completely contrast with each other in terms of subject matter. The earlier work depends on comedy while the latter on symbolist imagery. These two works are not only inventive but also quintessentially Ashton and provide clear examples of his style despite their disparate subjects.

In Chapter IV, I explore two of Ashton's non narrative dances: *Birthday Offering* (1956), and *Jazz Calendar* (1968). The one is a celebration of ballet as it stood in 1956, the other a slightly iconoclastic nod to Pop Art and popular culture. Made to celebrate 25 years of the Sadler's Wells Ballet, which soon after became the Royal Ballet, *Birthday Offering* comprises a series of solo dances with an introduction, coda and duet and showcased the talents and qualities of the Company's seven principal female dancers. Not only does it illustrate the kind of dance movement valued at that time but it also shows Ashton's respect for the work of Marius Petipa in *The Sleeping Beauty* (1890).[70] Indeed, the opening of the ballet is a quotation from the prologue of that ballet.

The work is a remarkable testimony to Ashton's interaction with his dancers for he focuses on their particular talents and abilities. Yet paradoxically, the solos, without having been adapted, have outlasted their original creators and the ballet is still in the repertory. *Birthday Offering* gives us another example of Ashton style. In both its choice of movement and choreography it shows how Ashton drew on the *danse d'école* and changed it to accommodate not only his own style but also that of the dancers. The ballet has not been studied in depth before and its fund of stylistic detail is ripe for analysis.

Jazz Calendar, given its jazz score and day-glo sets and costumes was surprisingly well received. Divided into seven sections, it too depended on the talents of its dancers. Considered to be Ashton's most trendy ballet with its atmosphere of the swinging '60s, it actually draws more from the social and stage dancing of 1930 than from that of the '60s. The talents of Jarman and Ashton merged to create an innovative and remarkable dance which has not been in the repertory for over two decades. Yet, I have decided to explore the piece in this book because it is an early example of Jarman's work and needs greater exposure. The stage scene is remarkable, with bright vivid colours, and it cleared the darkness from the January day of its first performance. But a major part of its interest lies in the choreography which seems closer to Ashton's 1930s work and so acts as a record for that era. If *Birthday Offering* epitomises Ashton's use of the *danse d'école*, then *Jazz Calendar* demonstrates how he made it into glitzy show business. Yet, Ashton's style is paramount.

His characteristic choice and assemblage of movement persists and his use of motif to structure the dances makes both tightly knit and succinct, despite their contrasting forms.

The narrative ballets in Chapter V have also been selected for specific reasons. They are both fine, if quite different, examples of his style in narrative dances. For Ashton the story itself was rarely a major concern.[71] Yet, narrative dances form a significant enough group. Just under half of his output uses narrative as a starting point, often with a very slender narrative thread and so it is the treatment not the story that is important in Ashton's dances.

Many claim Ashton was 'the great storyteller'.[72] Yet, paradoxically, he denied this, claiming that storytelling was not his primary objective. Writing in 1951 he observed that 'With every new ballet that I produce I seek to empty myself of some plastic obsession, and every ballet I do is, for me, the solving of a balletic problem'.[73] And even more emphatically he declares that he

> is not fond of the literary ballet, because it seems to me that there comes a hiatus always in which one longs for the spoken work to clarify the subject... And consciously, all through my career, I have been working to make the ballet independent of literary and pictorial motives, and to make it draw from the rich fount of classical ballet...[74]

So, for Ashton, the actual story is less important and was often only used as a stimulus to provide new movement and shape in his dances. Several of his narrative dances do not have stories in the sense of there being a sequence of events ending with a resolution.[75] In many, something happens but, while there can be a sequence of events, there is not necessarily a resolution. In addition, some of his dances depict character but do not have a narrative thread, such as *Enigma Variations* (1968).

The choice of ballet for discussion here had an element of inevitability. Many of Ashton's earlier narrative works before 1950 are now lost and, since I wanted to discuss more than one work, I discounted the two and three-act ballets because of their length. And so I have focused on *Daphnis and Chloe* (1951) and *A Month in the Country* (1976), each from a different era, made for a different range of dancers. Aspects of *Month* have been analysed in some depth, not least Jordan's analysis of the music but there is room for examining the work as a whole and beyond Jordan's focus on the choreomusical relationship.

Daphnis and Chloe, drawn from a story written in second-century Greece by Longus, is set in the early 1950s, rather than in ancient Greece, to the Ravel score originally composed for Serge Diaghilev's Ballets Russes (1912). Ashton had earlier bought Longus' book, translated by George Thornley and his copy (1947) is well thumbed and annotated throughout. As a resource, it provides excellent insight into Ashton's conception of the story and of his way of working. The ballet had Fonteyn and Somes as the main protagonists and Alexander Grant as the anti-hero Bryaxis. Something of the style of each dancer is present in the work though it is a potent example of Fonteyn at the height of her career. Importantly, it contains some very significant material for the corps de ballet which is well worth investigating in some depth. The groups are small, mixed gender groups, where, on the whole, male and female dancers perform the same movement. There are no set-piece standing positions framing the principal dancers, as found in the Petipa ballets, and the finale is a complexly rhythmic group for all, including the principal dancers.

Month has no corps de ballet. It is peopled with individuals and comprises a series of solos and duets with, at one point, a joyful quartet. These are linked by short silent acting sections and a brief mimetic interlude. Both Lynn Seymour and Anthony Dowell, the leading dancers, were in their prime as both actors and dancers. Ashton gave them movement which is a direct translation of each character and yet promotes the talents of the dancer. Coming near the latter part of his working life, it is, perhaps, his most sophisticated and mature narrative piece. A successful production is utterly dependent on the dancers understanding the movement, since it is through the movement that character is conveyed. Both of these works are stylistically significant. *Daphnis and Chloe* blends a mixture of the balletic code with ancient and contemporary Greek dance and these are tightly controlled by Ashton style. The latter work is also closely knit in terms of style. Motifs occurring in the first solo dance are developed in the second dance and variations of the early motifs are peppered throughout the work. And, as ever with Ashton, both his choice of movements and the ways in which they are assembled are typical of his style.

The range of works I have chosen to explore provides cogent examples of Ashton's style both in terms of movement and choreographically. Most of them have not been studied in depth, or even at all, and I wanted to demonstrate a significant range of his choreography. Clearly not every work he made could be included but I wanted to give examples of works that are interesting yet broadly cover each category of subject matter. Some of the pieces chosen are less well-known but deserve to be discussed because they are less conventional, yet, nevertheless, give a multi-faceted illustration of Ashton's style. The first four of these ballets are not generally given priority in discussions about Ashton's work but omitting them gives us a distorted and limited view of Ashton's work, let alone his style. I hope to alter that view in this book.

Sources

Larraine Nicholas, amongst others, has alerted us to the fact that the researcher is now central to research, in other words their modern prejudices guide their approach.[76] In this book, my own background as a member of the Royal Ballet, during the years Ashton directed the company, has directed my attitude to the dances. Deconstructive theories reveal the impossibility of presenting objective accounts of historical research and, indeed analytic discussion, and it is evident that most researchers' biases and preferences are reflected in their work. The perspective from which they are studying the work/event will dictate what sources to use and how to interpret them. As the theorist Linda Hutcheon puts it:

> What is foregrounded in postmodern theory and practice is the self-conscious inscription within history of the existing, but usually concealed, attitude of historians towards their material.[77]

Although this book is not a history of Ashton's dances, it draws on some aspects of historical research, such as gathering and analysing sources. My key sources are of course the dances themselves as seen on DVD/video recordings. While a filmed record can never replace a live performance, since the film flattens the movement and diminishes the dynamic or effort elements, it is nevertheless an important account of the dance. Recordings of several versions exist for the six works analysed in this book, showing different dancers' performances. They range from rehearsal footage to edited, broadcast recordings. Some of the earliest versions, housed in the archives of the Royal Ballet, are films made during rehearsal by Edmée Wood, the wife of the company manager Michael Wood. She had an interest in film and was determined to preserve these early versions of the ballets. The films are in black and white and some are silent, while others were recorded only to piano accompaniment, played and recorded during the rehearsal. Wood's films are invaluable since they usually show the earliest version of a work and, unless the dancer was injured, with the original dancer performing the work. They are however, problematic in that they are filmed from the centre of the auditorium and occasionally make sections of the stage difficult to see. The quality too is imperfect and some films have lines or white spots (dropout) due to age. They were subsequently transferred to video and ultimately to DVD and digitised but are still of enormous significance. For my research, I viewed *A Wedding Bouquet*, (in a recording from 1964) *Birthday Offering* and *Jazz Calendar* on DVD converted from Wood's films.

Later video tapes were made by ex-dancer and company archivist Robert Jude and are rehearsal performances. All were made as records for assisting in re-mounting the works and consequently have their limitations. For instance, in later recordings, in order to view the soloist, the screen shows a large square in the top right corner which displays a close-up of the solo dancer. Effectively, this reduces the size of the screen and diminishes the effect of the ensemble. To some extent, this can compromise the choreography. Earlier recordings, pre 1990, do not have this problem. Only the recording of the Royal Ballet's *Illuminations* was affected in this way. Some clear film, in the New York public library, of the Joffrey Ballet rehearsing *Iluminations* in practice clothes in 1980 was extremely helpful for viewing this work.[78] Although the same qualifications exist as those I mention below in connection with filmed material, this is one of the most easily readable versions of the work. It is filmed from the front and, as with those of the Royal Ballet, is for the purpose of recording and documenting. Alastair Macaulay's complaint that there is little formal dancing in the work can, as a result, be challenged because, without the costumes, it is easier to see the dance movement and choreography.[79]

There are also, however, two works filmed by the BBC: *A Month in the Country* (1978) and *Daphnis and Chloe* (2004). As films of a performance, they do not have the techniques available to a studio film, such as major editing and breaks for dancers to recover their breathing or even re-takes when mistakes have been made. So, from this perspective, they are closer to a live performance. They are of course of a much higher quality than rehearsal tapes but are also further interpretations. The director makes choices as to what is important and this can mean that the focus is shifted to that of the 'star' performer. As a result, valuable corps de ballet material, the 'unacknowledged armies' of ballet, is omitted or not seen by the camera.[80] By the same token, the director presents his own interpretation of the dance, which could be very different from that of the work's creators. Other problems we need to be aware of when viewing film are the effect of watching a three dimensional medium on a two dimensional screen: not only are the spatial elements flattened but also the effort elements are diminished. As dance scholar Sherril Dodds writes, this may be because the live body can be in the range of five to six feet in size, whereas the screen body is more like six to ten inches and this weakens the appearance of the body.[81] Equally, the extreme effort of the dancer is also modified. Yet the camera can also show us close-ups of the dancer and can focus on aspects not easily seen by the naked eye, such as muscular flexion. While filmed sources have to be analysed with these qualifications in mind, they are vital for understanding the choreography and for recording different performance styles.

I used a number of different paper sources: reviews, observations, articles and books. Reviews are contextually important because they show both the changing position of the critics, who over the years frequently alter their opinion, and the contemporary aesthetic. These vary geographically and invariably American reviewers such as Edwin Denby, Walter Terry and Arlene Croce regarded Ashton's work more favourably than did their English counterparts. It is interesting to find how often the English critics condemned his works for their lack of substance, for being out of step with the contemporary age and for lacking challenge or virtuosity. Critics were looking for innovation and some did not recognise that for Ashton, innovation lay in re-thinking the *danse d'école* as he understood it. Apart from the early 1950s, when he made works like *Illuminations, Daphnis and Chloe* and *Tiresias* (1952) that were more sexually explicit then was customary at that time, his dances were frequently discussed only in terms of the story and the choreographic treatment of it was ignored. The critic Richard Buckle who was prominent at the time complained that Ashton 'lives in a sort of nineteenth century dream world'[82] but while he initially disliked the sweet tunes, the story and 'the nostalgia for the nineteenth century' in ballets like *The Two Pigeons* (1961), five years later, Buckle accepted it as part of ballet's French inheritance.[83] In other words, works which were attacked for their anodyne qualities were later recognised for their place in Ashton's canon, for their stylistic context and for their relationship to ballet history. The *Dancing Times* provides another barometer of critics' views, since it was read by the majority of those in the ballet world and its editor, P.J.S. Richardson, was one of the main protagonists in pushing for an established training procedure. I consider his reviews and those of other contemporary critics in later chapters. Using these sources places the dances in the contemporary world and helps us to re-consider their stylistic value. Highlighting the ideologies and agendas of the critics is crucial to understanding not only the dances but also the context in which they were received and performed.

Lionel Bradley (1898-1953), assistant secretary and sub-librarian at the London Library was a ballet admirer and a meticulous ballet observer.[84] Between 1937 and 1953, he attended almost every ballet performance in London and kept a personal bulletin of these, commenting on every aspect of the performance and in particular on the décor. These bulletins were written for four or five other ballet fans who lived outside London and were unable to get to performances. He was well known for his painstaking attention to detail and as Cyril Beaumont observed, 'nothing roused his ire more quickly than to discover in a ballet book some mis-statement of fact'.[85] These unpublished bulletins are invaluable, not least because he returns to specific works over a period of several years, discussing his changing thoughts about a work and recording the moment when a new dancer takes over a role. Since he was not writing for publication, the material is frank and contemplative, very much a documentation and personal record of the works.[86] What is useful is that these are not memories but on-the-spot records. Bradley was known to write his reports on the ballets well into the night, so although the writing is obviously selective and reflects Bradley's biases, it is, on the whole illuminating. Bradley's overriding passion was for, what was then, the Ballet Rambert and he paid tribute to it in the book *Sixteen Years of the Ballet Rambert* (1946). This passion meant that he also had a high regard for Ashton. Of the works I discuss, he saw three: *A Wedding Bouquet, Illuminations* and *Daphnis and Chloe* and he details the choreographic changes made in these works, which are not recorded elsewhere.

The four autobiographies of dancers who worked with Ashton – Margot Fonteyn, Elaine Fifield, Lynn Seymour and Marguerite Porter – are notable for their focus on the dancer's private life rather than on their dancing and the works they performed, though both Fonteyn and Seymour do give some useful information about Ashton's creative process. The biographies of other dancers who worked with Ashton vary and need to be individually assessed. But they are not unbiased accounts of the dancers and the writers were often admirers and supporters. Equally, like the autobiographies, they are published for a public more interested in dancers' private lives than their dance life. Many do not deal with the choreography but some discuss how it felt both to dance in an Ashton ballet and to work with him, though frequently they are too anodyne and reflective of the ideological paradigms of the contemporary eras.

It is clear that these ballets were created by a range of people – artists, composers, writers and dancers. All of these fed into Ashton's style, so it is important to engage with material about or by these artists. Biographies of the musicians and artists, can be more helpful than those of the dancers as they present a perspective external to the dance world, giving an outsider's view on dance. My aim was to use only those resources relevant to Ashton's style, so each chapter varies. Because the work of Berners, Stein, Rimbaud, Britten and Beaton all impact on style in Chapter III, I have used more material. In Chapter IV, the dancers were the main stylistic collaborators in *Birthday Offering*, so material on their dance environment was relevant, while Jarman's input affected the style and appearance of *Jazz Calendar*. Different elements contributed to the style in Chapter V. John Craxton was an important collaborator in *Daphnis and Chloe*: he introduced Ashton to traditional Greek dance as well as designing the décor. In *A Month in the Country*, Ivan Turgenev's play was Ashton's main source for the work and an annotated copy exists in Ashton's library.

Two important books on Berners – a biography by Mark Amory and a more recent book by the musician and scholar Peter Dickinson – were used for information on *A Wedding Bouquet*.[87] The latter is a series of interviews with people who knew Berners and, although the book is well researched and sourced, it lacks substantial information on the Stein/Berners collaboration. Stein's own two autobiographies: *The Autobiography of Alice B. Toklas*

(1933) and *Everybody's Autobiography* (1937) although problematic, give some notion of her day to day domestic life. And the best scholarly material on Stein comes, as stated above, from the scholar Ulla Dydo. Her book is a detailed discussion of Stein's work and her use of language and syntax. [88]

Rimbaud's poem *Les Illuminations* is a vital source for the ballet as is Enid Starkie's biography from which Ashton took several images. Rimbaud was hugely admired by Ashton who found both the work and life intensely moving and his working library is testament to this: it contained several volumes of his poetry as well as volumes by Paul Verlaine, another symbolist poet and sometime mentor to Rimbaud.

Jarman's book *Dancing Ledge* (1984) gives some insight into his work on *Jazz Calendar*, not least the difficulties posed by Rudolf Nureyev over his costume. During my research I spoke to many who knew Jarman, and Keith Collins (his partner) allowed me to visit Prospect Cottage to view his photograph albums. Jarman's late musings on colour, written when he was going blind, have helped me realise how important colour was to him and how the colours chosen for *Jazz Calendar* reflected both the choreography and the fashionable jazz score. But I have been surprised by both the inaccurate picture labelling and comments on the ballet to be found in books focusing on his art and stage design. Jarman's work has posthumously been much praised but there is still a gap in the material on dance. I hope to rectify this in chapter IV.

My paper sources for the two narrative works were more limited. There is some writing on Craxton's collaboration with Ashton but the most significant information for this dance came from observing the choreography itself. It was helpful to know that Craxton had introduced Ashton to contemporary, traditional Greek dance and this alerted me to that element of the work. For *A Month in the Country*, Ashton's annotated copy of the play was vital because it identified his process and demonstrated from which sections of the play his idea of character had been drawn.

From these sources the picture that emerges is not the traditional linear impression of Ashton moving to a gradual development from his early days to become the 'lyrical English choreographer' that he is most noted for today. Rather, they show a more capricious Ashton, one who chose a remarkable range of material but was often viewed as a safe craftsman.

But before examining the dances, I investigate the various training styles employed during the early part of the twentieth century. In order not to misunderstand the dance movement style some notion of the training is vital. It was very different from that of today, with a focus on footwork and intricate steps. If Ashton's dances are to survive as interesting and profound works, an understanding of their development from early twentieth century training is needed, even though his style is distinct from the technical features of that training.

1. Ashton in Vaughan, David (1977) *Frederick Ashton and His Ballets*, London: Adam & Charles Black, 404.

2. I am not suggesting that he alone is responsible for the stylistic aspects of his choreography nor that style is constant. I deal with the notion of style later but my point is that the dancers he used in his work also contribute to the style and, at times the other collaborators. Such as the costume designers or the written text, in the ballets studied in Chapter III.

3. Vaughan (1977) xvii.

4. Kavanagh, Julie (1996) *Secret Muses: The Life of Frederick Ashton*, London: Faber and Faber, 607.

5. Such as, George Balanchine, Kenneth MacMillan and William Forsythe, to name but a few.

6. Dancers like Anthony Dowell, Margot Fonteyn, Alexander Grant, Nadia Nerina, Lynn Seymour and Antoinette Sibley amongst many others influenced his choice of movement and style.

7. This training is evident from performances by youngsters from these countries at the Prix de Lausanne. DVDs are available of these performances and I also spent time at the competition in 2009.

8. This is not stated in any of their advertisements or manifestos but it is clear from examining the dancers emerging from these schools that this is the case.

9. Ward Warren, Gretchen (1996) *The Art of Teaching Ballet*, Florida, University Press of Florida. This is a book which discusses the teaching of ballet with ballet pedagogues, many of whom use Vaganova's system.

10. Rudolf Laban (1879-1958) was actually born in Bratislava which was then part of the Austro-Hungarian Empire.

11. Preston-Dunlop, Valerie (1998) *Looking At Dances: A Choreological Perspective on Choreography*, Ightham: Verve Publishing, 95.

12. See, Clarke, Simone (2007) 'Talking Point', *Dancing Times*, 97, no1157, 11, Kavanagh, Julie (2007) *Rudolph Nureyev: The Life*, London: Penguin Books, 304 (attempting to protect his school), Kostrovitskaya, Vera and Alexei Pisarev (1995) *School of Classical Dance*, London: Dance Books in particular pages 19-23. All of these references, and there are more, suggest that the aim is to achieve technical perfection in the performance of the classical exercises.

13. In a recent DVD, Jordan, Stephanie and Geraldine Morris (2004) *Ashton to Stravinsky: A Study of Four Ballets*, Alton, Dance Books, the dancers found it impossible to perform the *renversé*. When attempting it, they executed it with completely upright bodies, making nonsense of the movement's title.

14. Glasstone, Richard (2008) 'Talking Point', *Dancing Times*, 98, no. 1174, 11.

15. See the following articles by Morris, Geraldine: (2000) The Role of Dance History in Performance Interpretation', *Dance History: The Teaching and Learning of Dance History:* Proceedings of the Society of European Dance History Scholars Conference, 92-102, (2003) 'Problems with Ballet: Steps, Style and Training', *Research in Dance Education*, 4, no.1, 17-30, (2004) 'Ballet as Sport v Ballet as Theatre: Is the Qualitative at odds with the Mechanical', *All About Ballet,Proceedings of the Society of European Dance History Scholars Conference,* www.eadh.com, (2008) 'Artistry or Mere Technique: The Value of the Ballet Competition', *Research in Dance Education*, 9, no 1, 39-54.

16. See Dowler, Gerald (2011) 'British Style RIP', in *Dancing Times*, June, 101, no. 1210, 27-29 and Glasstone, Richard (1994) 'The Royal Ballet School: A Neglected

Legacy', *Dance Now*, 3, no. 4, 50-53 amongst others.

17. 1995, 19.

18. 1995, 21.

19. Newman, Barbara (2004) 'Yuri Fateyev', *Grace Under Pressure*, Alton: Dance Books, 306.

20. Boos, Paul (1995) 'Teaching Balanchine Abroad', *Ballet Review*, 23, no. 2, Summer, 69-78.

21. Gottlieb, Robert (2004) 'Importing A Native Son: Honouring Balanchine in Russia', *The New York Observer*, 20th June (no page numbers available).

22. In the performance of Ashton's *The Dream* by American Ballet Theatre on DVD (1995), Alessandra Ferri, despite having been trained at the Royal Ballet School, ignores the emphasis on the downward dive in the final duet with Oberon. She makes a token bend towards the knee (Ashton required the dancer to bend right to the working foot) and emphasises a high *arabesque* instead. These are stylistic matters not technique.

23. By this I mean that the command is a how to achieve as opposed to describing a position, so in a glissade the command is to glide and is not a precise description of what to do.

24. Mears, Stephen (2007) 'Talking Point', *Dancing Times*, 97, no. 1159, March, 11 and the letters in the following months, April, May, June, November countered in July by Luke Rittner,

25. Challis, Chris (1999) 'Dancing Bodies: Can The Art Of Dance Be Restored To Dance Studies?', in McFee, Graham, ed. *Dance Education and Philosophy*, Oxford: Meyer & Meyer Sport (UK), 143-153.

26. Adshead, Janet ed. (1989) *Dance Analysis: Theory and Practice*, London: Dance Books

27. Adshead-Lansdale, Janet (2007) *The Struggle With the Angel: A Poetics of Lloyd Newson's Strange Fish*, Alton: Dance Books.

28. Eco Umberto quoted in Adshead-Lansdale, Janet (1999) *Dancing Texts: Intertextuality in Interpretation*, London: Dance Books, 17.

29. Rowell, Bonnie (2007) 'Choreographic Style - Choreographic Intention and Embodied Ideas', in Duerden, Rachel and Neil Fisher eds. *Dancing Off the Page: Integrating Performance, Choreography, Analysis and Notation/Documentation*, Alton: Dance Books, 108-117.

30. His comment that if he made a ballet dealing with Beatrix Potter's characters people would say 'the old man's gaga' is relayed in Vaughan (1977) 374. But it is also important to note that he only agreed to do the piece when it was decided to make it into a film.

31. His arguments are fully dealt with in Cavell (1969) and a discussion is beyond the scope of this book.

32. Beardsley, Monroe and W.K. Wimsatt (1954) 'The Intentional Fallacy' in Wimsatt, W.K. *The Verbal Icon*, Lexington: University of Kentucky Press.

33. Cavell, Stanley (1969/1976) *Must We Mean What We Say?*, Cambridge: Cambridge University Press, 236.

34. Cavell quoted in Rowell.

35. For further discussion on this point see Morris, Geraldine (2008) 'Artistry or Mere Technique? The Value of the Ballet Competition', *Research in Dance Education*, 9, no.1, 39-54.

36. Whatley, Sarah (2007) 'Issues of Style in Dance Analysis: Choreographic Style or

Performance Style', in Duerden, Rachel and Neil Fisher eds. *Dancing Off the Page: Integrating Performance, Choreography, Analysis and Notation/Documentation*, Alton: Dance Books, 118-127.

37. Whatley (2007) 124.

38. In modern dance, dancers trained in, for instance, Cunningham style will perform differently from those trained in Graham style and so their embodiment of the choreography will have quite a different focus. In ballet, the belief is that all dancers have a similar training and the differences between the training styles are not recognised and accounted for. While the choreographer is still there to supervise the work, these differences may not matter but when the choreographer is dead, the balletic training style takes priority and the choreographer's style is generally ignored.

39. Wollhiem, Richard (1987) *Painting As An Art*, London: Thames and Hudson and in (1979) 'Pictorial Style: Two Views', in Lang, Berel ed. *The Concept of Style*, Philadelphia: The University of Pennsylvania Press, 128-145.

40. Burgin, Victor (1986) *The End of Art Theory: Criticism and Postmodernity*, London: MacMillan, 202.

41. McFee, Graham (1992) *Understanding Dance*, London and New York: Routledge, 203

42. Adshead-Lansdale (2007), 81-85.

43. Blasis, Carlo (1968/1954) *An Elementary Treatise Upon the Theory and Practice of the Art of Dancing*, trans. Mary Stewart Evans, New York: Dover Books.

44. *The Video Dictionary of Classical Ballet*, there are no dates or film director available for this DVD but it is the version (still available) with the dancers: Merril Ashley, Denise Jackson, Kevin McKenzie and Georgina Parkinson.

45. There is an extensive range of ballet dictionaries see the following: Glasstone, Richard (2001) *Classical Ballet Terms: An Illustrated Dictionary*, London: Dance Books, Kersley, Leo and Janet Sinclair (1997) *A Dictionary of Ballet Terms*, London: A &C Black, Mara, Thalia (1966) *The Language of Ballet: A Dictionary*, New Jersey: Dance Horizons, Ryman, Rhonda (1997) *Royal Academy of Dancing: Dictionary of Classical Ballet Terms*, London: Royal Academy of Dancing and Ryman, Rhonda (1998) *Ryman's Dictionary of Classical Ballet Terms: Cecchetti*, Toronto: Dance Collection, Dance Press/es.

46. See Kavanagh 1996, particularly the account of Margot Fonteyn and Ashton, 184 and Sibley in in Jordan and Grau (1996), 157.

47. Sklar, Deirdre (2006) 'Qualities of Memory: Two Dances Tortugas Fiesta, New Mexico', in Buckland, Theresa ed. *Dancing From Past to Present: Nation, Culture, Identities*, Wisconsin: University of Wisconsin Press, 97-122, 99.

48. Rudolf Laban (1879-1958) Hungarian dance theorist, inventor of dance notation (Labanotation).

49. I am not suggesting it was the same aesthetic but in its opposition to the ballets of Petipa and in the ways in which Fokine wanted to emphasise the expressive aspects of the movement, it has similarities.

50. Garafola Lynn (1989) *Diaghilev's Ballets Russes*, New York and Oxford: Oxford University Press, 37

51. In her autobiography, Nijinska writes in detail about the influence of Fokine on her movement and how she changed her whole approach as a result. See Nijinska, Bronislava (1981) *Early Memories*, trans. Irena Nijinska, USA: Duke University Press, 334-5.

52. Hutchinson-Guest, Ann (1989) *Choreo-Graphics: A Comparison of Dance Notaion*

Systems from the Fifteenth Century to the Present, New York: Gordon and Breach, 181.

53. Bartenieff, Irmgaard, Martha Davis and Forrestine Paulay (1970) *Four Adaptations of Effort Theory in Research and Teaching*, New York: Dance Notation Bureau and Preston-Dunlop, Valerie (1983) 'Choreutics: Concepts and Practice', *Dance Research*, 1, no.1, 77-88

54. Sibley, Antoinette (1996) 'The Ballerina's Solos from *Scènes de ballet*,' in eds. Jordan, Stephanie and Andrée Grau, *Following Sir Fred's Steps: Ashton's Legacy*, London: Dance Books, 138-146.

55. Dowell in Jordan and Grau (1996), 150.

56. Jordan, Stephanie (2000) *Moving Music*, London: Dance Books, 84-86.

57. Topaz, Muriel (1988) 'Specifics of Style in the Works of Balanchine and Tudor', *Choreography and Dance*, 1, 1-36.

58. The term was coined by Henrietta Bannerman to describe frequently recurring motif's in Martha Graham's choreography. See Bannerman, Henrietta (1998) *The Work (1935-1948) of Martha Graham (1894-1991) with Particular Reference to an Analysis of her Movement System: Vocabulary and Syntax*, Unpublished PhD thesis, Department of Dance at Roehampton, University of Surrey, 51.

59. Somes, Michael (1961) 'Working with Frederick Ashton', in Haskell, Arnold, ed. *The Ballet Annual*, London: Adam and Charles Black, 50-54.

60. In Vaughan, David (1977) 9 n.

61. See Nears, Colin and Bob Lockyer (1988) *Dance Masterclass:The Dream*, BBC Production.

62. *The Fairy Queen*, in 1928 and again in 1946. The ballets: *Façade* (1931) (not performed to the words till 1972). *A Day in a Southern Port* (*Rio Grande*) (1931), *A Wedding Bouquet* (1937), *Illuminations* (1950) and *Persephone* (1961). He also directed and choreographed for six operas: the following had strong dance elements: *Four Saints in Three Acts* (Thomson, Virgil and Stein, Gertrude 1934) *Orpheus* (Gluck, Christoph, Willibald 1762/1953), *Death in Venice* (Britten, Benjamin 1973) and *Le rossignol* (Stravinsky, Igor, 1914/1981). The two remaining operas, *Manon* (Massenet, Jules, 1884/1947) and *Albert Herring* (Britten, Benjamin, 1947) were also highly choreographed.

63. Stuart, Charles (1947) *Observer* 2nd March, no page numbers available.

64. Dickinson, Peter (2008) *Lord Berners: Composer, Writer, Painter*, Woodbridge: The Boydell Press, particularly pages 97-101.

65. See Dydo, Ulla (2003) *The Language That Rises*, Illinois: Northwestern University Press amongst others.

66. See Kavanagh (1996), 596, his love of puzzle solving, particularly Chinese Checkers which reminded him of choreography.

67. Grant in Kavanagh (1996) 401.

68. Dydo in Neuman, Shirley and Ira B. Nadel (1988) *Gertrude Stein and the Making of Literature*, Hampshire and London: MacMillan Press, 45.

69. Percival, John, (December (1981) 'Sir Frederick Ashton', *The Times*, 28.11.81, no page numbers available.

70. Vaughan (1977), 284.

71. Crisp, Clement (2007) 'Into the Labyrinth: Kenneth MacMillan and his Ballets', *Dance Research*, 25, no. 2, winter, 188-195.

72. In Macaulay, Alastair (1983) 'Ashton our Contemporary: Trivia and Rhapsodies', *Dancing Times*, LXXII, no 874, 784-786.

73. Ashton, Frederick (1951/1992) 'Some Notes on Choreography', in Sorell,

Walter, ed. *The Dance Has Many Faces*, Chicago: Capella Books, 31.

74. Ashton (1951/1992).

75. Wake, Paul (2006) 'Narrative and Narratology', in Malpas, Simon and Paul Wake *The Routledge Companion to Narrative Theory*, London and New York: Routledge, 14-27.

76. Nicholas, Larraine (2007) *Dancing in Utopia: Dartington Hall and its Dancers*, Alton: Dance Books.

77. Quoted in Carter, Alexander (2004) 'Destabilising the Discipline: Critical Debates about History and Their Impact on the Study of Dance', in Carter, Alexander, ed. *Rethinking Dance History: A Reader*, London and New York: Routledge, 14 and in Hutcheon, Linda (1989) *The Politics of Postmodernism*, London: Routledge, 74.

78. Viewed in 2009 in the Robbins Dance Collection at the New York Public Library for the Performing Arts.

79. Macaulay, Alastair (2003) 'A Question of Balance"/ "Sur quel pied danser', *Conference on Dance and Literature*, Lincoln College, Oxford, April, unpublished paper.

80. Carter, Alexandra (2004) 'Destabilising the Discipline: Critical Debates About History and their Impact on the Study of Dance, in Carter, Alexandra, ed. *Rethinking Dance History: A Reader*, London: Routledge, 16.

81. Dodds, Sherril (2004) *Dance on Screen: Genres and Media from Hollywood to Experimental Dance*, Basingstoke, Hampshire and New York: Palgrave.

82. Buckle, Richard (1980) *Buckle at the Ballet*, London: Dance Books, 141.

83. Buckle (1980), 148.

84. Bradley, Lionel (1937-1953) *Ballet Bulletin*, in the collection of the Theatre Museum, Victoria and Albert Museum, London.

85. Beaumont, Cyril (1955) 'In Memoriam-Lionel Bradley', in ed. Haskell, Arnold, *The Ballet Annual 1955*, London: Adam and Charles Black, 46 and 49.

86. The Bulletins were sent on to a selection of friends outside London and then returned to him.

87. Amory, Mark (1998) *Lord Berners: the Last Eccentric*, London: Chatto & Windus and Dickinson, Peter (2008) *Lord Berners: Composer, Writer, Painter*, Woodbridge, Suffolk: The Boydell Press.

88. Dydo, Ulla (2003) *Gertrude Stein: The Language That Rises 1923-1934*, Evanston, Illinois: Northwestern University Press.

Chapter 2
The Foundations of Ashton's Style:
Training and Dance Influences

By the time Ashton started choreographing in 1926, the formalisation of training in the UK had just begun. Despite this, few of the dancers during the 1930s would have had the kind of intensive practice available to today's students. Given the eclectic nature of training in Britain before the 1920s and the fact that most dancers on the professional stage would have been trained in a number of genres, it is hardly surprising that the dancers Ashton worked with in his early choreography (pre-1940) had varied movement styles.

Dancers' style is not wholly personal but is largely shaped by their training. And because training in the first thirty years of the twentieth century was so different from that of today, I devote a large section of this chapter to a discussion of how that training evolved, to the aesthetic values inherent in it and to the other influences coming from contemporary stage dancing.[1] Because there were no companies devoted only to ballet, dancers had to perform for both genres, so an ability to switch between the two was vital. Choreographers too had to be expert in a range of genres and during the 1920s and 30s Ashton choreographed for the commercial stage and the ballet.[2]

I am less concerned with what was taught, than with the effect of that training on dance performance and how this informed Ashton's dance movement; the first part of the chapter explores this. Yet, Ashton's style was not only affected by the dancers and their training, it was also a product of his dance aesthetic, much of which was shaped by contemporary dancers and choreographers. His passion for Pavlova is well known but what he actually took from her less so, though his choreography manifests that he had a continuous conversation with her. The dancers Karsavina and Duncan also had a significant effect on his works. Despite maintaining that watching a ballet by Petipa was like having a choreography lesson, he was in fact more influenced by the work of Nijinska. From the commercial theatre too, there are traces of the style of the American dancer and choreographer Buddy Bradley. Perceiving how these elements, both dancers and choreographers, infiltrated and informed his style is the subject of the second section of this chapter.

Documentation of the training of the early part of the century is patchy and my findings are based on information from the written accounts of the dancers and the published syllabuses. The latter are contemporary but the accounts of dancers are written with hindsight and aimed at promoting the purity of ballet; few mention the hybridity which must have infused the English style during this era. The period after the First World War is more heavily documented. This was the era of formalised training and many of the controversies surrounding its inception take place in the *Dancing Times*.

This chapter is more historical in nature than those which follow and because it is dependent mainly on written sources and photographs, there is less dance analysis. Several dancers have written autobiographies and while these have been of some use, few discuss their classroom experiences or its effect on their dancing. The most analytic account comes from Ninette de Valois in her two books: *Invitation to the Ballet* (1937) and *Step by Step* (1977).[3] There is little film of the time and none which demonstrates classroom training. Even in 1948, when both Philip (P.J.S.) Richardson, the editor of the *Dancing Times*, and the dance historian, Cyril Beaumont, considered the development of training since 1914, they did not actually deal with how the dancers performed. But I believe that if we can somehow look at these accounts in a different way, we can uncover more about the training and how this affected the appearance and performance of the contemporary dancers and consequently Ashton's dance movement style. [4]

The context of that style and training can be found earlier, at the beginning of the twentieth century, in the ballets of the music hall. Today's ballet in Britain still owes something to those early dancers and teachers. The ballets of the era were short, presented alongside variety acts in the music halls and comprised a mixture of genres, choreographed from both the *danse d'école* and social dances.[5] They were rarely full evening works. Although the performances included both a large corps de ballet and star dancers, the intention was to mount a spectacle and entertain. The best of these took place in the variety theatres of the Empire and the Alhambra. Whilst the in-house corps de ballet was made up of English women, the principal dancers were engaged from abroad. In 1897 a Danish ballerina, Adeline Genée, was recruited to dance at the Empire Theatre where she remained until 1908 becoming one of the most popular dancers of the era. Later, she played a major role in training English ballet dancers. Genée's reign, which propelled the Empire into becoming the major ballet theatre of the Edwardian era, was followed by an influx of dancers from Russia, such as Lydia Kyasht and Adolph Bolm. Russian dancers also began appearing in other London venues: Karsavina performed at the Coliseum in 1909 followed by Ludmilla Schollar and Giorgi Kyaksht at the Hippodrome, while in 1910 Anna Pavlova and Mikhail Mordkin danced at the Palace Theatre.[6] It seems to have been the influx of these dancers together with the arrival of the Ballets Russes that led to the demise of music hall ballet, although not before the arrival of the first home-grown principal dancer at the Empire: in 1913 Phyllis Bedells was appointed to the prestigious role of première dancer.[7] Her reign was short-lived, however, because in 1915 the Empire disbanded its ballet troupe and Bedells moved on to perform in revues and the commercial theatre.

Dance Classes and Training in England before 1920

Bedells is a good example of the problems facing dancers of this period, in respect of proper training in ballet. Finding consistent training was difficult in these variety theatres, training was not always available and what little there was, was limited. As Ivor Guest points out, although discipline was strict it was not mandatory for the corps to attend a daily class and little of a technical nature was required of them.[8] Dancers who had some skills were trained in what became known as, 'the English school', a combination of step-dancing and skirt-dancing. Bedells started at an early age learning 'Fancy dancing' in Clifton with Miss Edna Stacey.[9] This comprised a mixture of social dancing and dances adapted from the stage for amateurs to perform.[10] In 1903, aged eleven, she began more 'serious' ballet lessons in Nottingham with Theodore Gilmer, who had been with the Paris Opera. After her appointment as a soloist at the Empire in 1907, Bedells began working with Malvina Cavallazi, an Italian who seems to have had a very rigid approach to training which led to Bedells becoming too set in the mode of the Italian School. The Empire management believed this impaired her spontaneity and convinced Alexander Genée, Adeline Genée's uncle and former teacher, to come out of retirement to give her three classes a week.[11] Later she worked with Bolm, Pavlova and finally Enrico Cecchetti. This diverse training seems to have been typical of the era, at least for those in London, able to afford the cost of the lessons. Intermittent classes did not allow the dancer to build a strong technique, though it may have led to a less rigid attitude to the *danse d'école*.

In addition to individual teachers, who only gave private lessons, there was an abundance of dance schools. The dance scholar, Theresa Buckland, notes that the teachers there gave lessons in the current social dances, in deportment, in callisthenics and in 'fancy dances'.[12] 'Fancy dancing' seems to have been the initial training for several of those wishing to become professional dancers. Many attended the classes of the fashionable Mrs Wordsworth, whose pupils included royalty and the aristocracy. De Valois' first dancing lessons were with Mrs Wordsworth, whom she described as an erect figure 'imposing, possibly modelled on Queen Victoria; resembl[ing] a neat little yacht in full sail'.[13] Olive Ripman outlined the content of her classes:

> skipping... Skipping was followed by Club Swinging. The class then formed

up in twos... March round doing a sort of 'goose step' up the centre in twos, divide up in fours. Then we did our spot of dancing, strictly fancy, starting with arm exercises done for some reason with a flower in one hand, and kneeling on one knee. The Steps!... for instance when what we call 'Changes' are correctly done, the feet are as close together as possible... In our 'Changes' we leapt into the air with, if possible, our legs spread to an angle of a quarter to three. The wider and higher the more Mrs Wordsworth shouted 'Beautiful'. There was also a sort of *coupé* step we called 'On it' done with a high kick in front and back with arms swinging in and out. Our *ballonés* were taken up to the knee, our Reel steps...were terribly incorrect. Cuts and Shakes all taken as high as possible. [14]

Ripman's description of the dancing class might fill today's ballet teachers with horror, yet it provided a good start and gave the children who attended a real joy of dancing. Even in the 1920s fancy dancing still held sway and if you wanted to learn to dance you might, as Leslie Edwards did, enrol in Mrs Hepworth Taylor's school. It did not help much with classical dance but as Edwards remarks, it was fun and enjoyed by all.[15]

That there was a reluctance to train in only one genre is shown by the response given to Richardson when he suggested establishing a society devoted just to ballet. Robert Crompton, the founder of the Imperial Society for Dance Teachers (ISDT, 1904), dismissed the idea on the grounds that most theatre managers preferred to engage dancers who could perform in a range of genres.[16] It may also have been because dancing, and ballet training in particular, was suffused in English class consciousness. Mrs Wordsworth would not countenance her students performing in stage dancing. She accepted young women to train as teachers, not as professional dancers. As Ripman writes, 'ballet was "taboo" and no one would think of learning it – the very lowest of Cinderellas in the world of the arts'.[17] De Valois supports this comment, remarking that Mrs Wordsworth had 'a puritanical loathing of dancing as a profession [and] regarded it the duty of anyone under her tuition to eschew the theatrical profession at all costs'.[18] It was probably its place in music hall that brought ballet into disrepute, but the arrival of Serge Diaghilev's Ballets Russes in 1911 changed this perception.

Diaghilev's company prompted several English men, in particular Richardson and Beaumont, to become involved with ballet in Britain and most noticably with the development of a training system devoted only to ballet. They were also instrumental in promoting individual teachers. Richardson was particularly keen to support the many foreign teachers that held private, and sometimes group, classes in London and it was with these teachers that those few English dancers like Hilda Bewicke, Hilda Butsova, de Valois, Anton Dolin, Vera Fredova (Winifred Edwards), Alicia Markova and

THE

DANCING TIMES

A SOCIAL REVIEW OF DANCING AND MUSIC.

New Series.
No. 55.   APRIL, 1915.   Monthly,
                                                          Threepence.

SHE TAKES THE RING.

YVONNE MEHRO,

to whom Madame Genée has awarded the Prize in our " Arabesque "
Competition.

She is a pupil of Miss Flo Martell.

Courtesy of the *Dancing Times*

Lydia Sokolova (Hilda Munnings) trained.[19] The dancers reached an acceptable standard, enabling them to join both Pavlova's company and that of the Ballets Russes. The varied training styles of these teachers coupled with schools like the Alison Steadman Academy and Lila Field's Academy gave the early twentieth century dancers their movement style. It was eclectic, drawn from a number of training systems as well as from other genres and it was from the aesthetic and value systems embraced by this style that the ballet training drew. In 1920 when Ashton started taking ballet classes, first with Léonide Massine, briefly, and then with Rambert, these were the prevailing values and hence the ones which coloured his dance movement style.

Ballet Training in England before 1920

Edouard Espinosa's (1871-1950) contribution to the development of ballet-only schools is important.[20] His autobiography (1946) is a first-rate source for this period, even if at times it may not be wholly accurate. His was one of the few voices to be heard clamouring for training to be formalised and was supported in this by Richardson. Espinosa began his training late, aged eighteen, with his father, a famous dancer and teacher. By his own account, Espinosa learned quickly and although critical of 'his terrible feet' his father praised his 'knees and ballon'.[21] The Reichshallen Theatre in Berlin was the scene of Espinosa's first ballet performance but he was dismissed soon after the opening of the show. Clearly, he still had much to learn and his dance style was mixed, enhanced by movements picked up from the wide range of dancers he met when performing in opera, pantomime and the music hall. He appropriated some 'special steps' from two Italian dancers in New York and, in pantomime in Dublin, he learned buck dancing and the American cakewalk from two African American dancers.[22] His performing career was not extensive though continued during the early part of the twentieth century. To supplement his earnings, he opened a school in London in 1896, apparently his first incursion into teaching ballet.

One of his major interests was in codifying the *danse d'école* and in 1909, he began writing a '*Technical Dictionary of Dancing: The Theoretical Analysis of the Art of Operatic Dancing, The Training and Reproducing of all the Authentic Mediaeval Dances.*'[23] He devised a syllabus for his school, The British Normal School of Dancing, which had both the French terminology for the steps accompanied by the English words, which were not always a direct translation. As he put it 'The French nomenclature of steps superseded the words "kicks", "twist", "bas pas", "stay turns".'[24] The latter terms were also used in social dancing. Despite having been described by de Valois as a representative of the French school, it seems that Espinosa's background was more diverse and unlikely to have been purely balletic.

By the second decade of the twentieth century, he had become a revered figure in London ballet and, as Richardson believed, placed British ballet on a sound basis.[25] Having pestered Richardson for some time to publish his recommendations to teachers, this advice finally saw publication in 1916.[26] It was in the form of a syllabus headed 'What every Teacher of Operatic Dancing Ought to Know and Be Able to Teach', and later it formed the basis of the AOD's (Association of Teachers of Operatic Dancing of Great Britain, established in 1920, becoming the Royal Academy of Dancing in 1935) syllabus and first examinations. Both the AOD's syllabus, and the examinations based on it, were devised by Espinosa and drawn from those he had used in his British Normal School in 1908.[27] De Valois regarded him as a formidable pedagogue, arguing that his terminology is still the basis of the English technical school.[28]

Others, such as the dancer Lydia Sokolova, did not encounter Espinosa but Sokolova's account gives some idea of how early English dancers achieved enough technical ability to join ballet companies like the Ballets Russes. Her training came from a number of Russian dancers who visited London in 1909 and 1910. Beginning at the Steadman Academy, she then moved on to work with Mikhail Mordkin.[29] It seems Sokolova was good enough to join his company because she was summoned to accompany the troupe for the 1911 American tour. By the time she joined the Ballets Russes in 1913, she had encountered a range of different training styles: those of Pavolva, Alexander Shiraiev (a character dancer), Ivan Cloustine and Theodore Kosloff, all of whom were Russian.[30] Later in the Ballets Russes she studied with Enrico Cecchetti, who, she claims, was the most meticulous and exacting teacher she had yet encountered. When Cecchetti returned to Italy in 1926 Nicholas Legat, a Russian dancer and teacher replaced him. Legat's method, writes Sokolova, was 'lighter, much less strict and accurate than Cecchetti's, so although [the] classes became gayer, [they] lost strength and precision'.[31] Sokolova, who was most lauded for her character dancing, remained with the Ballets Russes till Diaghilev's death in 1929.

The dance teachers of the early part of the twentieth century were more than a mere conduit to the institutional systems started in the 1920s, their multi-stranded approach formed the stylistic basis of English ballet. Training youngsters in a range of different styles generally leads to more adaptable bodies but can also affect their embodiment of the *danse d'école*. Ashton used these bodies with their diverse training and performance repertoire in his choreography. Because of this, the dance values inherent in the stage dancing and other dance genres of the era fed into his choreography and these are particularly evident in his works from the 1930s, though they have never been wholly absent even from his later works.

Whilst there was no agreed national system for teaching ballet in England before 1920 there were, as suggested earlier, several acclaimed teachers. Because of the First World War, many foreign dancers were trapped in London, and, for financial reasons, opened studios. Calling herself Madame Karina, the Danish dancer Karen Lindahl opened a school in 1914 and the Russian dancer Seraphine Astafieva opened hers in Chelsea in 1915. The Italians, Lucia Cormani and Francesca Zanfretta, were also teaching in London in 1915[32] and when Russian dancers, both from the Imperial theatre and the Ballets Russes, came to London, many of them gave classes during their visits, both before and during the war.

There are no accounts of how or what these foreign dancers taught but they came from different schools and their perception of the technical vocabulary was far from uniform. Indeed, Astafieva was celebrated more for her knowledge of mime than her toe dancing.[33] So too was Zanfretta, whose method was recorded for the Vic-Wells school by Ursula Moreton during the 1920s and so fed into the training at the Sadler's Wells School. Yet, Astafieva became the most celebrated teacher, probably because of her role in training Dolin and Markova.[34] Richardson praises Astafieva's attention to detail[35] and later, in an article written in 1948, puts her on a par with Nicholas Legat. In spite of this reputation, she is not mentioned in de Valois's books, neither was she engaged by her to teach at the Sadler's Wells School or asked to be part of the group that formed the Association of Operatic Dancing.[36] Indeed none of these teachers became involved with that, or any other, association probably preferring to remain independent and thus unrestricted in their approach. But it must be assumed that they provided a significant portion of the training in London in the late teens and that their attitude towards the technical vocabulary coloured the way in which it was interpreted by later dancers (for instance, Fonteyn occasionally visited Astafieva during the 1930s).

The Establishment of Institutional Training: Forging Dance Movement Styles

Editorials and other published material in the *Dancing Times* show just how much Richardson (the editor) assisted the formation of institutionalised technique and his contribution, along with that of Beaumont, is, in effect, as important as those of the teachers. During the teens and twenties, brief articles on technique accompanied by excellent photographs appeared in the *Dancing Times*. These give some notion of the aesthetic values of the period. While the underlying anatomical principles are in line with those of today, the style was quite different. Espinosa's discussion on arabesques and attitudes with accompanying pictures in 1914 shows how the aesthetic has altered; the shape is quite different.[37] An acceptable arabesque had a lower leg extension; the torso was flatter, the hips in line with each other and the arms more relaxed; it was altogether less athletic looking. Genée's demonstration of *port de bras* 1922 is another example.[38] The arms are rounder and placed more in front of the body than we are used to seeing today and the look is almost cosy. These photographs are an excellent source but they show only static poses, so both dynamic and flow are absent. And yet more pictures, ostensibly depicting movement, omit other vital elements. In a later (1916) discussion of the *coupé-posé* and *coupé-jeté* from Espinosa, the photographs show only the end pose and the legs from the knee down, so the positioning of the torso and arms is left out.[39]

Richardson was determined to establish a recognised English ballet culture and was largely responsible for guiding and generating interest in technique. Reflecting on his early work in 1948, Richardson commented on the early pictures, claiming that they were a necessary teaching tool because before 1920 the teaching of classical dance technique had been a closed book to most English dancing schools. Not only did Richardson encourage teachers to gain knowledge of 'correct technique', he also increased his own by watching the classes of various pedagogues, including those of Cecchetti.[40] His mission to improve training was constantly hampered by a lack of unity amongst the teachers and he proposed the formation of a society which could award certificates of competence to knowledgeable teachers.[41] His goal was achieved in 1920 with the foundation of the Association of Teachers of Operatic Dancing (AOD). Of almost equal significance to his cause were the Dancers' Circle dinners which he initiated in 1919.[42] These encouraged greater communication amongst teachers and others in the profession and paved the way for the AOD. They also gathered a substantial section of the amorphous dance world into a coherent group.

Through publishing photographs of the stylistic and technical elements of ballet, Richardson significantly influenced the appearance of early twentieth century English ballet. Though supported by a commentary, the photographs tacitly excluded any other way of performing the movements depicted. The following brief comparison between a series of *arabesques*, published in Beaumont's edition of Cecchetti's work (1947, plate VIII), and those of Espinosa demonstrates the aesthetic differences between the two approaches.[43] Allowing for the fact that they are presented in different forms – drawn and photographed – they look quite different. Cecchetti's first *arabesque* is shown with a more vertical back, while the dancer in Espinosa's version is almost horizontal. Cecchetti's second *arabesque* has a much greater pull of the shoulders, which form a straight line, from front to back, in contrast to Espinosa's squarer version. Espinosa has no third or fifth *arabesque* equivalent to those in the Cecchetti manual and in fourth *arabesque* the arms are shown forward and to the side, while in the Cecchetti work, they are in

Courtesy of the *Dancing Times*

one long line. When carried throughout a syllabus, or system of training, these subtle differences between two systems lead to distinct ways of moving and dancers trained only in one system will not necessarily be able to adapt to choreography made on dancers trained in another.

Beaumont, the champion of the Cecchetti method, also left a distinctive mark on twentieth century training, although his influence was not as far-reaching as Richardson's. Beaumont published extensively on dance but his major contribution to training was his book: *A Manual of the Theory and Practice of Classical Theatrical Dancing* (1922) which set out Cecchetti's teaching method and interpretation of the classical vocabulary. That same year, he established the Cecchetti Society, the founding committee of which included Margaret Craske and Derra de Moroda and the Society became a branch of the ISDT/ISTD (Imperial Society of Dance Teachers (1924) which was changed to Imperial Society of Teachers of Dancing in 1925).[44] The examination system based on Cecchetti's method was presented in *The Dance Journal* which Beaumont edited during the 1920s and 1930s. Publishing articles on all its branches, the magazine also regularly contributed items on ballet's technical vocabulary and its relationship to classroom training. In 1925, it printed the first Elementary Cecchetti examination syllabus which entailed adapting Cecchetti's system. This infuriated Cecchetti who believed his method was only suitable for professional dancers.[45] Children's examinations and an Advanced syllabus followed in 1927.[46] This swift formation of examination syllabuses may have been issued as a challenge to the AOD. The first Cecchetti syllabus stresses small details such as the dynamic use of the head, body and arms.[47] This contrasted with the information published by the *Dancing Times* for AOD examinations, which was, on the whole, confined to footwork. But as Beaumont later argues the Cecchetti syllabus was designed to develop the whole body 'harmoniously'.[48] Unlike the AOD examinations, which were initially designed to instruct teachers on the correct method of teaching ballet, the Cecchetti examinations were aimed at aspiring professionals, since they required a high level of technical competence. For instance, despite knowing the daily *enchaînements*, candidates had to respond to unprepared *enchaînements* and were also required to execute a previously prepared dance based on the Cecchetti method.

Both magazines discussed faulty technique but Beaumont's analysis includes a discussion of the qualitative elements: flow in the *port de bras*, rhythm and timing, and contrast between *grande allegro* and *terre à terre* work.[49] Despite promoting Cecchetti examinations, the ISTD also retained its own ballet branch, complete with examination syllabus. Each year guests were invited to give masterclasses in both styles. Karsavina occasionally gave the ISTD class and, as published in the *Journal*, hers is significantly different from Cecchetti's, although she had frequently studied with him.[50] Contrary to his approach, she gave an almost choreographed barre, combining different exercises and introducing pointe work. Her centre practice included a repeat of the barre, though with longer and more varied combinations. While this is probably not an ideal class for training, it is more exciting to dance. And though it may not improve the technical elements, it would help with the qualitative.

By looking at the early syllabuses of the AOD it is possible to gauge some of the characteristics of the dancer trained by this method and of its aesthetic values. The syllabus details lists of steps, showing that much emphasis was placed on *terre à terre* work. Details of head movements, of how to interpret *épaulement* or of ways of combining arms with the technical steps were omitted from the published syllabuses, as were instructions for the use of music. Perhaps the founders of the syllabus believed these to be too familiar to be described or they felt them to be unimportant. Either way, it must have led to great variations in their execution. Neither were the exercises defined by gender, so in all probability the same material was taught to and by both men and women. Ballet training appears to have placed less emphasis on gender, possibly because fewer men attended the classes. Physical accomplishment of a given list of the codified movements was required at all levels and, because no set *enchaînements* were given, teachers must have been free to invent their own.

These early syllabuses are likely to have produced dancers who had mastered the exercises in the Advanced syllabus but this did not necessarily allow them to develop strength and precision. That this was the situation is confirmed by De Valois who argued that because of the brevity and speed of the training in early twentieth century Britain, the dancers were rarely able to achieve good *ballon* or a sound *adage*.[51] The open-ended nature of the syllabus may also have led to significant variations in standards across the country. According to Pamela May, the AOD was the main source of training during the twenties and thirties, so the majority of youngsters entering the Sadler's Wells School would have had a background in the system.[52] But there is little more concrete material available beyond photographs in the *Dancing Times*. Clearly the presence of the examinations helped teachers and their pupils to understand the anatomical details of the body but they did not give enough qualitative instructions. This is not to suggest that teachers ignored these but that they are not stressed in the printed texts and so perhaps are considered unimportant.

Cecchetti's system, as is evident from the manuals produced by Beaumont with Stanislav Idzikowsky and later by Beaumont with Craske, was prescriptive and, according to Beaumont, recorded so that the exercises could only be performed in one specific way.[53] It was more detailed than those of the AOD, since each day's class was prescribed and these were reiterated weekly. The constant repetition can, as de Valois found out, elicit an automatic response. Commenting on the ritualistic aspects of the system, de Valois considered that despite producing great strength and harmony, it was ultimately limiting. Her praise is reserved for Cecchetti's abilities as a pedagogue and, in her opinion, it was 'his special system [which]... possibly cramped his full powers'.[54]

There are discrepancies in the accounts of the way he taught and as to which values dominated his teaching. Some former pupils indicate that precision was all important, while others insist that it was the quality of the movement that was significant.[55] What emerges is that there are different versions and interpretations of his method and, not surprisingly, these have changed even more through time. According to those dancers who trained with Cecchetti himself, his teaching gave dancers a fluid, mobile torso. This was because he emphasised the postural muscles of the stomach, allowing the torso to move with more freedom. As the Cecchetti scholar, Toby Bennett, argues, the method is characterised by a 'rich use of the back and harmony of line, the play of weight, the use of the ground and a generous use of space'.[56] Molly Lake remembers 'flow, continuity and coverage of the ground' to have been the most significant features, while Laura Wilson argues that the focus was more on 'spatial pattern and dynamic change'.[57] Bennett analysed the system in some detail and found that Cecchetti-trained dancers not only have strength and flexibility in the torso, they also have an appreciation of the subtle rhythmic variations between different steps, coupled with a profound understanding of *épaulement*. As with any of these systems, it depended on teachers' interpretations and several dancers suggest that, even in the early days, quite significant variations occurred.[58]

Ashton's Dancers

Sources from the ISTD do not identify the numbers of teachers who taught the system, so it is difficult to find out how many of those entering the Sadler's Wells School in the thirties had a Cecchetti background. Undoubtedly the dancers Ashton worked with between 1926 and 1935 in the Rambert school were trained in the style and film footage from that period shows dancers with a capacity for rapid movement, combined with fluid, mobile upper torsos, though they often lacked articulate feet. In any event, it was the system most familiar to Ashton and he attached great importance to it, believing it 'to be the best system of training' and one that had given him an excellent grounding.[59] But most importantly he loved the Cecchetti *port de bras* which, he felt gave dancers a sense of line, and variations of these frequently appear in his dances.

The other important influence on Ashton's dancers was the training at the Sadler's Wells School. De Valois' training is not documented until the

1950s but before that, magpie-like, she employed a range of teachers at the School. May, who joined as a student in 1933, remembered learning with Nicholas Sergeyev, Craske, Idzikowsky and, for a short time, Anna Pruzina. Both Craske and Idzikowsky taught versions of Cecchetti's system, while Sergeyev seems to have been working within the old Imperial Ballet tradition. Much of his centre work comprised solos from the nineteenth-century ballets, chiefly *Swan Lake*, *The Nutcracker* and *The Sleeping Beauty*. These were used for training purposes and their use seems to have been common practice amongst teachers of the Russian Imperial Ballet. May did not comment on de Valois's own teaching and it is possible that by then she played a much smaller role in the day to day training at the school.

Because they were also used in training, these Petipa/Sergeyev dances from *The Sleeping Beauty*, particularly in the performances of the Royal Ballet, give some idea of the values of the Imperial Russian Ballet and hence of the Vic-Wells Ballet. Films from the 1950s feature dancers trained in the Sadler's Wells School during the 1930s. What stands out is the speed at which the dances are performed. Today's slightly slower tempo gives rise to an alteration of the choreography. While the steps are ostensibly the same, their appearance is not. What is lost is the sense of dancing. The poses, moments of stillness and turnout are emphasised in the later versions but the sense of motion is absent and the dances are seen more as a set of links between positions.

The bodies too are dissimilar, not simply in their appearance but in the way that they move. In 1950 and before, there is a sense that these dancers are three dimensional. There is none of the flatness and openness of today caused by greater turnout and higher extensions. An example is the high *arabesque*. Earlier both hips were level (or almost) and consequently the leg was lower, the body more angular and the back curved. Today's high *arabesques* are the result of lifting the hip of the working leg so that the extension is almost in second position and the legs are in a straight, vertical line, making them appear flat, while the torso is more upright forming a U shape. This is a complete contrast to the earlier aesthetic. Turnout too is flatter, more pronounced in later pictures. In some Ashton dances turnout can be sacrificed to achieve suppleness in the upper body. For example, in a *retiré* position, the body bends right over the working leg, though the knee can point forward rather than sideways; this would not be acceptable today. Something too is lost by the change in qualitative elements. Most of today's dancers, even in a gentle work like *Les sylphides*, have much stronger projections. Sparks fly from the finger tips and the tips of the toes, everything in the body extends beyond its physical extreme, so that the effect is one of brilliance and of athleticism. The need for display permeates all dances, irrespective of choreographic style. Earlier, the dancers were more contained and the patterns made around the body more complex; this leads to a greater range of light and shade. In a 1953 film of *Les sylphides*, the dancers give an impression of effortlessness. They seem lighter and less athletic, more in keeping with Fokine's aesthetic and the ethos of the work.[60]

The picture that emerges from this examination of the available training during the twenties and thirties is mixed. Those in de Valois' school generally arrived with a basic knowledge of ballet and received what seems to have been a strong if rapid training before being whisked into the company; many attended the school for only a year before joining the company at seventeen. Some, like Fonteyn, were even younger. So in general, they had four to five years of training before becoming professionals. This compares unfavourably with today's training; youngsters now are required to have had at least eight years of daily lessons before joining a professional ballet company. Rambert, with whom Ashton trained, frequently took older pupils, particularly if they were male. These were encouraged at any age, even when they had had no previous training.

The dancers of the era probably lacked the strength of today's dancers and they certainly had less flexibility in the limbs; today's hyper-extensions were not valued then. But, in contrast, they had lithe torsos, an ability to change direction rapidly and faster footwork. But ballet did not exist in isolation; despite the efforts of the AOD and the Cecchetti Society, from Russia through Europe expressive modern dance was deemed to be as important.[61] Something of the grounded nature of this dance found its way into ballet movement, as evidenced in de Valois' choreography. And although there is little evidence that Ashton was influenced by expressionist dance, the choreography of his ballet *Dante Sonata* (1940) bears a striking resemblance to aspects of that genre.

This divide between the two systems, advocated by the AOD and ISTD is replicated by the training in the schools of Rambert and de Valois. De Valois, shrewdly recognising the power of publicity and self-promotion, aligned herself firmly with Richardson and the Association; she even took their examinations in 1929.[62] Whereas Rambert does not seem to have been much involved with it and fully promoted Cecchetti's system. Through the 1930s, 40s and 50s de Valois was in close contact with the Royal Academy and in 1955 they used most of her method as the basis for their new exams.[63]

These two institutions (AOD/RAD and ISTD) acted mainly to ensure that teachers knew what steps to teach and how to teach them, while the schools founded by both de Valois and Rambert in 1926 and 1920 respectively were not examination based and not for the once-a-week child who wished to learn deportment.

Marie Rambert

Rambert has written about her school but what is not discussed beyond the cursory, is how she taught and the kind of dancer that emerged from her teaching. To understand her attitude to training, a glance at her dance background and her teaching manner is instructive. According to Arnold Haskell, Rambert was a fanatic,[64] which may be why Agnes de Mille described her as:

> Madame Wasp, queen hornet, vixen mother, the lady boss of Notting Hill. Knobby knotted with passion... she scrabbled from side to side in the room, pulling pushing poking, screaming and imploring'.[65]

Alexander Bland is a little kinder but the picture of a fanatical character emerges from his description. Yet, she had an 'uncanny eye for detail... [and the ability to] cajole, trick and magnetise her little team into enthusiastic and self-sacrificing collaboration'.[66] She was obsessive about ballet, helping her pupils by drawing out and nurturing their sometimes limited talents.[67] Most writers seem to agree, however, that Rambert was more interested in individuality than in turning out hugely technical dancers. Haskell, the dance critic and friend of Rambert, admired her dancers for their 'marked individuality and not simply the competent performers of classroom steps'.[68] It was this individuality and enthusiasm for dancing as opposed to executing the steps correctly that Ashton took from Rambert. He did not condone sloppy dancing but neither did he applaud technical fireworks.

Rambert's early preference for non-balletic dance attracted her to individualism and initially engendered in her a distinct lack of interest in ballet, both the technique and the choreography. She found it stiff and without expression:

> The bodies of the dancers had seemed so rigid, their movements so stilted with their formal poses and fixed smiles. They had stirred in me no desire to dance. It was only much later that I understood what classical ballet meant and what a powerful means of expression it could be.[69]

She preferred the exuberance and communicative powers of Duncan, which not only made her 'mad with joy' but also strengthened her resolve to learn to dance.[70] A turn-of-the century combination of Émile Jaques-Dalcroze and Duncan promoted her individuality and probably resulted in her later innovative approach to training and choreography. She learned to dance with Raymond Duncan but joined Dalcroze in 1909. Dalcroze was a musician, composer and educator, who pioneered a method of teaching music concepts through movement. His approach to rhythm and music was still in its early stages when Rambert first joined his school but he had already introduced the notion of unequal beats and changes of bar-time. These were a characteristic of his improvisations and helped students to understand complex rhythms. According to Beryl de Zoete, he may well have been inspired in this by the African drumming he heard and the musicians he worked with during the year he spent as a conductor in Algiers.[71] Dalcroze recognised that understanding rhythm for music students was as important as achieving perfect pitch and that the most informative way to do this was through dance. As he put it:

> I came... to seek the connexion between instincts for pitch and movement, between harmonies of tone and time, between time and energy, between dynamics and space, music and character, music and temperament, finally between the art of music and the art of dancing.[72]

Marie-Laure Bachmann has argued that the turn of the century coincided with the return of notions of individuality. For Dalcroze too what was important was the uniqueness of the person. He aimed to free individuals, making it possible for them to achieve fulfilment.[73] Bachmann notes that he strove to give the individual total control over their actions, so that whatever the situation, they could be free to choose their own response. Understanding and physically responding to musical rhythms, could, he believed, enable the individual to achieve this but even more important was his belief that every part of the body could contribute to expression. This is also a characteristic of Ashton's choreography and it may well have been something he absorbed from Rambert and her approach to training.

Rambert's own ballet training was limited. She first encountered ballet when she joined the Ballets Russes to help Vaslav Nijinsky with the Stravinsky music for his ballet *Le sacre du printemps*. After spending a year with the company, taking class with Cecchetti, she became what can only be described as a fanatical ballet enthusiast. Later in London, she spent several more years taking classes with Cecchetti and, according to her ex-pupil Brigitte Kelly, she also adopted his manner of dealing with his pupils, which could be both brutal and harsh.[74] She never became a great ballet dancer but she could recognise talent in others and, most importantly, she did her utmost to preserve her dancers' individuality.[75] She opened her school in 1920 to teach ballet but not surprisingly, given her background, she wanted to teach her students to dance, not just to perform exercises.[76] She taught a version of Cechetti's system but as Maude Lloyd remembered, 'she tended more and more towards personal amendments'.[77] As a teacher Rambert had limited skills, often unable to communicate to her students how to achieve what she required of them but whatever else might be said about her teaching abilities, as a producer of young choreographers she was unparalleled.[78] Her diverse background may well have contributed to this because it had given her a much wider attitude to dance that came from outside the narrow confines of ballet and could appreciate that the ballet aesthetic was not appropriate for all choreography. Ashton, Antony Tudor and Andrée Howard, were goaded and cajoled by her when taking their first steps as choreographers and, because she recognised the need for students to perform, as early as 1926, she encouraged those choreographers to make dances for revues and plays. Not everyone was praising of the performances but as Bland succinctly puts it, even 'her critics... admire the way she can extract a genuinely theatrical performance from inexperienced dancers'.[79]

Photographs of the dancers from Rambert's school during the 1920s and early 1930s show dancers, mainly dressed in long skirts, posing in fluent groups, linked by arms or legs. Their upper bodies seem more pliant, more curved than the taut stretched bodies of today's dancers. Apart from supported arabesques, there are fewer balletic poses, such as in a *retiré*, *posé* or *grand jeté* and in the pictures of Ashton's *Leda and the Swan* (1928) the dancers' torsos bend back and rotate. Rambert may not have encouraged fine footwork, her own feet were always a problem, but what her students lacked in steely feet, they more than made up for in the fluidity and the scope of their upper bodies.[80] And this is probably the result of a training derived from the aesthetics of her three mentors: Duncan, Cecchetti and Dalcroze.

Frequently losing her dancers and choreographers to the Sadler's Wells Ballet because of her inefficiency as an organiser, she, nevertheless, had the necessary vision and background to encourage the emergence of a generation of British choreographers. Despite his leaving for the Vic-Wells Ballet in 1935, the years Ashton spent with Rambert were happy ones and he recognised that she was the one who had instilled confidence in him and launched him on his career, commenting that

> Her tremendous energy was both inspiring and an irritant: together we managed to produce many works. Her great sense of humour... and her wide culture, past-associations, and her incredible memory... together with her great critical qualities and resourcefulness; all these were wonderful standbys when there was no money and not much else.[81]

Ninette de Valois

As noted earlier, de Valois began her dancing lessons with Mrs Wordsworth and at the age of twelve, entered the Lila Field Academy, a general theatre school, where she was singled out to specialise in ballet.[82] She does not describe the training she received at the Field Academy nor the classes she took from Madame Rosa, a celebrated Italian teacher whom she encountered in 1914 at the Lyceum Theatre, when performing there in pantomime.[83] Her first 'serious' training began with Espinosa, whom she saw three times a week for two half-hour sessions and one longer class. Out of her weekly salary of £5, she paid him one guinea, an exorbitant amount in relation to her earnings.[84] She claims that his classes were fast, focusing on *terre à terre* work, which eventually strengthened and saved her feet. But when Espinosa left to tour South Africa in 1920, she joined Cecchetti, who had opened a studio in London.

Without a doubt, Cecchetti helped her technique and strengthened her dancing, yet she is strangely ambivalent about his approach. She found it a useful method to study for a short time but believed it to be too autocratic 'as taught in the days of the Maestro', too heavy in general, but valuable to choreographers, possibly because of Cecchetti's inventive and complicated *enchaînements*.[85] Questions must also arise concerning his musicality because of his practice of 'whistl[ing] his way through class... with a fixed tune for each particular step or exercise, [a] tune [that] was whistled week in and week out'.[86] De Valois found this tedious and in later years, banned those particular melodies in class.[87] Despite her reservations, she was praising of some of his material, claiming that she learnt about the meaning of symmetry and the harmony and meaning that can be achieved in the *port de bras*.[88] Tellingly, her remark, that the choreography of Léonide Massine is really only understandable with a Cecchetti training, is significant for Ashton's work, since his first lessons were with Massine.

After Cecchetti left London in 1922, de Valois benefited from working with Legat. She found initially that his classes made her stiff and tired, which she believed to be the result of her three years with Cecchetti's repetitious classes; the same sets of exercises were repeated weekly and created a habitual way of moving. Legat taught her to expand her movement, making it more fluid and relaxed. She names two other teachers from whom she benefited: Nijinska and Olga Preobrajenska. From the former she learnt to breathe easily but it was the latter's classes that she found to be the most useful overall in strengthening her technique; unfortunately she does not reveal how.[89]

Like other dancers of her time, for the first eighteen years of her life, arguably the most formative years, her training came from an eclectic mix of teachers and as she rightly points out, it is impossible to change one's earliest training, the 'deep-rooted, fundamental approach' which ties 'your body by force of habit and development', though it is of course possible to eliminate weaknesses caused by the earlier training.[90] But the habitual stylistic aspects of the training persist.

De Valois opened her *School for Choregraphic Art* (sic) in 1926 (becoming the Sadler's Wells School in 1930/1). It advertised itself as teaching the Cecchetti method but as Kathrine Sorley Walker observed the School was never in fact confined to one system. Because de Valois frequently changed her mind about training, it is not possible to establish exactly what she was teaching in 1926, in terms of the *danse d'école*. If her aim was to establish an English School distinct from that of the Russians, French and Italians, it was not to ignore the best features of these. She drew from each taking what was most useful for the establishment of a distinctly English style.[91] But she also believed that the ballet dancer should not be confined to one genre and her curriculum included traditional mime, taught by Madame Zanfretta, character dancing taught by de Moroda and Plastique which May believed was a form of Dalcroze eurhythmics used to encourage her pupils to choreograph. She does not seem to have regarded the ballet class as an inspirational basis.[92] Her pupils had also to become knowledgeable about design: Vladimir and Elizabeth Polunin taught stage craft, also with a view to encouraging choreographers.[93] De Valois, keen to find a specifically English traditional dance, was in touch with the Cecil Sharp House, where she learnt of a particular Morris dance which women were permitted to perform and which she performed as a solo from time to time.[94] She wanted her English school of ballet to be drawn from English traditional dancing roots, although, she also conceded that the

> style and type of country will come out mainly in our choreographers. And we've got to back their work with the 'stiffest' technique we can find from everywhere, moulding in to our natural movements and roots.[95]

Was she in fact shaping the training to suit the demands of all choreographers or merely her own?

Despite admiring Legat's training and Cecchetti's pedagogic skills, de Valois always remained loyal to Espinosa. She suggests that not only had he significantly influenced her dancing, he had also informed her approach to training. Both his teaching of the balletic poses, like the *attitude* and the *arabesque*, and his approach to footwork contributed to the style of the English School. The training which emerged from the Sadler's Wells School from this early period was finally crystallised and documented in 1950. Covering an extensive range of steps, the syllabus had an emphasis on *terre à terre* work and *petit batterie*. The *enchaînements* usually comprised four different steps and they demand rapid alterations in weight and change of spatial orientation from movement to movement. For instance, an *enchaînement* involving *jeté en tournant* at 90 degrees is followed by an *assemblé* and *sissonne en tournant* and the whole is repeated.[96] This sequence sends the dancer whirling into space but she has to sharply adjust to the full stop of the *assemblé* before turning again. When teaching these movements de Valois drew attention to the contrasting elements of each movement, to spatial orientation and to the dynamic emphasis of the whole *enchaînement*.

Much of the teaching in her school was devoted to developing the leg from the knee down and to producing strong feet. But the strength of the school lay in the fact that she did not establish, in written form, a strictly codified notion of each step. This meant that the teaching retained flexibility and was able to change and adapt to the choreography of the day. These classes seem primarily to have been designed to suit her own needs and those of Ashton, since both choreographers demand rapid alterations in direction and weight and an ability to articulate the feet.

As well as establishing an English School of technical training, she wished to link English choreography with the dramatic theatre, in order to generate 'a revival of the more dramatic form of ballet... [through creating] a sound body technique of expressive movement'.[97] All her own ballets are dramatic and, as Beth Genné notes, de Valois saw her company as an integral part of the repertory theatre movement.[98] That she made no plotless works is hardly surprising; that she was dismissing of ballets that had no dramatic content is more so. She had no respect for or faith in plotless works believing that

> the fundamental business of the theatre is to portray a state of make-believe. It is mainly a fantastic representation of the realities of life through dramatic rendering. The major channels most commonly used are the play, the opera, and the ballet and their derivations.[99]

The notion of abstract ballet is, she argues, misconceived and the cry for 'a purely abstract rendering... divorced from a literary source [is] inconsistent'.[100]

The solo from *The Rake's Progress* (1935) made for Markova embraces many of de Valois' principles and demonstrates how her training and choreography were linked and thus in its dance movement style bears some relation to Ashton. While her choreography is quite different from that of Ashton, the skills needed to perform it are, to a large extent, similar. For this reason it is worth looking briefly at one of her dances. Unlike Ashton, she was not influenced by the abilities or qualities of the dancer; she simply expected them to reproduce her choreography. When asked whether she ever changed anything for a dancer, she responded with an emphatic 'no', adding that, if forced to do so, she would have been most upset.[101] She made no secret of the disdain she felt for choreographers who depended on their dancers for inspiration because she believed that ballets using dancers for inspiration would date.

The Betrayed Girl's solo in Scene V of *Rake* highlights the dramatic elements of the Girl's predicament and draws covertly on English traditional dance. As it is performed in front of a drop curtain, the stage space limits the use of motion from one side to the other: the dance speeds rapidly back and forth between the two sets of wings, reinforcing the Girl's dilemma. The movement too reflects her difficulties; it is grounded and tortuous, using a limited vocabulary. Dominated by a toe-stabbing motif which develops into a series of toe-heel actions, the lower body is confined to sharp movements which pierce the floor with strong pointes. The Girl steps on to pointe, though it is more of a trudge than a step, and remains on pointe as she performs *pliés* and *glissades* without ever returning to the flat. Complimenting the lower body, the arms and hands gesture despairingly upwards, sideways and towards the back with clenched fists and drooping head. This expressive gesture, derived from conventional gesture, is a major element of the dance. And, as observers, our focus is drawn towards these features. The solo is thus strongly dramatic and connects the ballet with the expressionist drama of the period. The dancer needs strong secure pointe work for this solo and, because she stands mainly on one leg, a firm central core is also essential.

Having these technical abilities is at the heart of de Valois' values and her teaching and classes developed both of these: a firm body core and strong footwork.[102] These, together with an ability to alter both weight and direction quickly, are characteristic of the dancers of the era and the teaching in the schools of both de Valois and Rambert encouraged these skills. Since this was the raw material from which Ashton drew inspiration, these abilities and the qualities associated with that kind of dancing body form a significant element of his style.

Both of these women influenced Ashton and the dancers they produced affected his style. But perhaps the most telling difference between the attitudes and approach of the two women is reflected in their comments about Ashton's musicality. Rambert points out that:

> Although he had no technique yet, he had unfailing grace even when he was making mistakes in movement. He found it very difficult to copy my *enchaînements*... to music, though he was genuinely musical. Later I realised that as he was himself creative, the music probably suggested to him subconsciously much more beautiful *enchaînements* than the purely educational ones which I combined.[103]

De Valois, however, had a very different perspective finding him deaf to the music:

> There was never as much as a hint of lethargy about his dancing. When young, his weakness lay in a difficulty in keeping time with the music – and the clock. Eagerness and intense nervous energy (his natural reaction to movement) made him deaf to sound; one would hold on to him grimly and at the same time experience something of the trouble encountered by anyone involved in the capture of a Dartmoor pony.[104]

Plainly, the values of the two women were different but both played a role in

Ashton's development as a choreographer. De Valois' emphasis on creating a technical style affected that of Ashton and it is probably safe to assume that she consciously arranged her training to suit his choreography.

Influences on Ashton: Choreographers

Bronislava Nijinska and Marius Petipa

> The thing that a choreographer really needs is an eye. He has to do his training through an eye... if someone has the desire to express himself in this way he should work under other choreographers... just like the students did with Michelangelo and Raphael. I think that I learned to be a choreographer through watching other choreographers at work. And Nijinska in particular, helped me tremendously. I never took my eyes off her when I was with Rubinstein... I used to sit in the corner all day long, just watching her.[105]

Ashton paid tribute to Nijinska throughout his life. He once observed that everything he learnt came from her and although he never imitated her, except perhaps in his first ballet, *A Tragedy of Fashion* (1926), both his movement style and choreographic style owe much to her work.[106] Ashton had seen Nijinska's works with the Ballets Russes during the mid 1920s but only began working with her when he joined Rubinstein's Company in 1928. He spent almost a year there and danced in virtually all the ballets she created at that time. Traces of her movement theories, dance movement style, class work and choreography can be found throughout his dances; this becomes clear in the chapters which follow. His debt to her was repaid when he brought two of her most lauded works into the repertory of the Royal Ballet: first *Les biches* in 1964 and then *Les noces* in 1966. Not only did this return Nijinska's work to mainstream dance theatre, it also revived interest in her choreography as a whole.

Ashton learnt much from Nijinska's classes and during his year with Rubinstein, Nijinska gave the company class. As he noted, these were more like choreography classes.[107] She probably based these on the theories she had developed for her Ecole de Mouvement. Her principles and attitude to dance movement and choreography can be found in an essay written by her and reproduced in Nancy Van Norman Baer's catalogue (1986).[108] Focusing on the relationship between the classroom training and choreography, Nijinska argues that when new choreography emerges, the classroom training should be altered to accommodate the new movement. In essence, her arguments concern the education and training of dancers, who are so conditioned by their training that all they are able to do is to replicate it, despite the needs of the choreography. Dancers still training in the 'old' school, she complains, 'know how to force their bodies into [the new] *pas* and even to link them into a series but the quality of their movement does not correspond in the least to contemporary dance technique'.[109] Nothing is allowed 'to affect the quality of movement of these mechanical *pas*'.[110] The dancers turn everything into what they can already do and consequently 'falsely transmit the choreographic score, utterly destroying the particularity of the work'.[111] Nijinska believed that the classroom training, based on the *danse d'école* and unchanged since Petipa's time, was detrimental to the dancer because it omitted motion, encouraging the dancer to strike one pose after another. She observed that in Petipa's time his interpretations of the steps were the material the dancers had learned in the school and she advocates that the *danse d'école* should adapt itself to the needs of the contemporary choreographer, just as it had during Petipa's reign. Her criticism seems to be aimed at the Ballets Russes, but probably too the Russian Imperial Ballet, neither of whose primary aim was to support classroom innovation. She did not accept that a single system of training provides the dancer with all the skills needed and believed that training is something that should continually change and adapt to new demands. Her classes, as a result, were designed specifically to prepare dancers for her own choreography.

Supporting these principles in her choreographed dance movement, Nijinska created continuous strands of steps so that the dancer has no time to rest from one to the next. Poses and positions are not central and when they do occur, as in *Les noces* (1923), they are for a specific reason, creating tableaux to help reinforce the ritualistic aspects of the marriage of the Bride. They comprise angular shapes, flexed feet and broken *arabesques* in which the arms, bent and curved, cut off the line. Ashton understood her emphasis on motion, commenting in later life that he had inherited her wonderful sense of movement.[112] Both *Les noces* and *Les biches* amply illustrate Nijinska's main tenets; the phrases have continuous strands, stopping the dancer from emphasising the positions. So there are no 'dead and unconscious space[s]' that lack plasticity.[113] Generating the actions from the torso also prevents this and creates the sense of motion. As Georgina Parkinson put it, 'You can't just arrive at a position, you have to get there'.[114] As Parkinson found to her cost, Nijinska removed preparations from jumps and turns and while this adds to the momentum, it also forces the dancer to the limits:

> what she really enforced from our technique was movement. She made me understand what dancing was all about… it was something that Sir Fred had tried to make us understand but we didn't quite and it was only when Bronislava came and taught us *Les biches* that we realised what breathing

was and what actual body movement was. So much had been said about it, but we had to pick this out of her.[115]

Ashton believed that her classes were based on Cecchetti, at least in part, though this is unlikely and, in any case, Ashton's knowledge of Cecchetti was limited, having only encountered a version filtered through Rambert.[116] Nijinska's classes are more likely to have come from her theories developed before she re-joined the Ballets Russes in 1921 and, as previously mentioned, the class movement was designed to support her own work. Nijinska took a great interest in Ashton believing that he had an excellent understanding of choreographed movement. At the time he danced for her, though, he lacked a solid technique.

> He was not completely ready for classical dancing, but in character dances he was among the best. He stood out by his exact rendering of style and his flawless accuracy in the details of my choreography, Ashton did not dance solo parts when he was with the Ballets Ida Rubinstein but he knew how to render individual what he did in ensembles.[117]

Most of our knowledge of Nijinska's movement style comes from the dancers who were taught by her and through her choreography of which *Les noces* (1923) and *Les biches* (1924) are the most performed examples. Although their choreography is quite different from each other, there is much that links the movement style. In both works the *pas de bourrée* is a major motif, repeated in a variety of different ways: on pointe, on demi-pointe, with parallel feet and with long strides. For the ensemble and soloists, the arms are generally fixed, either with the clenched fists placed next to the cheek or held by the side of the body, as in *Les noces*, or on the shoulders, or with palms pressed against the cheek, as in *Les biches*. Restricting the use of the arms means that the dancer is forced to generate the movement from the torso – the limbs cannot help. A phrase of movement from the opening of *Les biches* illustrates the point. A single woman performs a series of turns across the front of the stage (SR to SL) to end with an open *chassé* to *arabesque temps levé*. The impetus for the *chassé* comes not from the working leg but from the torso with the shoulder thrust forward and upwards. This creates a series of different body transitions in a single jump and is typical of the way Nijinska introduces multiple *épaulement* in a single action. As the curtain rises, the dancer seems to explode into this effervescent phrase, which sets the tone for the ballet.

Introduced at the start, the fixed arm position continues in different ways throughout the whole work. At one point in the dance, the group of women perform a *bourrée couru* in which the shoulder leads; the arm is bent at the elbow, with the hand resting on the shoulder. The fixed position of the arms of the Garçonne, one at the side of her body, the other one bent with the palm placed against her cheek, is something which Ashton picked up on, though he used it slightly differently. For example, in the Friends' dance in scene I of *Persephone* (1961), both arms are placed by the side of the body. And in other dances he restricts the arms, so that there is a need for more activity in the torso. For example, the women in the hunt in *Sylvia*, Act I, hold bows throughout that dance. This proved to be particularly difficult, even uncomfortable, for the current dancers in the revival of that work in 2004.

Les biches is a highly accomplished work, so beautifully crafted that it could act as teaching aid for choreography. But the real marvel of the work is the simplicity of its motifs. Walks become swaggers, delicate steps, stomps, struts, and little runs as in the Hostess' dance. And the *bourrée couru* is stretched, rushed, shortened and used to taunt and ridicule the three men. She wanted the dancers to communicate through the movement and not through the dancers' own emotional feelings. Her choreography forced the dancer to move in a certain way and, as a result, communicate the expressive elements to the observer, without adding fake facial expressions. Maria Tallchief puts it succinctly when discussing Nijinska's *Etude*: 'there was no great emotion in it, but it was very emotional because of the demands on our breathing and the way we held our torsos'.[118]

Nijinska's approach to movement is very different from that of today. She emphasised a continuous flow of movement, whereas today priority is given to positions and shape. If anything, we have eliminated the sense of motion from the classroom.[119] The shoulders, upper back and pelvis play a much greater role in Nijinska's movement, than today's training allows, with force coming from the pelvis. Her attitude to space is also different. Nowadays, in the classroom, students are taught to move the arms peripherally, going directly to a position but in Nijinska's dances the focus of the arms is more flexible; the limbs form curved and zig-zag lines around the body. The arms are treated not as separate entities but as part of the torso and are rarely used simply to frame or elongate it. In *Les biches*, the arms move centrally, advancing close to and up and down the body rather than peripherally. This diverts attention to the upper body and away from the feet. Nijinska's positions are more curved and convoluted as opposed to the symmetrical poses of the classroom. Ashton's approach to dance movement is similar in principle to that of Nijinska and it is evident that he used her work as a model for his choreography.

Although having a private lesson is how Ashton described watching *The Sleeping Beauty*, it was not until the 1940s with *Scènes de ballet* (1948) that there is any evidence of a link with Petipa.[120] Ashton regarded Petipa's choreographic craft as supreme and *Scènes* has some obvious references, such as the geometric patterns made by the corps de ballet and of course the 'Rose Adagio' quintet for the four men and the Ballerina. In his book, Vaughan identified most of the Petipa references but whereas aspects of Petipa's structure are evident in some works, there is little that reflects his dance movement. In Chapter IV I consider more fully Petipa's influence because in *Birthday Offering*, Ashton consciously paid homage to him. The opening ensemble for the seven couples seems to have been based on the prologue in *The Sleeping Beauty* and the variations for the women, although quite different in terms of their movement choices and arrangement, hint at the dances for the Fairies. Of the other works I deal with, there is less evidence of Petipa's influence.

Buddy Bradley

Surprisingly, the other choreographer whose dance movement can be detected in Ashton's work is that of Buddy Bradley, who met and worked with Ashton during the early 1930s. Bradley, an African American dancer, arrived in London in 1930 to choreograph the dances for *Evergreen* and this was so successful that he was asked to collaborate with Balanchine for a Cochran revue the following year. Constance Valis Hill, who has written on Bradley's choreography, notes that they shared the same dancers, with Bradley making twenty nine numbers and Balanchine just two.[121] This pattern continued when Ashton began working for Cochran the following year. Tantalisingly, Ashton's choreography for the revues and shows in the commercial theatre is unavailable. Yet his work for these stage shows was substantial and aspects of it have crept into his ballets. He made dances for 19 revues and musical shows during the 1930s – short ballets often danced by what the programme describes as 'C.B. Cochran's Girls', with Ashton and dancers from the Ballet Club. He also made dances which can be described as 'stage dancing', in works like *Magic Nights* (1932) which included a rumba and a tango, in *Nursery Murmurs* (1933), *Jill Darling* (1934). *Round About Regent Street* (1935) and *Home and Beauty* (1936). Though not called musical theatre, these works have a close relationship with that genre.

The jazz craze had already captivated Paris in the 1920s with many European choreographers creating jazz ballets (Massine, *Crescendo*, 1925, Nijinska, *Jazz*, 1925, Jean Borlin, *La création du monde*, 1923, amongst others). Though as Valis Hill argues, because the jazz elements were interpreted through non-American eyes, the dances demonstrated little understanding of real American vernacular dance. What she means by this is the dance created in uptown New York by African American tap dancers who invented intricate movements with complicated rhythms. Their dancing was different from the simpler steps of the white performers in Broadway musicals.

With the exception of the *Foxtrot* (1940) from *Façade* (1931) which has obvious references to stage dancing, such as the exit step at the end of that dance and the high backward kick when all four dancers move in a semi-circle upstage, there is no other concrete evidence that Ashton put actual stage dancing in his ballets.[122] Yet, just as he infused his dances with the characteristics of Pavlova, Duncan and Nijinska, so too are the qualities and features of stage dancing present in his works. He coaxed his dancers to create a relaxed, easy upper body, particularly evident in the dances he made during the 1930s, and he encouraged a kind of Fred Astaire-like attitude to the movement. It is more important in an Ashton dance to perform it like Astaire did by showing the dance rather than showing the dancer. On a number of occasions, Fonteyn stresses the importance of relaxation. When coaching the Bride's variation from *Le baiser de la fée* (1935), she insists that the dance 'mustn't [appear to] be hard work' and that attention must be deflected away from the technical elements.[123] An unrestrained backbend is evident in *Apparitions* (1936) in a series of lunges into fourth position, combined with a low backbend.

Bradley worked with Ashton on six works between 1932 and 1937 and it was as a result of their first collaboration, *Magic Nights*, in which Ashton performed in one of Bradley's tap routines, that Ashton invited him to collaborate on a Camargo Society production. *High Yellow* (1932) had music by the English jazz composer Spike Hughes and although Vaughan indicates that Bradley choreographed most of the movement, he believes that Ashton shaped the piece as a whole.[124]

Bradley's specific talent was for arranging new foot-tailored routines for star performers. Notable aspects of Bradley's dance style are the polyrhythmic effects. The head, shoulders and feet move in different rhythms and this is evident in some of the numbers in the film *Evergreen* (1934) also choreographed by Bradley. There are other moments when a plastic fluidity in the torso contrasts with the sharper, faster rhythm of the feet. Throughout Ashton's choreography there is evidence of polyrhythmic movement and of low, grounded movement in which the lower half of the body is heavily weighted. The group dances in *La valse* (1958) are a good example. in *Cinderella* (1948) he clearly refers to some of Jessie Matthews' steps in *Evergreen* in his own dances as the Ugly Sister. In the film Matthews executes a high, sideways kick in which the torso bends slightly at the waist and the shoulder is raised to accentuate and allow for a very high kick. Ashton, as the timid Ugly Sister, imitates this several times with the same torso and shoulder movement, but because the kick is low, though the bodily exertion is similar, the movement appears comic. The pelvis coiling, snake-hips movement, derived from Earl Tucker and used by Bradley in *Evergreen*, also found its way into several Ashton dances, including *Four Saints in Three Acts* (1934), Walter Gore's dances in *Les masques* (1933) and the Foxtrot in *Façade*. But it is also there in *Daphnis and Chloe* (1951) when Chloe, from a fifth position on *pointe*, makes a *plié* on *pointe* and performs the snake hips movement simultaneously.

Ashton's acute eye for movement probably led him to use some of the stylistic aspects of Bradley's dances. The loose plasticity of the upper body, a centring of the weight in the pelvis area and the apparently relaxed approach to movement are all evident in Ashton's dances and are likely to have been the result of the many revues he worked on with Bradley. Though not generally collaborating, Ashton allowed some of Bradley's choreography and dance movement to seep into his own work. He admired Bradley and that influence plays a small though not insignificant role in Ashton's style.

Influences on Ashton: Dancers

Anna Pavlova

That Anna Pavlova was Ashton's ideal is well known but that he also drew extensively on his knowledge of other dancers, particularly, Karsavina and Duncan, is recognised but less frequently discussed. Ashton was propelled into dance after watching Pavlova perform in Peru, where he lived until the age of 14. He particularly admired her theatricality and ability to mesmerise an audience. It is almost impossible to understand now the experience of seeing Pavlova dance but those who saw her remembered a 'melancholy sentiment of unforgotten loveliness, bygone moments of delight'.[125] And her technique was impalpable, 'like air in motion; it is fluid as water; as swift as fire'.[126] It was for her 'a means to an end, so successfully achieved that... few are the initiated in choreography who would be able to discern the technical elements in Pavlova's dancing'.[127] Her attraction came purely through her dancing since she rarely created new choreography and as Ashton observed, she 'just danced to teashop music'.[128]

For Ashton she was undoubtedly 'the greatest theatrical genius he had ever seen' and despite having, what he oddly described as a poor technique, through her theatricality, she gave the impression of being significantly more accomplished than she was.[129] This ability to enchant an audience is not easily analysed from the scraps of film that exist but certain features do emerge and it is these which Ashton seems instinctively to have admired and incorporated into his dance movement style. Ashton, in conversation with Natalia Makarova, talks about her magnetic qualities, describing her vibrancy and theatricality. He remembered that before she emerged, a 'spotlight trembled across the stage and hovered until she appeared' and this theatricality was carried into her everyday life. Ashton mentioned how she emerged from the stage door to her waiting car; standing for the applause, she pulled apart her bouquet of flowers and threw handfuls to the crowd of admirers. Ashton's dances are supremely theatrical and he must have learnt this aspect of his craft from Pavlova.

Pavlova made a series of films in Hollywood in 1924, of which there are only fragments left, and while it is difficult to get a real impression of her dancing, they do give some idea of her theatricality and of the abandonment with which she moved. *Le cygne* (1907), also known as *The Dying Swan*, the dance with which she is most associated, provides a good example of her movement qualities. When compared with other dancers, such as Maya Plisetskaya and Galina Ulanova, it conveys a mysteriousness which is absent from their performances.[130] Most evident from the filmed material, particularly in *Le cygne*, are the speed and fluidity of her *bourrées*. Her movement radiates outwards with a sense that the movement flows from the *bourrées* into her body and exits through her fingertips into the space. Her feet are not turned-out but this is irrelevant since her feet are fast and furious, yet appear to glide. Her arms do not seem to be separate from her body and their flexibility, extending through to the hands, makes them seem like limp, broken wings. The dancing of Plisetskaya and Ulanova, however expansive and technically accomplished, is controlled, even when they kneel, and it just does not have the expressive, even expressionist, qualities of Pavlova. She never kneels but falls, even collapses, as she ends the dance. The final *port de bras* is generated from the middle of her body and although controlled, she conceals this. Few would describe her as expressionist, and most of her work is not, but if expressionism is partially about revealing the inner condition of the subject's mind, then in *Le cygne*, she conveys it.

Another feature of her dancing is the continual sense of movement; she is rarely still. This may be because her dances involve long threads of movement rather than short phrases. She only just achieves a position before she moves on. There is an extravagance in her dances, a sort of indulgent quality, which creates the sense of abandonment. This sense appears again in a solo described as *Night after Music*.[131] The dance is made up of running, *bourrées* and several *grandes jetés en tournant*. The *grandes jetés* end in a backwards/ sideways bend on the knee but because of the violence of the flow, which projects into the ground, a sense of total freedom is created. This aesthetic is quite different from that of today: Pavlova's limbs are more abandoned than placed and she has a gift for resisting control or at least this is how it seems.

Beaumont described her dancing as having vitality, luminosity and incandescence but he found that her feet surpass those of most dancers.[132] Both he and de Valois praise her superb feet 'with highly arched insteps, delicately wrought as a cast-iron piece of tracery'.[133] Ashton too was enthralled by her feet and loved the way in which she drew attention to them, showing off their delicacy and power. Whenever Ashton worked with dancers whose feet he admired, he made fleeting, rapid *bourrées* and movements which highlight the feet whenever possible.

Ashton's dislike of stiff dancers probably derives from his passion for Pavolva. He associated stiffness with lack of plasticity and immobile shoulders. Pavlova's fluidity seemed to circulate through her whole body and not merely from her arms and hands. This meant that she was totally committed to the movement as opposed to the steps. As Ashton observed:

> She was a rule unto herself, she didn't bother about turning out or any of those things and she had... wonderful nobility of stance... that I haven't seen equalled in anybody.[134]

Ashton was also, at times, a rule unto himself and was less concerned about the actual step, if performing it according to the syllabus impinged on his dances. He was insistent that expressiveness should take precedence over technical achievement. As he put it 'You must use your technique in order to help you with your feelings not to smother them'.[135] As I explore Ashton's choreography in the following chapters, it becomes apparent that his tribute to Pavlova's dancing was constant, colouring almost every aspect of the dance movement. These are found in the actions of the arms which originate in the centre of the back, sequences which articulate the feet, rapid actions and references to the steps she most frequently used, particularly the *bourrée*. The phrase known as the 'Fred step' comes from her *Gavotte Pavlova* (1913) and acts, like Whistler's butterfly, as Ashton's signature.[136] It occurs in almost all of his ballets, from *Les masques* (1933) onwards and was both a tribute to her and acknowledgement of her role as one of Ashton's muses.

Tamara Karsavina

Few useful descriptions of Karsavina's dancing exist but, as Nijinsky's partner, she must have had equally striking qualities and comparable technical abilities. She performed as leading dancer in the majority of Fokine's ballets and as one of the two women in Nijinsky's *Jeux* (1913). Most who have written about her praise her looks and beautiful eyes and according to Peter Lieven, she 'developed into a ballerina of the first magnitude, technically perfect and a true dramatic artist'.[137] The short extract of film that does exist shows her exceptionally light jump, in which she appears to soar.

Karsavina's conception of dance was as much intellectual as it was physical. She demonstrated that most of the assumptions made about dancers' intellectual abilities were false, writing copious articles about dance and technique throughout her life. Her articles on technique, written between 1920 and the late 1960s, give some notion of her attitude to dance as does the Karsavina Class held by the Royal Academy of Dance, devised by her in 1954. It is a synthesis of her own dance training background, stretching back to her days in the Russian Imperial Ballet School and suggests that one of the most important qualities acquired there was *ballon.* This was attained through understanding the difference between a 'soft and a sharp take-off'.[138] Writing in the 1930s she gives priority to expression over classroom movement, explaining how differently the arms and legs can and should be used in a ballet like *Giselle* (1841).[139] Later, in 1953 she returns to the problem caused by interpreting the dances in *Giselle* without understanding the expressive requirements of that work. She complains that the dancers of the 1950s lack understanding of contrast, of being able to highlight one movement at the expense of another. What is needed is more emphasis on some steps at the expense of others, more clearly defined *épaulement* and a greater breadth of movement.[140] And when discussing technique in general, she writes:

> that before one begins to memorise [the breakdown of] a given enchaînement, one should visualise it first in line and movement. In other words, one should try to grasp the spirit of the movement and the pose. A perfect dance is an animated drawing in space. [141]

How this should be achieved is not clear but the spirit of what she is communicating is that expressiveness should take priority over technique, but this has nothing to do with the dancer's personal feeling.

Her advice and coaching inspired Ashton and her effect on him is most strongly revealed in his own comments. He first met and danced with Karsavina at the Ballet Club in 1930 and in an article written in 1954, he describes how informative that had been. 'We watched her every movement, admired her discipline, her exquisite manners, her humility and her approach to the public'.[142] But most of all he learnt from dancing with her, partnering her in *Les sylphides* and in several other works, including some of her own choreography. Writing of this experience, he remembers her patience and encouragement and her help with his technical problems. 'These were days of inspiration and absorption on my part, and the knowledge I acquired of the real meaning of dancing was invaluable for my future work'.[143] When later he danced the waltz from *Sylphides* with Pamela May, he encouraged her to imitate Karsavina, forcing her to balance without his support; the only assistance he gave was to take the tips of her fingers very lightly to create the appearance of weightlessness.[144] According to Fonteyn, he 'adored Karsavina as much or more [than Pavlova]', coaxing her to copy Karsavina's dignity, her command of the stage and the way in which she used her eyes.[145]

While Pavlova's influence is relatively clear in Ashton's dances, it is more difficult to discern that of Karsavina. In addition to the attention he paid to the use of the eyes, it is possible that some of the arm movements in his

ballets were also taken from Karsavina. She taught him the mime for Act II of
La fille mal gardée (1960) and it is likely that gesture, and his use of it,
throughout most of his other works, was also gleaned from her. But perhaps
the most lasting element was his knowledge of style. Working with her in
Sylphides was formative, not only did she help him with partnering but she
also instructed him in Fokine's style. Dancing in the Royal Ballet's production of *Sylphides*, I was struck by the care Ashton took with it, even for the
corps de ballet. In fact he thought it so important that he frequently brought
in Serge Grigoriev, Diaghilev's ballet master and the dancer, Liubov
Tchernicheva, Grigoriev's wife, to coach us.

Isadora Duncan

The other dancer Ashton admired was Isadora Duncan, whom he found
'very considerable... as an artist and as a dancer'. He loved her 'enormous
grace', her power and quality of repose. She had an ability to cover the stage
and a wonderful way of running, in which she made you believe that she had
'left herself behind, and you felt the breeze was running through her hair
and every thing else'.[146] When he agreed to choreograph the first of the *Five
Brahms Waltzes in the Manner of Isadora Duncan* (1975), simply called
Brahms-Waltz, he explained to Lynn Seymour, who danced it, that he would
not recreate Duncan's choreography, rather, he would aim to 'emulate the
atmosphere she exuded, the aura she spun and the innovation that so captured and enthralled her followers'.[147] And it was these aspects of Duncan
that he also brought into his dances, seen most clearly in sequences dominated by running. For example, there are long threads of stage-covering
running in *Symphonic Variations* (1946), in *Monotones II* (1965) in *Scènes de
ballet* (1948) and in Beliaev's first solo in *A Month in the Country* (1976).
Natasha's sudden slump at the beginning of the duet with Beliaev in the
same ballet, as danced by Seymour, also has that feeling of abandon, of giving in to gravity and in the context of the ballet to the inevitable.

As with Pavlova, Duncan too had a theatricality and Ashton loved it.
Seymour describes how when he came to choreograph the next four dances,
his fascination for Duncan came through. It was

> our great good fortune for it provided us with endless inspiration and in-
> formation. Fred would also regale me with his memories of Isadora's one
> woman show... She would frequently break off mid-performance to chat
> with the audience... and once the music was (sic) begun she would inspire,
> extemporise and, as Fred said, 'squeeze your heart' with the purest ges-
> ture or simplest turn of the head.[148]

Ashton's choreography did not duplicate what these dancers had done but it
was saturated with memories of their movement, their theatricality and, in

the case of Pavlova and Duncan, their apparent abandonment. These elements have become part of its style infusing both the movement and the choreography, a point I return to in later chapters.

Influences: Ashton's Dialogue with the Past

Classroom styles, choreographers and dancers were all part of Ashton's heritage and all find their way into his choreography. Ashton knew that he was drawing on all of these but he pulled them together, moulding them to become Ashton style. To understand this style and allow for its specificities, it helps to identify the various elements that contribute to the overall dance movement. From the classroom, Ashton used the short *enchaînements* of the Cecchetti style. These demand simultaneous actions of the limbs, torso and head as well as multi-directional floor patterns. Dancers used to moving like this adapt easily to the short intricate phrases of movement that also require the ability to make rapid changes of direction. From Nijinska, he learned the importance of motion, achieved through torso initiated movement, and phrases in which transitions between steps are fluid and frequently concealed. This aspect of mobility appeared too in the dance movement of both Pavlova and Duncan but he also made use of their theatricality and their skill with dynamic, creating light and shade. Ashton absorbed all of this, suffusing his dances with these elements. What their presence shows is the difference between Ashton's dance movement and that of the *danse d'école*, even if some of the conventions and values of the classroom are evident in the style.

Moving on to the ballets, discussed in the following chapters, there is the presence of more collaborators. Some were genuine collaborators, present and in discussion with Ashton, others were long since dead. With the latter, they are part of the work because Ashton chose them, distilling the meaning to suit his choreography. How we interpret the ballets will vary and depends on our knowledge and theoretical stance. This does not mean that there are indefinite meanings but that within the boundaries outlined in Chapter I, there are several meanings.

In looking at the works in the following chapters, I try to show that not only are these multi-authored dances but that they are also susceptible to change, though not any change. Acknowledging this reveals different and new insights. Just as the dance movement comprises a range of sources, so do the works themselves. Ashton himself rarely attributed definite meanings or styles to the works, suggesting that meaning lay with audiences.

> If people can receive different impressions from the same series of movements and all enjoy them in their different ways, why should I need to pin them down to one interpretation by saying I meant such and such?[149]

Ashton's works are made up of multiple sources, drawn from different genres. He does not see himself as the overall authority and this leaves the question of meaning open. I hope to show in the following chapters that Ashton's work is not merely classical ballet, but also has a definite style which, if ignored, could result in the loss of the dances. It is also less conventional than is sometimes suggested and as much part of the contemporary dance world as works being made today. The painter Nicolas Poussin understood the meaning of innovation and how it depends on form as much as subject matter:

> Novelty in painting does not consist above all in choosing a subject that has never been seen before but upon a good and novel arrangement and expression, thanks to which the subject, though in itself ordinary and worn becomes new and singular.[150]

There is a significant time lapse between Poussin and Ashton but they were both intent on making new art works, using a formal style as a basis, and both drew on the past for inspiration.

1. Carter, Alexandra (2005) 'London 1908: A Synchronic View of Dance History', Dance Research, 23, no.1, 36-50.

2. I use stage dancing to describe the dance of the commercial theatre. Balanchine too choreographed for the commercial theatre and de Valois for drama.

3. De Valois, Ninette (1937) Invitation to the Dance, London: The Bodley Head and de Valois, Ninette (1977) Step by Step, London: W.H. Allen.

4. I do know of the short extract of film which shows Karsavina practising at the barre but it is too brief to glean much.

5. Guest, Ivor, (1992) Ballet in Leicester Square, London: Dance Books, passim.

6. Guest, Ivor, (1992), 143.

7. Guest, Ivor, (1992), 139.

8. Guest, Ivor (1992), 131.

9. Bedells, Phyllis (1954) My Dancing Days, London: Phoenix House, 10.

10. Buckland, Theresa (2011) 76.

11. Bedells, Phyllis (1954) 33.

12. Buckland Theresa (2011) Society Dancing: Fashionable Bodies in England 1870-1920, London: Palgrave, 76.

13. De Valois, Ninette (1957) Come Dance With Me, London: Hamish Hamilton, 28

14. Ripman, Olive (1974) 'Wordy', Dancing Times, LXIV, no. 766, July, 581.

15. Edwards, Leslie (2003) In Good Company, London: Dance Books.

16. Buckland (2007) 'Crompton's Campaign: The Professionalisation of Dance Pedagogy in Late Victorian England', Dance Research, 25, no. 1, 22.

17. Ripman, Olive (1974) 'Wordy', Dancing Times, LXIV, no. 766, July, 581.

18. De Valois, Ninette (1957) Come Dance With Me, London: Hamish Hamilton, 29.

19. Their training was not wholly with these teachers as the autobiographies of Sokolova and de Valois make clear but both worked one or more in the early part of their careers.

20. Although the word hubris is not mentioned, his row with the RAD caused many to fall out with him and accuse him of taking the law into his own hands: see Richardson, P.J.S. (1950) 'Espinosa', Dancing Times, no. 476, May, 483-485 and see too Bedells, Phyllis (1954) My Dancing Days, London: Phoenix House, 213.

21. Espinosa (1946), 19.

22. Espinosa (1946) 36.

23. Espinosa (1946), 113.

24. Espinosa (1946), 118.

25. Richardson, Philip (1950) 'Espinosa', Dancing Times, no. 476, May, 483-485

26. Quoted in Parker, Derek (1995) Royal Academy of Dancing: The First Seventy Five Years, London: The Royal Academy of Dancing, 2.

27. Espinosa (1946) 153.

28. De Valois, Ninette (1977) Step By Step, London: W. H. Allen, 11.

29. In Bedells' book (1954), she claims that Cecchetti only charged her a guinea (£1.05) a lesson.

30. Shiraiev was later co-author of a Russian book on character dance.

31. Sokolova, Lydia ed. Buckle, Richard (1960) Dancing For Diaghilev: The Memories of Lydia Sokolova, London: John Murray, 235.

32. Anon, 'Sitter Out', Dancing Times, 53, February (1915) : 184.

33. Anon, 'Sitter Out', Dancing Times, 55, April (1915) : 236.

34. Amongst several English critics such as Haskell (1943) and Richardson (1948).

35. Anon, 'Sitter Out', Dancing Times, 55, April (1915) : 236.

36. It is not clear why de Valois appears not to admire Astafieva but Pamela May in an interview with the author (1999) did indicate that de Valois never allowed any of them, apart from Fonteyn whose mother controlled her, to attend Astafieva's classes.

37. Espinosa, Edouard (1914) 'Attitudes and Arabesques', *Dancing Times*, no.51, December, 76-81.

38. Genée, Adeline (1922) 'Correct Arms', *Dancing Times*, no.139, April, 595-599.

39. Espinosa, Edouard (1916) 'Some Errors in Tuition', *Dancing Times*, no. 73, October, 79-85.

40. Genné, Beth (1982) 'PJS Richardson and The Birth of British Ballet', *Dance History Scholars Proceedings*, Fifth Annual Conference, Harvard University, February, 94-101.

41. Anon, 'Sitter Out', *Dancing Times*, 76, February (1917) : 156-7.

42. Anon, 'Sitter Out', *Dancing Times*, 106, July (1919) : 423.

43. Espinosa, Edouard (1914) ' Attitudes and Arabesques', *Dancing Times*, no. 51, June, 76-81.

44. Anon (2004) *100 Years of Dance: A History of the ISTD Dance Examinations Board*, London: ISTD, 36.

45. Anon, 'Elementary Syllabus', *The Dance Journal*, 1, 3, June (1925): 41-43.

46. Anon, 'Advanced Syllabus', *The Dance Journal*, 1, 9, February (1927): 41.
Anon, 'Children's Syllabuses Grades 1 and 2', *The Dance Journal*, 1, 10, June (1927).

47. While the *Dancing Times* published a series of arm positions posed by Adeline Genée in April 1922, these were posed and the dynamic elements were not detailed or outlined.

48. Beaumont, Cyril. no title but article comments on differences between the Cecchetti method and other schools, *The Dance Journal*, 1, 9, February (1927) : 33.

49. Beaumont, Cyril. 'On examinations in the Cecchetti Syllabus', *The Dance Journal*, 1, 9, February (1927) : 41, 43, 44.

50. Anon, no title, *The Dance Journal*, 1, 11, September (1927) : 29-30.

51. De Valois (1977) 12.

52. Author's interview with May, July 1999.

53. Beaumont, Cyril (1945) *The Diaghilev Ballet in London*, London: C.W. Beaumont, 180.

54. De Valois (1957/81) 45 See too my article (2008) 'Artistry or Mere Technique? The Value of the Ballet Competition', *Research in Dance Education*, 9, no.1, March, 39-54.

55. Bennett, Toby (1998) 'Cecchetti Movement and Repertoire in Performance', *Twenty First Annual Conference*, Oregon: Society of Dance History Scholars, 203-209.

56. Bennett, Toby (1997) 'Cecchetti and the British Tradition', *Dance Now*, 6, no.3, Autumn, 55-59.

57. Both quoted in Bennett, Toby (1998) 206 and 207.

58. See, for example, Kersley, Leo (1993) 'Stanislas Idzikowski', in Bremser, Martha, ed. *International Dictionary of Ballet*, Detroit, London, Washington: Saint James Press, 687-690 and Newman, Barbara (1982) *Striking a Balance*, London: Hamish Hamilton, 113

59. Pritchard, Jane (1996) 'Two Letters', in Jordan, Stephanie and Andrée Grau, 101-114

60. Simpson, Christian (1953) *Les sylphides*, London: BBC.

61. Konecny, Mark (2004) 'Dance and Movement in the Cabaret', *A Journal of Russian Culture*, 10, 133-146.

62. Parker, Derek. *Royal Academy of Dancing: The First Seventy Five Years*, London:

Royal Academy of Dancing, 1995.

63. Author interview with Pamela May, (1999).

64. Haskell, Arnold (1930) *The Marie Rambert Ballet*, London: British-Continental Press, 17.

65. De Mille, Agnes (1958/1982) *Dance to the Piper* and *Promenade Home*, New York: Da Capo Press, 184.

66. Bland, Alexander (1955) 'Marie Rambert', *The Ballet Annual*, no. 9, London: Adam and Charles Black, 58-63.

67. Kelly Brigitte (2009) *'Mim': A Personal Memoir of Marie Rambert*, Alton: Dance Books.

68. Kelly, (2009) 66.

69. Rambert, Marie (1972) *Quicksilver*, London: MacMillan, 36.

70. Rambert Marie (1972) 35.

71. De Zoete, Beryl (1950) 'The 1,000,000 Mile Journey: V with a reminiscence of Jaques-Dalcroze', *Ballet*, 10, no.2, 34-38.

72. Quoted in de Zoete (1950), 37.

73. Bachmann, Marie-Laure (1991, reprinted 1993) *Dalcroze Today: An Education Through and Into Music*, trans. Parlett, David, Oxford: Clarendon Press, 11-12.

74. Kelly, Brigitte (2009).

75. Haskell, Arnold (1930) 13.

76. Williams, Peter (1976, revised 1981) 'Movement is my Element', *Ballet Rambert: 50 Years and On*, London: Scolar Press, 10.

77. Bland, Alexander (1955) 62.

78. Kelly, Brigitte (2009) 38.

79. Bland, Alexander (1955) 62.

80. Kelly, Brigitte (2009).

81. Ashton in eds. Crisp, Clement, Anya Sainsbury and Peter Williams (1976) *Ballet Rambert: 50 Years and On*, London: Scolar Press, 34.

82. Morley, Sheridan (1969) *A Talent to Amuse*, London: Heineman, 14.

83. I have not been able to discover much about Madam Rosa.

84. De Valois (1957/1973) 38.

85. De Valois (1977) 16.

86. De Valois (1977) 17.

87. When I studied with her at the Royal Ballet School in 1963-4, Hilda Gaunt used a tune which Cecchetti had whistled, de Valois immediately stopped the class and commanded her never to play it again!

88. De Valois (1977) 18.

89. De Valois (1977) 24.

90. De Valois (1977) 17.

91. De Valois (1937) *Invitation to the Ballet*, London: The Bodley Head, 252.

92. De Valois (1976) 19.

93. Sorley Walker, Kathrine (1987) 64.

94. Sorley Walker, Kathrine (1987) 64.

95. Interview (1988).

96. This comes from Pamela May's unpublished material.

97. Quoted in Sorley-Walker (1987) 62.

98. Genné, Beth (1996) *The Making of a Choreographer: Ninette de Valois and Bar aux Folies-Bergère*, Wisconsin: Society of Dance History Scholars, 35.

99. De Valois, Ninette (1937) *Invitation to the Ballet*, London: John Lane, The Bodley

Head, 176.

100. De Valois (1937) 176.

101. Interview at Royal Ballet school (1988).

102. The classes, which became known as 'Madam's Classes', were developed during the late 1940s and early 1950s and core strength and strong footwork are central.

103. Rambert, Marie (1972) 120.

104. De Valois (1957/1981) 181.

105. Ashton in Dominic, Zoë and John Selwyn Gilbert (1971) *Frederick Ashton: A Choreographer and his Ballets*, London: Harrap, 31.

106. Wohlfahrt, Hans-Theodore (1996) 'Ashton's Last Interview', *Dance Now*, 5, no.1, Spring, 25-30.

107. Pritchard, Jane (1996) 'Two Letters', in Jordan, Stephanie and Andrée Grau eds. *Following Sir Fred's Steps: Ashton's Legacy*, London: Dance Books, 101-114.

108. Van Norman Baer, Nancy (1986) 'On Movement and the School of Movement', *Bronislava Nijinska: A Dancer's Legacy*, San Francisco: Publications Department of the Fine Arts Museums of San Francisco, 85-87.

109. Nijinska, Bronislava in Van Norman Baer, Nancy (1986) 87.

110. In Van Norman Baer, Nancy (1986) 85.

111. In Van Norman Baer, Nancy (1986) 87.

112. Wohlfart, Theodore (1996) 'Ashton's Last Interview', *Dance Now*, 5, no. 1, Spring, 25-30.

113. Nijinska in Van Norman Baer, Nancy (1986) 85.

114. Parkinson, Georgina in Remine, Shields and Jacqueline Maskey (1990) 'Bronislava Nijinska: Dancers Speak', *Ballet Review*, 18, no.1, Spring, 15-35.

115. Parkinson in *Ballet Review*, (1990) 24.

116. Pritchard, Jane (1996) 107.

117. Cited in Dominic, Zoë and John, S. Gilbert (1971) *Frederick Ashton: A Choreographer and his Ballets*, London: Harrap, 10.

118. Tallchief, Maria in *Ballet Review*, (1990) 26.

119. See my article on the subject (2008).

120. Vaughan, David (1977) 231.

121. Valis Hill, Constance (1992) 'Buddy Bradley: the Invisible Man of Broadway Brings Jazz Tap to London', *Society of Dance History Scholars*, California: University of California Riverside, 77-84.

122. The *Foxtrot* was added later in 1940.

123. Foy, Patricia (1988) private video made in Panama, showing Fonteyn teaching the solo to a Panamanian dancer.

124. Vaughan, David (1977) 78.

125. Lieven, Peter (1936) *The Birth of the Ballets-Russes*, London: George Allen and Unwin, 336.

126. Holmes, Olive ed. (1982) *Motion Arrested: Dance Reviews of H.T. Parker*, Connecticut: Wesleyan University Press, 32.

127. Quoted from Svetloff, in Williamson, Audrey (1943) 'The Dancer as an Artist', *Dancing Times*, no. 398, November, 56.

128. Ashton quoted in Wohlfart (1996) 30.

129. Ashton quoted in Kavanagh, Julie (1996) 1.

130. All three of these can be seen on youtube .

131. This dance appeared on Italian television and was recorded for me. I have no other information as to the producer or director. The dance too remains obscure and could well have been danced under a different title in live performances.

132. Beaumont, Cyril (1945) *Anna Pavlova*, London: C.W. Beaumont, 21.

133. Quoted in Sorley Walker (1987) 51.

134. Quoted in Doob, Penelope (1978) 'A Conversation with Sir Frederick Ashton', *York Dance Review*, no.7, Spring, 16-25.

135. Quoted in Wohlfart (1996) 29.

136. That is the painter James Abbott McNeil Whistler (1834-1903).

137. Lieven, Peter (1936) 329.

138. Karsavina, Tamara (1953) 'Second Act of Giselle', *Dancing Times*, no.518, 75.

139. Karsavina, Tamara (1930) *The Dancing Times*, quoted in *Dancing Times*, (1995) January LXXXV no. 1012, 419.

140. Karsavina, Tamara (1953) ibid.

141. Karsavina, Tamara (1930) *The Dancing Times*, quoted in *Dancing Times*, (1995) January LXXXV no. 1012, 419.

142. Ashton, Frederick (1954) 'Marie Rambert: A Tribute from Frederick Ashton', *Dancing Times*, no. 412, January, 151.

143. Ashton quoted in Vaughan, David (1977) 59.

144. Author's interview with May, July 1999.

145. Fonteyn, Margot (1975) *Margot Fonteyn*, London: W.H. Allen, 52.

146. Interview in NYPL, recorded 8th May 1969.

147. Seymour, Lynn (2002) 'The Isadora Dances of Sir Fred', *Dancing Times*, 93, no. 1106, October, 50, 51 and 53.

148. Seymour, Lynn (2002).

149. See Buckle, Richard (1947) '"Abstract" Ballet', *Ballet*, 4, no.5, November, 20-24.

150. Cited in Blunt, Anthony (1967) *Nicolas Poussin*, Phaidon, 365.

Chapter 3

Unconventional Dances:
Ashton's Style in Ballets with Words

In the years following the death of Diaghilev, British ballet was still finding its feet; new works were essential to the health of the fledgling Vic-Wells Ballet. Bringing Ashton into the Company in 1935 increased the repertoire and encouraged fashionable artists to become involved.[1] The first of the two ballets discussed in this chapter was more than merely fashionable, it was a remarkable work, bringing together three renowned artists, Gerald Berners, Gertrude Stein and Ashton. Both Berners' music and Stein's words had a subversive quality which Ashton used as a basis for the characters. Originally a choral work, the ballet has been described as 'a satire on weddings by way of *Les noces*[2], and, when heard with the chorus, as opposed to the speaker, it resonates with that work. The ballet is set in the Ain region of France and looks back to the Edwardian era, its backcloth depicting a well-ordered house, harmoniously set in the landscape.[3]

A Wedding Bouquet was not Ashton's first ballet to have words nor was it his first encounter with Stein. In 1934 he had choreographed the dances for Virgil Thomson and Stein's opera *Four Saints in Three Acts*, working in New York with a group of singers and dancers with limited training.[4] He had also already choreographed for a production of Purcell's *The Fairy Queen* (1692) in 1928 and to Constant Lambert's *Rio Grande* (1931), set to a poem by Sacheverell Sitwell. Berners' music was not unfamiliar to him either; he had previously used it in *Foyer de danse* (1932).[5]

In the other work I discuss, *Illuminations* (1950), the choreography uses the words to structure the work and create the imagery. Made for New York City Ballet, with unfamiliarly trained dancers, it is one of Ashton's more unusual works. It is similarly structured to *A Wedding Bouquet* in that the dance phrases are fragmentary, the set-piece dances are woven into the fabric of the whole, and are barely perceptible. The music for *Illuminations* by Benjamin Britten, was written earlier in 1939. Ashton first heard it in 1945 at a performance conducted by Britten after which he was invited to choreograph the piece. Cecil Beaton's costumes and sets, however, were designed in conjunction with Ashton. The work comprises a series of songs taken from a much longer group of poems by the French symbolist poet Arthur Rimbaud. The two works are very different in their subject matter and *A Wedding Bouquet* provides an out-and-out contrast with *Illuminations*. Despite being grounded in comedy it has dark undertones, while *Illuminations* in spite of its violent undertones, has moments of light relief.

A Wedding Bouquet

From its first performance, Ashton's ballet was regarded as 'a fine example of team-work.'[6] During the 1930s, collaboration was considered to be the essential ingredient of a ballet, a notion generated by the Ballets Russes and Diaghilev. Central to Diaghilev's thinking was the belief that the arts of music, design and dance should be linked to form a single unit and the Vic-Wells Ballet followed this assiduously.[7] To what extent the makers of a dance collaborate varies but since choreographer, designer, composer and writer in this dance worked closely together, their contributions need to be considered in some depth.

In London's artistic circles Stein and Berners, while not exactly celebrities, were well known.[8] Both were, to some extent, almost as celebrated for their eccentricities as for their work, yet Berners had already composed music for a ballet for Diaghilev's Ballets Russes, *The Triumph of Neptune* (1926),[9] and Stein's *Autobiography of Alice B Toklas* (1933) and her opera *Four Saints in Three Acts* had both been widely acclaimed in the USA.[10]

She was an American writer living in Paris, who also became renowned as a collector of paintings and for living in a fairly open relationship with Alice B. Toklas. As part of an avant-garde artistic circle, she was one of the earliest collectors of the work of Pablo Picasso. Recognising the value of cubism, she tried, in a sense, to adapt its principles to her writing, breaking up the words and re-assembling them into a more abstract form. Reading her work is taxing, and as the scholar Ulla Dydo points out, Stein challenges our conception of reading, and our assumptions as to what sentences, and words should do.[11] Despite the abstract quality of her writing, her material was taken from everyday life. *A Wedding Bouquet*, adapted from one of her plays, deals with the goings-on of the local French people in a village, near Aix-Les-Bains, where she had a country house. This relationship between the more conservative Ashton and the unconventional Stein was a surprising one, yet her collaboration with him and Berners produced a dance which was both avant-garde and enduring.[12]

In the 1930s there were many who found Stein's work virtually impenetrable and even today, some still find it 'unreadable'.[13] Stein, though, was a serious writer and we know this from examining her other works and from the fact that she spent a life-time writing books, plays, articles and autobiographies: in other words, her work is decipherable, created within artistic concepts. According to Sarah Bey-Cheng, Stein is 'the first genuine avant-garde dramatist,' without her work, experimental drama in the USA would never have happened.[14] But she points out that the works are better understood in relation to three artistic trends of the twentieth century: the avant-garde, the development of cinema and 'the emergence of homosexuality as an identity'.[15]

Berners was a multi-talented artist who not only composed music but also wrote novels, several volumes of autobiography and painted a significant number of oil paintings. These were mainly landscapes, modelled on the work of Jean-Baptiste Corot, the nineteenth century French artist. Like his backcloth for *A Wedding Bouquet*, they were gentle, possibly even conservative, paintings of the countryside.[16] Unfortunately his eccentricity sometimes clouded appreciation of his work, particularly his music, and he did little to challenge this image. One of his most ardent admirers and friends was Igor Stravinsky who, it is thought, recommended his work for publication to J. and W. Chester.[17] Berners' earliest music was considered avant-garde and described as having 'originality in the writing [and] a true sense of irony in the music itself, not just in the humorous titles and amusing commentaries'.[18] He was, and still is, frequently compared with Erik Satie and his music is quite unlike other English composers of the time, such as Edward Elgar and Ralph Vaughan Williams.[19] By the time he started work on *A Wedding* Bouquet, his score for the Ballets Russes, *The Triumph of Neptune*, had been highly praised and *Luna Park; or the Freaks* (1930) was also well regarded. This was a ballet, choreographed by Balanchine, in a revue of Cochran's. Set in a fairground, each character had distinctive music and that for the adage section mimicked Pyotr Ilych Tchaikovsky's *The Sleeping Beauty* (1890).[20] Although succinct, the music drew on several genres and because of its Broadway style reprise, Philip Lane suggests, it is Berners' *Scènes de ballet*.[21]

Although Berners liked to present himself as an eccentric, he was a serious musician. After falling into obscurity for some time, his work gained fuller recognition during the celebrations of his centenary in 1983.[22] His approach to Stein and the writing of *A Wedding Bouquet* was both meticulous and professional; he spent over a year writing the score. Berners first encountered Stein during the 1930s and Dickinson, in his illuminating collection of interviews, claims that he 'liked her because she was fashionable, modern...and she did disconcert people'.[23] Further plans had been made for an opera but the Second World War intervened and Stein died in 1946

The following table provides a brief outline of *A Wedding Bouquet*. It is approximate and not meant to constitute all the movement but it gives some idea of the fragmentary nature of the work.

Table 1

Section	Characters	Words	Movement/ dynamic	Music
Beginning to end of ensemble (6mins 30)	Webster; peasants; Josephine; John and Paul; Violet; Ernest; Thérèse All join in the ensemble section at end	'This is now scene I.' Also discusses the characters and their problems Ends with 'there shall be no hesitation'	Small footwork and gestural upper body. *Pas de bourrée; bourrée couru, glissade; arabesques; chassé; walks*	Opening is vivacious replaced by anxious sounding music (Webster) followed by a *Tranquillo,* busy music returns and ends with ostinato
Approximately 5 mins 30	Julia enters alone, Josephine returns; Bridegroom enters is shooed away by Pepé; Arthur enters also attacked by Pépé; Guy; Pépé and Arthur again; 4 Guests; Julia and Bride Groom duet	Language coincides with action as description of wedding given: 'she may be wearing a gown newly washed' Pépé section refers to action; 'this would make a dog uneasy' long section without words	Julia enters with a *bourrée couru,* dynamic is varied between undulating and strong sudden bends then (broadly) returns to crisper footwork and gestural upper body; duet is more vigorous with bigger jumps and lifts, and big jumps and turns occur in Guy's virtuoso dance	An *Andantino* follows and then an *Allegro* Ends with the *Tranquillo* heard earlier
Approximately 8 mins 30	Wedding: entrance of Bride and two gendarmes. All now present. Ensemble dancing into Bride's solo, interrupted by Josephine's drunkness . Paul has solo dance then group dance and Josephine is expelled	'Charming' for wedding and this is now Scene IV language reflects dance and Josephine's portrayal of drunkenness. 'Bitterness' repeated ends with 'Josephine will leave'	Some replica- tion of social dancing in form of a waltz. Ensemble in pairs. Alternates between some large jumping, small footwork and paired dancing.	Waltz tune interspersed with mutterings from chorus about Josephine

Section	Characters	Words	Movement/dynamic	Music
Approximately 4 mins. 30	Divertisse-ments: Bride and Bridegroom duet trio: Webster, Paul and John and Pépé, Guy and Arthur	Much of this is in silence and comments about the characters and weddings; 'they will come together to vote as to whether they will be without weddings'	Duet : conven-tional pas de deux adage turned back to front and often upside down First trio fast with individual footwork in one section Second trio has much in common with trio from *Les rendezvous*	Mainly waltzes
Approximately 3 minutes (finale)	Bridegroom and 4 Guests joined by Arthur and eventually Bride, Violet, Thérèse and Julia, during waltz all enter and exit off stage leaving Julia alone with Pépé	Names are reiterated but used for rhythm ends with repetitions of 'bitterness'	Stage dancing in tango though when bride enters she and others perform *fouettés* ends with waltzing step	Tango ending in a waltz

Stein's Play and its Metamorphosis into a Ballet

A Wedding Bouquet is a shortened adaptation of Stein's one act play *They Must. Be Wedded. To Their Wife*, completed in 1931.[24] Stein divides the play into four acts and numerous scenes, although not in the conventional use of these divisions. According to Marc Robinson these 'Acts' and 'Scenes' ' function like frames around paintings, directing and focusing our attention on discrete sections of the perceived world'.[25] Similar, seemingly arbitrary, framing is found in several other Stein plays. In *They Must. Be Wedded. To Their Wife*, Act III comes after Act IV and then is followed by a second Act IV. This habit of disturbing and fragmenting the narrative has analogies with other writers like James Joyce and Virginia Woolf and with film technique and Stein was hugely influenced by film.[26] Writing in 1935 she observed that

A Wedding Bouquet, showing chorus on stage (1937). © Felix Fonteyn. Courtesy of Mrs Hookham.

anyone is of one's period and this our period was undoubtedly the period of cinema and series production. And each of us in our own way are bound to express what the world in which we are living is doing.[27]

In the ballet, the narrator or chorus names the scenes, so they are incorporated into the music and narrated text. This helps structure the text, dividing it between discussion of character and description of place. Time and place are mentioned in Scene I: 'Scene one is a place where they are' which occurs before Act I is mentioned. Scenes occur somewhat randomly, not necessarily following each other logically. There are no Scenes II or III. The wedding occurs in Scene IV (the play's divisions are a little different). Regarding the short scenes and fragmented sentences as cinematic provides a structure for our understanding of the ballet: each section is short, often fragmented and has no standard variations or set-piece group dances. The narrative has a filmic quality, edited into a series of cuts, small slices of action.

Dydo, one of the leading Stein scholars, argues that Stein never used words as signs, in the semiotic sense, and, 'once embedded in the text, [they] are no longer a reference to the existing world'.[28] She claims that Stein's work is, in one sense, about the act of writing and, as with cubism, was concerned with structure. She sought to make the works self-contained; the words 'point inwards to the piece', rather than 'pointing outward to the world'; they are there because of the rhythm or texture or because Stein has played with them.[29] Freed from their conventional meaning, words can have new forms, as can ballet steps. Nouns can be broken up into verbs and nouns, thereby altering their function; for example, selfish can be separated into two new words sel(l) fish, so these are not nonsense as some critics suggested when *A Wedding Bouquet* was first performed.[30]

As Stein deconstructed the word and changed its grammatical function, so Ashton changed the function of the ballet step: he made linking steps important and frequently the main focus of the dance. Yet, Stein insisted that she did not invent but used what she observed.[31] Dydo claims that because of this, reading Stein involves both an examination of the text's internal composition and the external references to Stein's own world. 'The two are in constant creative opposition. The references make us attend to the world while the composition asks us to attend to the design'.[32] The same can be said of Ashton's choreography: the characters in *A Wedding Bouquet* are recognisably human but the tightly constructed choreography puts dance at the centre.

In 1929, Stein acquired the lease of a country house, Bilignin, in Belley, in south eastern France and her move to the country had a considerable impact on her writing. Dydo argues that some of the writing of the early 1930s not only incorporates the daily life of the countryside but is also a reflection of her life there with Toklas. There is mention of country elements in *They Must. Be Wedded.*, such as the importance of the harvest and the problem of rain, but more significantly, there is an important event, weddings were central to country life of the time.[33] Making a good match was crucial within that bourgeois society, because it preserved property, allowed for the provision of extra indoor and outdoor help, extended the family and provided care for elderly relatives. Stein hints at the necessity for marriage throughout the play and mentions the duties and the worries inflicted by this need. So, phrases like 'Thérèse will always hear that she is not a disappointment Nor whether there will be her share' and 'John an elder brother who regrets the illness of his father because it deprives him of travelling as a vacation' are not just platitudinous comments but seem to reflect the anxieties of the characters, possibly caused by the French system of inheritance.[34]

Ashton uses the words to depict the characters and to give the ballet a hint of anxiety. Paul 'has charm'; Josephine is 'tall and true' and 'married', though evidently not happily as she ends up tipsy and is ousted from the party: 'Josephine will leave'; Violet is slightly spinsterish and desperate to marry: 'Violet oh will you ask him to marry you'. Ernest, whom Violet approaches, is well-mannered, finicky and dapper: 'Ernest Politeness' and he 'may be a victim of himself'; Julia is 'forlorn'. Neither the Bride nor Bridegroom is mentioned by Stein but Ashton conceives of the one as dotty and the other as a rake. Sometimes he uses the text literally as when Pépé, Julia's dog, attacks Arthur: 'Julia could be called Julia Arthur Julia Arthur only this would make a dog uneasy'; or when Violet mimes that she is 'older than a boat'.

Berners' Contribution: Music, Text Adaptation, Design

The text, the choreography and the music are closely linked throughout and because it was first set to a chorus, there are times when the repetitions of the chorus are manifest in the dancing; as lines repeat over and over, so do dance phrases. These links are lost when the text is narrated. The choral version was performed until 1940 when, because of the Second World War, the company had to tour England as part of their war-effort contribution. As it was too costly to tour with an orchestra, all dances were performed to two pianos. A chorus was also out of the question; so Constant Lambert (the musical director of the Sadler's Wells Ballet) became the narrator. The speaker remained until 1983, when for Berners' centenary, the chorus was reinstated for a few performances. At the Ashton centenary revival, in 2004, the narrator returned.

Stein stayed with Berners in March 1936 and it was then that he agreed to add music to one of her plays.[35] His initial decision was to set the whole play as an opera but by 18 July 1936, he had asked Ashton to choreograph the piece as a ballet.[36] In a letter to Stein, just after he had visited her, in August, Berners mentions that the music is nearly finished and includes 'a fugue, a waltz, a tango and a very moving adagio on the theme, "Josephine will leave".'[37] The fugue is not in the final score, though Bryony Jones, the music scholar, mentions that there are fugal entries, such as when the chorus' overlapping entries for 'Josephine will leave', create the impression that everyone is talking at once.[38] With the narrator this disappears. According to Jones, the rhythm of the music is largely dictated by the speech patterns, though occasionally Berners changed the words to suit the musical rhythm.[39] The score also has some typically humorous features; the passage, 'It is going on nicely', is ironically underscored by harmonies which seem to suggest that quite the reverse is taking place.[40]

Berners later informed Stein that he would do the décor himself, describing it thus:

> The backdrop is an oval landscape of a house a little like Bilingin only simplified and I have put it on the banks of a river and reflected in the water (sic). The costumes are of no particular period – if anything slightly 1900 and the principal characters, Josephine Therese etc I have given a rather 'endimanche' air. The curtain (shown during the overture) is an immense bouquet with a wedding couple standing on either side of it.[41]

It could be set in either England or France, though the characters behave in ways that are assumed to be French. Yet the overlay is English. The other characters' reaction to Josephine's drunkenness and Julia's erratic behaviour has a kind of English stiff-upper-lip quality, generated by the dance movement. The main focus of the movement is on the lower body and the expressive gestures are stiff and comical, not generous and extravagant. Neither are there exaggerated leg extensions or extravagant turns, everything is understated, if at times somewhat eccentric.

During his visit to Bilingin in August 1936, Stein drove Berners out in her car to show him things of interest. Tellingly he records that 'the neighbours are interesting and curious. Gertrude had a knack of dramatising them – and perhaps it [was] she who [made] them interesting and strange'.[42] It is likely that some of these characters found their way into both the play and the ballet. From one reference in the text, Berners added the dog Pépé. It was based on Stein's Mexican Chihuahua and Stein sent Berners a photograph of her dog to help Berners construct the dancer's mask. Just before the opening, in a letter dated 17 March 1937, Berners discusses Pépé.

> Pépé's part is getting larger and larger. He now appears for a moment in a

white gauze tutu and a wreath and does a short classical dance with pointes and entrechats and all that. As the English are a race of dog lovers it ought to have a great success...[43]

The *entrechats* are a reference to a phrase, performed by Giselle in Act II of the ballet, another of Ashton's covert references. Although Giselle's tragic plight is burlesqued here by Pépé, the reference could also be seen as a warning. Like Albrecht, in *Giselle*, the Bridegroom is a man with secrets. Observed by four Guests, hidden behind a table, he has a topsy-turvy duet with Julia whose forlornness has clearly been the result of a prior relationship with him. It ends in an embrace from which she is reluctant to disentangle herself. Contemporary audiences would have known that Fonteyn, who played Julia, had recently taken on the role of Giselle. The allusion to *Giselle* and perhaps Fonteyn's new role is ambiguous, partly playful and partly serious but it could also be satirical.

It is likely that Berners had reduced Stein's play to a suitable length before he wrote the music and before inviting Ashton to choreograph. The 1949 printed version of the play is part of an anthology of Stein's work. It is much longer, thirty-four pages, in contrast to the ballet script's ten. The ballet uses virtually all of the text from the first six pages and also includes lines from three later pages: 'Let no one deceive. By. Smiling.' (in the ballet as, 'Let no-one be deceived by smiling'); 'Thérèse Crowned with lace. With grace... In place of lace' (in the ballet as 'Therèse is crowned with lace and crowned with grace in place of lace'); and:

Josephine May she be tall. And true.
[and Julia] may she also. Be new.
May she. Also. Be. One of few.

(Square brackets denote what is in the ballet but not in the play.)
There are some places where Stein's text has been moved a couple of lines up or down but, apart from a few word changes, the text of the play and that of the ballet are very close. Stein seems not to have been bothered by Berners' changes to her play, writing to Berners that 'Anything you want to do will be what I want you to do'.[44]

A major feature of the ballet's text is the use of repetition, which is not in Stein's play. Berners continually repeats phrases and frequently stresses each syllable of each word, fragmenting the word. He threads these repetitions throughout the score and they are sometimes picked up by Ashton who parallels the musical repetition by repeating the dance phrases. Jones argues that Berners' musical style favoured repetition in preference to variation and development and the repetitions are not Stein's and must have been added by Berners. She notes that Berners must have written the music before meeting Ashton and Lambert and had probably already constructed the libretto.[45]

Ashton picks up on Berners' waltzes and tangos. He uses the waltz to celebrate the marriage, though the movement burlesques the traditional waltz and he adds movements from those performed by 'chorus girls' in the stage dancing of the era. Later the waltz is used for a display of *grands jetés* by several of the Guests and in particular to show off those of Julia, who, with one of the men, makes a circle of *grands jetés* around a group of guests. At the ballet's conclusion, the cast exits to the waltz which gradually tails off to leave Julia alone, 'forlorn' with her dog Pépé. Although it has been clear right from his first entrance that the Bridegroom is not to be trusted, his participation in the tango quells any doubts we may have had. His persona reminds us of that of the Dago in the tango from *Façade* (1931); the latter is undoubtedly seedy.

Ashton's Choreography

Aspects of Nijinska's dance movement style figures in this work, for there are numerous references to *Les biches* in both the dance movement and the choreography. Ashton frequently reclaims dance movement material, both his own and that of others. Sometimes the quotations are used ironically as in the Piglet duet in *The Tales of Beatrix Potter* (1971) and sometimes to create a dialogue between two works as with *Les biches*. There are of course some very individual features but the work has several key stylistic characteristics found in other, both earlier and later, Ashton dances.

Like the play, the ballet is peopled with friends and relations of the Bride and Groom and, like Stein's words, and Berners's costumes, Ashton attempted to capture the distinctive elements of a French country wedding. All the locals are there, the peasants, the two Gendarmes and the men 'according to their social status, [wearing] dress-coats, frock-coats, jackets or waistcoats' and the ladies supporting 'town-style dresses'.[46] Each character enters and leaves before gathering with the others for the wedding ceremony, a disparate collection of very ordinary people made eloquent by Ashton's choreography and Stein's words and just like at any wedding, we only hear half finished phrases and see scraps of dance. Nothing is complete and, at the end, we are aware that this is not the whole story, nor the happy-ever-after affair that weddings are supposed to anticipate.

Webster, the Edwardian housekeeper, manages the country house where the wedding takes place. She opens the ballet, performing one of the longest dances in the piece (almost two minutes). She then beckons on the four peasants and eventually joins in with them. As Josephine enters, and the music changes to a more legato phrase, the peasants carry Webster off in a mock

funeral lift, holding her flat and high above their heads. Various characters
are then gradually introduced in ones, twos and fours. In the first ten minutes of the ballet, apart from Webster's solo, no dance lasts more than twenty
to thirty seconds. Each character enters with a brief dance only to be interrupted by the arrival of the next. Ashton hurries the dancers on and off the
stage, treating us to all the furore and general confusion that precedes a
wedding. The Bride and Groom enter through a guard-of-honour-like group-
ing of the guests. Photographs are taken; then the whole group dances. As in
Aurora's wedding, from *The Sleeping Beauty*, there are divertissements but
everything is in a jumble; the Bride's solo starts off the divertissements and
comes before the main *pas de deux*. Two trios ensue before the tango brings
the Bridegroom back on and marks the beginning of the end.

Each individual has a distinctive motif, a key to their character, none more
so than Webster. She scurries from side to side, hands joined and held high to
show sharply pointed elbows. Evidently, she is something of a tyrant and the
jabbing, spiky nature of her runs on pointe and picked-up *pas de bourrée* (a
step unit containing three changes of weight) make this clear. The movement creates an image of a driven, frenetic persona, amplified by the way in
which the arms, bent at shoulder height, are occasionally flung from side to
side; the movement is emphatic, focused and forceful. With elbows akimbo,
she scolds and gestures to no one in particular but at times streaks of mis-
chief and affection shine through too, such as when she rushes to take the
photograph of the wedding. In the trio with John and Paul, she is frisky, even
perhaps seductive, collapsing every now and then in order to be revived by
the two men. This trio recalls a similar one involving the Hostess in *Les biches*,
which Nijinska danced but choreographed on de Valois, the original Webster
in *A Wedding Bouquet*, and the quick, sudden *saut de basque en tournant* are
surely allusions to the Hostess's solo dance. Contemporary audiences might
well have also recalled the other trio in *Les rendezvous* that Ashton did for de
Valois in 1933.

Ashton uses the *danse d'école* in Webster's opening dance to convey her
personality but without abandoning his familiar stylistic characteristics. He
elevates linking steps, like the *pas de bourrée*, making them major motif in the
dance. Ashton transforms the balletic *pas de bourrée* into a running, series of
triplets. The feet are almost parallel and Webster remains on pointe, virtually
throughout the cluster of phrases (de Valois was known for her precise footwork). To convey character, the phrases initially depend on gestural arm
movement, though for the rest the arms are kept close to the body, encouraging activity in the upper torso; this too is a feature of Nijinska's movement
style.

Picking up on de Valois'/Webster's resourcefulness, Ashton provides her
with a multitude of ingenious *pas de bourrée*: [47]

A Wedding Bouquet. David Drew as Paul, Deanne Bergsma as Josephine, Kenneth Mason as John. © Roger Wood. Courtesy of the Royal Opera House.

Phrase a) moving in a circle and remaining on pointe, she performs three *pas de bourrée*, as if running, each ending or beginning with a kick into a low attitude.

Phrase b) two and a half repeats of the same *pas de bourrée*, travelling from side to side with larger steps.

Phrase c) a high kick and shouting gesture before a jumped turn, repeated.

Phrase d) a parallel *bourrée couru* with two *relevés* into the low attitude.

Phrase e) a flat footed *pas de bourrée* from side to side.

This cluster of triplets is eventually completed by the 'Fred step' using only the first four steps, and then replacing the *pas de chat* with eight *ronds de jambs en l'air*. These are performed hopping on pointe, to *effacé*, and draw attention to the aggressive, industriousness of the character.[48] Throughout the ballet the *pas de bourrée* and *bourrée couru* (a running, gliding movement on pointe) recur; every female character has her own individual version. This echoes *Les biches* where walks on pointe, off pointe and performed with long strides are used to distinguish each of the different persona.

Josephine, the first guest, enters backwards, performing a lazy, languid, parallel version of the *bourrée couru*. Her elliptical pathway and eye-shading gesture emphasise her indolence. Her next phrase has a sliding movement into *arabesque* and a *pas de bourrée*. The contrast between these *pas de bourrée* and those of Webster is palpable: where Josephine's are languid and lazy, Webster's are strong and purposeful. Described by Stein as a 'ça va bien' type, Josephine is almost too sophisticated to attend a country wedding.[49] When she engages with the smartly attired Paul and John, who interrupt her dance, she leans seductively from one to the other, anticipating her subsequent drunken behaviour. Violet and Ernest enter next in a flurry of runs/ *bourrée couru* and fast *sauts de basque* (a low turning jump on one leg) type of step, two more recurring signature movements. The last to enter in the opening section is Thérèse, who crosses the stage, diagonally entering from upstage left, with a fast backwards *bourrée couru*; she ends by bumping suddenly into Violet. Almost immediately, the characters re-enter and this first introductory section is completed by a short ensemble dance. They exit, one behind the other, performing a staccato dance phrase of *chassé*, (a sliding movement) *pas de bourrée* with upper body comically twisting from side to side.[50]

Ashton does not show off the technical talents of his dancers, at least not their virtuoso talents. The opening section is almost shockingly limited with its brisk *terre à terre* steps and fragmented phrases. If the ballet is not a showcase for technical exploits, it is undoubtedly an essay on intricate footwork. The intricate steps and complicated use of the torso in the opening section set the tone and stylistic pattern for the rest of the ballet. Key movements are revealed: the *bourrée couru*, *pas de bourrée*, low *arabesque* and *pas de chat*, just the kind of steps that de Valois was interested in developing as characteristic of an English ballet style.[51]

The short ensemble dance that ends the opening section gives further clues to Ashton's movement style and highlights Ashton's use of music and text. In it all the characters who have already been introduced perform the sequence, comprising six phrases of repetitions and no breaks:

Phrase cluster a) eight hip thrusting, jerky walks which accentuate the 'there' and 'no' of the text.

Phrase cluster b) ten small *entrechats* performed in a circle with arms rising to fifth.

Phrase cluster c) an *épaulement* rich combination of *glissades* ending in a hop to one leg with an extra *glissade* in the last phrase (Ashton uses this again in *Tales of Beatrix Potter* (1971) for Mrs Tiggywinkle).

Phrase cluster d) a *pas de bourrée* with two *entrechats*, repeated four times, though in the final phrase of the quartet an extra two *entrechats* are slipped in at the end. During both the *entrechats* and *pas de bourrées* the shoulders change, moving in the direction of the front foot, making the phrase highly active.

Phrase cluster e) combines a turning jump with two *petits jetés* re-peated twice, ending with four little *jetés*. The *petits jetés* end heavily with a jolt, not the usual light classroom movement.

Phrase cluster f) is a recurring *chassé*, *pas de bourrée* with changing *épaulement*, travelling in a curve and taking the group off stage.

These are all nursery steps, as the critic Luke Jennings points out, but not the classroom version.[52] They are too fast, follow each other without prepara-tion and are performed as a single long sequence. The constantly changing *épaulement* makes them lively, even effervescent. Although taken from the *danse d'ecole*, the steps break the rules in several ways. The arms are not used as in the classroom and the speed at which they have to be performed pre-vents them from being textbook copies. Instead, they are clipped, sharp versions of the original, not bothered by the need to close in an exact fifth position.

The movement too is clipped, echoing the sounds of the sentences: 'There can be no hesitation', which is broken up between the bars into two halves 'there can be' and 'no hesitation'. Musically, the first bar has two quavers and a crochet with a word on each note while the second bar has five notes, a quaver, two semiquavers and two quavers, with 'no' on the quaver and 'hesi-tation' divided along the remaining four notes. This division places an emphasis on each of the notes. The sentence, repeated throughout the section, is interrupted by a repetition of the phrase 'they all wish that they had been there' which occurs on the turning and *jeté* step just before the final phrase.

To follow the notes exactly could be boring and Ashton's phrases do not quite do this. While the words are given rhythmic emphasis through the variation in notes, some of the dance phrases slip over the notes and coincide with the bar. In the first phrase (see above) the musical phrase coincides with the dance phrase but in phrases b and d, the dance phrase spills over into c and e catching up again at the end of e. This is because Ashton slips in an extra step, within the same musical span at the end of phrases b and d. As Jordan notes in her analysis of Ashton's musical style, this slipping in of extra steps is a feature of his approach to music.[53]

The vocal repetitions differ between the choral and spoken versions; the chorus sings the phrase fifteen times but the Speaker only four.[54] The singers are heard throughout, fading as the group exits but because of the Speaker's silence, a long orchestral passage is heard instead. The waning effect of the exit is lost. Ashton of course choreographed to the chorus and the Speaker creates a different effect and influences how we see the dance. The spoken voice is declamatory and more nuanced, changing the tone and making the text sound ridiculous. We therefore do not experience the dance in a similar way. The tone of the Speaker can also encourage the dancers to falsify the characters. Ashton follows the words of the chorus, although in the final exit, he draws attention to the mechanical beat of the base line ostinato with the rapidly changing *épaulement*. The continuous nature of the cluster of phrases responds to the sense of the words, 'there can be no hesitation'. Indeed, there is no hesitation between each phrase. This close relationship between words and movement is much more evident in the choral version. The comedy depends on the speed of performance and the incessant quality of the group of phrases. The humour is reinforced by the reference to stage dancing; the exaggerated entrance comes from the chorus line, the steps in Phrase Group c also appear in the Popular Song in *Façade* (1931), itself a reflection of the dead-pan, soft-shoe music hall duet.

Arms, apart from one incidence, are kept low or held behind the back. Restricting the use of the arms so that the movement has to be initiated from the torso is something Ashton learnt from Nijinska but in *A Wedding Bouquet*, he uses it to comic effect. The impetus for the movement comes from the torso forcing it to work harder; this creates a look of frenzy and underpins the comedy. There is no need to add funny faces, or a raised eyebrow, the sequence itself is humorous and reflects the gossipy excitement of those arriving for a wedding.

This long, unbroken group of phrases is unusual in Ashton. The only other examples are in *Le Rossignol* (1981) and in the solo for the Queen of the

Air in *Homage to the Queen* (1953) but long phrases are otherwise rare. Ashton's phrases and phrase clusters usually come in bite size pieces and each has a single defining feature.

Ashton's signature steps in this work are interspersed with conventional, everyday gesture. Just before the ensemble scene for example, Violet performs quick, travelling *sauts de basque* which interrupt the flow of her *bourrée couru*, performed more like a fleeting run than a *bourrée*. Her phrase is accompanied by gesturing, pleading arms and, in response, Ernest occasionally covers his ears with clenched fists, a characteristic Ashton gesture.[55] But unaware of Ernest's feelings, Violet coyly turns away from him and with arms stretched down and fingers entwined, she declares her love. During this plea, Ernest tiptoes off stage, shaking his finger. This is both witty and poignant. Throughout Violet's dance phrase, the narrator, or chorus, insistently chants, 'oh will you ask him to marry you' and makes clear that she is not young any longer.

> Thérèse I am older than a Boat
> And there can be no folly in owning it.

Violet is dressed in a lavender gown with a high neck decorated with lace, accoutrements of the older Edwardian woman. Ashton does not present her as elderly, only as rather sad. According to Dydo, Stein was very conscious of the unfair status of women in France, in particular of unmarried women, who in the early twentieth century had little power and social standing.[56] French women did not have the vote till 1944. Married women, while also restricted, had control over their husbands.[57] So, whatever power women had, it was invested only in those who were married. While Ashton may not have been aware of this, Stein certainly was and although Violet's plight may appear amusing, the reality is more chilling.

Stylistically, Violet's dance phrase is typical of Ashton's altered codified steps. Like Stein's words, these steps are detached from their referents. In Violet's phrases, the change is caused by the *saut de basques'* position in the dance phrase, because they are interspersed with a running *bourrée couru* and gestures. The effect is both to diminish the jump's virtuoso qualities and its codified correctness and to disturb the *bourrée*. The whole phrase serves the plight and temperament of the characters; the fussiness of the Edwardian spinster in the fast *bourrée couru*, her desperation in the gestural movement and the horror of Ernest as he clutches his temples and tip toes off stage.

These Chaplinesque elements are created by Ashton. For he makes the characters seem silly but forces us to sympathise with them because they are so human, mundane even. The references to *Giselle* and *Les noces*, both disturbing works, help to reinforce these comic overtones. Is Ashton and perhaps Berners too, suggesting the Bride and Groom in *A Wedding Bouquet* are in an arranged marriage, like the couple in *Les noces?*

In Julia's dramatic entrance Ashton alludes to Pavlova's theatricality. On an empty stage, she enters from stage left with a rapid *bourrée couru*, eerily twisting her long hair in her fingers. This dramatic moment and the darkness of her dress cast a note of gloom over both the character and the occasion. But Ashton also uses the entrance for comic effect.With a clear stage, we expect a grand entrance; yet, Julia enters in silence. Her movement, weighted and tortuous, lacks the energy of the exiting group. She collapses forward from time to time confirming her hopelessness. This is not the entrance expected of ballerinas, quite the reverse in fact. Julia's movements are exaggeratedly tragic, although unlike Violet, she is young and beautiful. The comic character, explains John Vorhaus, has four notable features: a comic perspective, flaws, humanity and exaggeration.[58] Julia sees her situation as supremely tragic and this is divorced from reality and the normal. She is full of self-pity but sympathetic to Josephine when she is drummed out of the wedding; all of this is encapsulated in her exaggerated movement. Pavlova's presence is sensed even if Ashton uses the grand ballerina entrance as a comic device.

At this stage in his career, Ashton was still under Nijinska's influence. In *A Wedding Bouquet*, he drew extensively from her and one of his more significant quotes demonstrates his ability to tease his audience through movement. The phrase, adapted from *Les biches*, occurs in the dance of the two Bridesmaids who, like the Grey Girls in *Les biches* are joined together but here beneath a veil. A repeated phrase in the *Chanson Dansée* (Grey Girls) – *glissade, jeté en avant, demi contretemps, glissade pas de chat, pas de chat, glissade assemblé* – is picked up by the Bridesmaids and becomes the repeated phrase, *assemblé, sissonne* step across and two *pas de chat.*[59] The *glissades, jeté en avant,* and *demi-contretemps* are missing from the Bridesmaids' dance and the Grey Girls do not do the *sissonne* but the rhythm and continuous quality of the two phrase clusters are similar. In neither phrase do the dancers have time to think; the phrases need to be deeply-rooted in muscle memory. The reference is also clear because in both, the women are physically attached to each other and the series of phrases follows a semi-circular path. Nijinska hints that the women in the *Chanson Dansée* are lesbians and the dance ends in a sudden embrace. It is quite likely that Ashton was making reference to this and perhaps even to the relationship between Stein and Toklas. The dance occurs just after the wedding has taken place and it would be easy to miss the moment.

Threaded through the ballet are other references to *Les biches*. The repetitious *entrechat quatre*, the *bourrée couru,* the exaggerated emphasis on *épaulement* and the mass of small footwork are found throughout *Les biches* and there can be little doubt that Ashton was referencing that work. The moment, when the four unnamed guests dive behind the table, observing Julia and the Bridegroom, is reminiscent of a similar incident in *Les biches* when four women hide behind the blue sofa to spy on two men. London audiences in 1937 would have recognised this reference. Beyond Ashton's admiration for Nijinska, his referencing of *Les biches* suggests more than covert borrowing. In alluding to it, Ashton links the characters of both works. The sexuality of those in *Les biches* is unclear, even the title has two possible interpretations: the deer or the prostitutes. Their behaviour is also risqué. In *A Wedding Bouquet*, apart from the Bridesmaids, sexuality is not a major issue; yet the behaviour is. The Bridegroom has clearly had love affairs with several of the women attending the wedding and his effect on Julia and Josephine has apparently been quite shocking.

In *A Wedding Bouquet*, there is an abundance of signature steps, so, contrary to what the writer, and early historian of the Vic-Wells Ballet, H.S. Sibthorpe suggests, lots of dancing.[60] There are references too to stage dancing and, most prominently, to both the dance movement style and choreography of Nijinska. Phrases are repeated and refreshed and picked up and used by other characters and despite its fragmentary nature, it has vague structural similarity with *Les biches*: characters entering in small groups or alone, followed by a group dance and a series of short divertissements.

The Dancers

Ashton's dancers also play a part in his dance movement style and this work's original cast included dancers from a range of different dance backgrounds, trained by early twentieth century pedagogues, such as Bedells, Espinosa, Craske and Astafieva. As noted in Chapter II, the training at the Sadler's Wells School was, at this time, equally eclectic, drawing on Sergeyev, Idizikowsky and occasionally other Russian immigrants like Anna Pruzina. There was nothing uniform about these teachers, quite the reverse in fact since their dance experience was drawn from the music hall, revues, musical theatre and the Ballets Russes, reflecting the dance world in Britain during the 1930s, as made clear in the book *Who's Who in Dancing 1932*.[61] Typified by such artists as Astaire, Jessie Matthews and Bradley, the appearance was of an effortless nonchalance and in ballet this translated into less emphasis on turnout than there is today and more on having a relaxed, flexible, natural looking upper body, though an ability to perform intricate footwork was also important.

Tap dancing and the intricate footwork of the social dances figured prominently on most teachers' CVs and it is likely too that the skills encouraged by these dances found their way into the ballet training. Certainly it is fair to say that the emphasis on beaten jumps and intricate, rhythmic *pas de bourrées* was an aspect of the early Cecchetti syllabuses and these features were emphasised in the classes of de Valois during the 1930s and later. Equally, learning tap dancing improved rhythm and encouraged fast footwork. Ashton's passion for fast intricate footwork was clearly echoed in this training and may also have been influenced by it and the dancers were well equipped for these demands.[62] By the same token, Berners' long costumes, covering most of the body, dictate that footwork and gestural movement should dominate.[63] High extensions in long skirts look incongruous; Julia has high *arabesques* but when The Bride performs the same movement, she has changed to a short tutu.

There is no account of the making of the choreography, though it is unlikely Ashton drew on the individual talents of the dancers because the ballet is more dependent on group dancing but their specific personalities are indeed evident. Sorley Walker believes that Ashton cast his dancers carefully so that the characteristics of each dancer suited the role they were given.[64] Fonteyn, at the time a rather legato dancer, had less footwork as the 'forlorn' Julia, while Robert Helpmann, an excellent actor, as the Bridegroom was described by P.W. Manchester as having 'captured exactly the spirit of burlesque...[he] never attempts to win any sympathy for this frustrated would-be-rake'.[65] And, of course de Valois was wickedly typecast as the formidable Webster, ruling sternly over the proceedings, just as she did over her company. Mary Honor, The Bride, was a virtuoso dancer who had performed in musical theatre until 1935. Her technical strength surely encouraged Ashton to include not only a series of fast turns but also some *fouettés*. The choreography for The Bride demands technical skill, since despite ending upside down and back to front in most of the *pas de deux*, she needs to be in control of it all without looking ruffled by the experience. The teenage Somes, whose high jumps were very much admired, has several displays of big jumping movements in his role as Guy.[66] It is the only obviously virtuoso dancing in the ballet and probably because Somes wanted to show off his abilities, Ashton made use of them. Of the other dancers, June Brae's languid movement may well have inspired the character of Josephine, though as she grows more intoxicated, her movement becomes gracefully slurred and unsteady. Brae's celebrated elegance probably came from her time in Paris studying with Mathilde Kschessinska, a teacher renowned for her attention to the upper body.[67] For Ashton the dancer was the catalyst whose presence stimulates the dance movement and despite the ensemble nature of *A Wedding Bouquet*, Ashton drew on and enhanced not only the technical abilities of the dancers but also their approach to movement. As with his other works, their dance movement and that of the era is inextricably linked with the choreographic style of this ballet. In spite of the eclecticism of the training, the dance movement has unity, probably because the choreography embraces the *zeitgeist* of the 1930s.

The Ballet's Reception

Throughout its history *A Wedding Bouquet* has given rise to controversy, some critics found the words unintelligible while others were amused and charmed and it still produces mixed responses. As Mary Clarke observed, 'there are people who detest the whole affair, "don't understand it" and think it an absurd waste of time and talent'.[68] After the initial performance in 1937, the writer and diarist, Lionel Bradley found it amusing but unlikely to last beyond ten years.[69] The anonymous critic of *The Bystander* regarded it as a Berners ballet and wondered if he should

> call Lord Berners a fifth Marx Brother or a Lewis Carroll of ballet? His 'Wedding Bouquet' is glorious nonsense, more witty than farce. His period is Edwardian, his theme is a French provincial wedding, set to his own music and words by Gertrude Stein, decorated by his own setting and dresses.[70]

Arnold Haskell, writing in the *Dancing Times*, made the point that the artists have been true to their intentions, that the ballet 'was light, but never flippant, and Berners, both in setting and music, showed a deep understanding and sympathy for the Edwardian period'.[71] He regarded it as a burlesque of the Edwardian music hall but did not believe it to be an enduring masterpiece.[72] Sibthorpe, whose unpublished manuscript on the Vic-Wells recounts the early years of the company, was less enthusiastic. He argues that

> Ashton's choreography refuses to allow anyone to do much dancing, the Stein-song is intoned by a group of singers... and there is a further gratifying touch of differentness-at-all-costs in the allusive comments printed below the name of each character in the programme.[73]

James Monahan in *The Manchester Guardian* remarked that 'the most observable nonsense came from Miss Stein', although he did regard the ballet as funny.[74] Haskell in *The Daily Telegraph* praises Stein's words and suggests that they are not 'unintelligible or deep in their hidden meaning, they are just excellent theatre and their rhythm forms an admirable accompaniment to the dancing'.[75] In general, the critics did not find Stein's writing comprehensible and none seemed to realise that the material came from her play *They Must. Be Wedded. To Their Wife*. In these early reviews, the focus was on the humour and wit and on the contributions of Berners and Stein, Ashton's choreography is hardly mentioned. Occasionally, a critic refers to the dance movement. Haskell in another review mentioned that 'Ashton never relied on mime or knockabout comedy alone, but provided much that was interesting as pure dancing.'[76] Richardson also comments on the choreography praising Ashton for 'the brilliant arrangement of Pépé's dances. Pépé could have been a nuisance and ridiculous – instead Pépé is welcome and really funny'.[77] Beyond comments like these, little is written about the choreography.

In revivals, critics still admired the ballet but generally focused on the dancers' performances rather than the work itself. They found the performances poor and Monahan argued that the Stein words were dated and 'a bit of a private joke', with 'the choreographic action... imprisoned in those words'.[78] This may well have been because of the change to spoken narrative with different Speakers imposing meaningless intonations on the words. When the ballet was revived in 2004, for the centenary of Ashton's birth, the critics were more positive, both about the ballet and the performances. Judith Mackrell in the *Guardian* regarded it as an *'amuse-bouche'* that would 'whet... appetites for the rest of the season',[79] while Clarke found the performance 'lighthearted, witty, funny, sometimes a little sad'.[80] But it was Jennings, the *Observer's* critic, who recognised the sophistication and seriousness of the choreography, despite finding Stein's words unsophisticated. He argued that while the choreography appears straightforward with 'nursery steps... match(ing) the libretto's simplistically prepared phrases', it comprises 'pared-down *enchaînements* [which are] an essential stroke of the portraitist's pen'.[81]

Conclusion

In *A Wedding Bouquet* Ashton handles the witty subject matter with care. His choreography treats dance very seriously and the movement is tightly-knit, drawn from a small pool of steps (see Chapter I). Like Stein's sentences and Berners' music, the structure is fragmentary. The solos have short scraps of dance and even the pas de deux and trios are brief. Yet it was one of the works for which Ashton felt most affection. In conversation with Clement Crisp in 1963, he observed that

> although it is a humorous ballet, it's rather Chaplinesque in the sense that it has an underlying sadness. And... I think all the characters are very well rounded, and what humour there is is almost a tragic humour in a way.[82]

Throughout this chapter I have shown the integrated nature of this work; Stein's sparse, fragmented, internal-looking prose influenced the musical, dance movement and choreographic styles but without destroying the individuality of choreographer and composer. Believing that one thing is as important as another, she never valued one word more than another and this is reflected in Ashton's dance movement. He does not emphasise the virtuoso steps or give them prominence over linking steps; all are treated equally. Each of the three artists made compromises for the sake of the work as a whole: Stein allowed her text to be cut, Berners agreed to cuts in the music and Ashton worked within parameters set by both text and music, adjusting his style accordingly. The ballet emerges less as a light and frothy confection and more as a work which focuses self-reflectively on dance, music and literature.

The analysis also shows that dancers interpreting the piece need to focus carefully on the dance movement itself and that the comedy comes from understanding the impulses of the movement, not from facial contortions, and that the steps cannot be executed with classroom precision. Speed and mobility are valued above turnout and limb flexibility. If Ashton was not a radical, this ballet with its mix of high art and popular culture shows him to be hugely inventive and no one can watch the work and fail to be touched by the humanity of the characters and the ingenious use of the *danse d'école*. Its dance movement presents a prime example of Ashton style: intricate steps, joined to others that force the dancer to change direction rapidly, short dance phrases, movement initiated from the torso and restless spatial floor patterns.

Illuminations

Ashton and the dancers from the New York City Ballet might be thought of as the originators of *Illuminations* (1950) but although neither Britten (1914-1976) nor Rimbaud (1854-1891) directly collaborated with Ashton, they are equally as important and a vital part of the ballet and to understanding the ballet's style. The ballet was inspired by the poetry of the French poet, Rimbaud, and his life, as described in Enid Starkie's biography. Ashton sought to be true to the spirit of Rimbaud's poems and was keen too to include aspects of Rimbaud's life. Having read the poetry and then Starkie's biography, he was gripped by Rimbaud, whose life he found both moving and profoundly sad.[83] And when in 1945 he heard Britten's music for *Les Illuminations* (1939) he promised the composer that he would use it for a ballet.[84]

Rimbaud and *Les Illuminations*

I'm now making myself as scummy as I can. Why? I want to be a poet, and I'm working at turning myself into a seer. You won't understand any of this, and I'm almost incapable of explaining it to you. The idea is to reach the unknown by the derangement of all the senses. It involves enormous suffering, but one must be strong and be a born poet. It's really not my fault.[85]

This extract comes from a letter Rimbaud wrote to his teacher Georges Izambard on 13 May 1871. It reads like a manifesto for symbolist poetry, since it expresses an attempt to write about reality in a way that is almost wholly oblique. Symbolism is regarded as a reaction to the realism of the earlier nineteenth century poetry and a return to writing that fore-grounded mystical and religious matters. Rimbaud's poems are not descriptive, neither are they narrative. Rather they comprise imagery and symbolic references, making them highly complex and difficult. Writers on Rimbaud often highlight his debauchery, yet he was also a serious and profound writer. Starkie clams that Rimbaud's mystical poems, of which there are several in *Les Illuminations*, 'are a manifestation of an experience trying to find expression in a medium which cannot contain it'.[86] Fantastic and exquisite images are at the heart of *Les Illuminations* and in the ballet Ashton attempts to capture these; the work is suffused with potent imagery. Rimbaud achieved cult status in France in the late nineteenth century and ten years after his death a monument was erected to him in his home town of Charleville, near the Belgian border. Quite apart from his extraordinary writing, his tumultuous and often chaotic life puzzled biographers and literary critics. Starkie argues that there are major problems confronting anyone trying to get to grips with Rimbaud. He is a difficult artist to understand given the contradictions and complexities of his life.

Ashton did not just use the poems chosen by Britten, he also took images from the whole work and from Starkie's biography. So Ashton's interpretation is coloured by Starkie's portrayal of Rimbaud's life. In his early years, Rimbaud was a brilliant student, a model pupil who won all the school prizes. By the time he reached sixteen, however, he had become defiant, unruly and rebellious. This may have been caused by the departure of his teacher, Izambard, who had been both mentor and friend. Not long before his eighteenth birthday, he moved to Paris where he met the poet Paul Verlaine. Verlaine became his lover, champion and supporter for the next two years (1871-73). But their relationship was tempestuous and difficult and ended with Verlaine shooting Rimbaud in the arm. Starkie believes that they never met again. A year later, Rimbaud ceased writing and spent the rest of his short life in North Africa as a trader, writing no more poetry.

The poems in *Les Illuminations* have been described as an evasion, 'something to help him to escape from sordid reality and to find his own form of life'.[87] For Rimbaud, childhood seemed to have been a world of virtuousness and purity and when his debauched life became too sordid, he longed to return to the innocence of this world. Starkie argues that *Les Illuminations* is full of remembered images from childhood, both from his own and in general, presented without any attempt to analyse them. Combined with elements from his study of magic and alchemy, the images are hallucinatory and at times mystical, though mysticism derived more from alchemy than Christianity. Throughout the poem Rimbaud creates a made-up world, the poet's ideal world, consisting of a series of contrasting images which Starkie considers are an attempt to recapture the intensity and magic of childhood. Rimbaud believed that the child receives sensations directly, without analysing them and thus could create a more profound world, a world of limitless possibilities. According to Ernest Delahaye, his closest school friend, Rimbaud once observed that in childhood;

> The whole of poetry is there. We have only to open our senses and then to fix, with words, what they have received. We have only to listen to our sensitiveness to everything that we feel, whatever it may be, and to fix with words what it tells us has happened.[88]

Rimbaud was also concerned with dreams. To capture the sensation of dreams he created his own dream world through smoking hashish, which produced hallucinatory images and, for a time, allowed him to be in a state of unreality. In *Les Illuminations* he tries to create the sensations, the wonder and innocence of childhood with the contradictory and dream-like images that hallucination produces.

Poetry, for Rimbaud was a way of exploring the infinite; it was spiritual and mystical.[89] He delved into notions of virtue and evil, or as Starkie puts it, the struggle between the angel and the devil. For not only are the poems about the sensations of childhood, they are also concerned with the experiences of evil and goodness, emanating chiefly from questions of religion. Several readers have found the poems truly profound and have been awed by the transcendental experience expressed in them. Some have even believed that reading Rimbaud restored them to religious conviction. Paul Claudel, the French Catholic philosopher, claimed that he owed his return to the faith to Rimbaud, *Les Illuminations*, he declared, brought him 'the tremendous revelation of the supernatural everywhere around [him]'.[90]

Britten and *Illuminations*

Britten (1913-1976), the English composer and conductor, was a major figure in twentieth century British music. He composed operas, orchestral, choral, chamber and film music as well as songs for the solo voice. He too was fascinated by the wonder and magic of childhood and it was probably this that drew him to the poems.[91] Like Rimbaud, he believed children were capable of experiencing sharper feelings and of appreciating natural beauty more intensely than adults.[92] According to Christopher Palmer the links between Rimbaud and Britten are palpable.[93]

Britten was also drawn to the idea of composite arts. During the 1930s he had collaborated with the poet W. H. Auden on several films, particularly documentaries, for the GPO (General Post Office) film unit in Blackheath and this allowed him to work with a variety of other artists.[94] Possibly because of his friendship with Auden, he became involved with Rupert Doone's Group Theatre, a collection of individuals, established in 1932 with the express purpose of co-operative training, in music dance and drama.[95] They performed at the Mercury, Rambert's small theatre in Notting Hill Gate, where Ashton began his choreographic career. Doone was a dancer and choreographer and had been in Ida Rubinstein's company. Difficult, though innovative, Doone's work embraced the notion of total theatre and Britten's involvement can only have reinforced his view that theatre should combine all the arts. Britten made the music for seven of Doone's productions, from *Timon of Athens* in December 1935 to Auden and Christopher Isherwood's *The Ascent of F6* in June 1939.

Of *Les Illuminations*' forty-two poems, Britten chose eight. Peter Porter points out that Britten's selection shows just how skilful he was at knowing which text is most suited to music.[96] Most of the music was written when Britten was living in New York in 1939, though he had composed *Antique* before leaving England. Made for string orchestra and voice (originally soprano but later sung by the tenor Peter Pears), the music could be seen as responding to the dichotomy in the poetry between innocence and experience, between good and evil. This is manifest early in the opening fanfare, where there is a tension in the orchestra caused by an opposition between the violas and the violins: the former enter in E Major whilst the latter are in B Flat.[97] As Charles Hazlewood suggests, Britten seems to be considering musically the opposition between youth and experience.[98]

Ashton and Rimbaud

If Britten was hugely attracted to Rimbaud, so too was Ashton. For Ashton, Rimbaud's life was intensely sad and his poems immediate and sensational. He read them in French, although his working library also had translations, along with six volumes of Rimbaud poems, two biographies and five volumes of writings by Verlaine. Ashton's reading of Rimbaud's poems during the Second World War and Starkie's biography in 1947 left a deep impression and the former may well have encouraged him to read other spiritual literature. At the beginning of the war, he had made a pact with Lambert to read the whole of the Bible and in 1944 began studying the works of the Spanish mystics, St Theresa of Avila and St John of the Cross.[99] Although not deeply religious, Ashton did have some religious convictions. He had attended a Catholic school in his youth in Lima and had served as an acolyte to the Archbishop in Lima's cathedral. Kavanagh maintains that he retained something of this Catholicism throughout his life.[100]

Given the material he was reading, it is hardly surprising that several of the works Ashton made during the 1940s deal with, or make reference to the mystical. If not directly concerned with mysticism, they are works which have religious overtones, and *Illuminations*, though made in 1950, is really part of that group. One piece in particular, *Symphonic Variations* (1946), although non narrative, had a scenario based on mystical notions of love.[101] We cannot know what Ashton gained from reading the work of the mystics but there are moments in *Symphonic* which suggest ecstasy. In the duet when the central woman is lifted just above the floor and then is progressively lifted till she reaches high above the man, she appears to have reached a moment of deep spiritual bliss, particularly as the moment is accompanied by a section of soaring music. While *Illuminations* does not have the serenity of *Symphonic*, nor the ritualistic elements of *The Wise Virgins* (1939) or even the fierce despair of *Dante Sonata* (1941), there are moments in the *Being Beauteous* section which recall *Symphonic*. Sacred Love enters with other-worldly, gliding *bourrée couru* and later is lifted just off the ground in low, hovering lifts. Even her exit, in which she is held high by the men in wide scissor split legs, has an air of serenity and spirituality.

Illuminations comprises a series of fragments infused with images from the poems; some refer to the hallucinatory sections, others are more mystical. Ashton also tries to reflect some of the conflicts of the poetry. In a letter to Beaton, he observes that 'Rimbaud was not afraid of the most penetrating and excruciating metaphors'.[102] Although concerned not to make the dance obvious, Ashton found it difficult to transfer the imagery, commenting that

> there cannot be characters in a ballet (as in drama or the novel) the figures must appear must, of necessity be archetypical... *Illuminations*, dealing as it does with the most fantastic poetry and poet in the history of literature must of necessity avoid the obvious yet the ballet must be a ballet.[103]

In the ballet he vacillates between the more debauched imagery and those of childhood and yet is keen to retain subtlety. But the imagery that Ashton quotes later in this letter does not come from the poems in Britten's *Illuminations* but from other poems in the work. Lines like the 'parlour at the bottom of the lake' come from Rimbaud's later poem *Une Saison en Enfer*.[104] So when Ashton wrote the following lines to Beaton, he must have been familiar with most of Rimbaud's work.

The major effect in Rimbaud is reversal. 'the drawing room at the bottom of the lake' – the cathedral on an iceberg surrounded by fire – the 'alchemy of the word' – everything becoming something else.[105]

Initially he wanted these scenes, or something like them, to be part of the ballet.

> Through a change of light could Charleville become something else? Can the whore change into an angel? Can the dandy be a child playing diavolo? Can the goose girl become a princess – and the princess a charwoman? The birds might be mechanical – the baker's loves might be guns or swords; a bird on the hat maker's head might be real and fly away. These should not be merely symbolical activities. Symbols tend to contract. Evocation is what is needed.[106]

Some find their way into the choreography, giving it a contradictory and dream-like quality, supported by the costumes.

Cecil Beaton's Role

This was a ballet which was fervently discussed before a single step was formed. 'No ballet upon which I have ever worked has entailed so much investigation and thought as *Les Illuminations*' (sic) recalled Beaton.[107] Beaton and Lincoln Kirstein started work on the designs before Ashton's arrival in New York in early 1950. Writing about their initial discussions in the British *Vogue* before the ballet travelled to London Beaton explains that

> Kirstein and I agreed on certain essentials for the ballet. It must have a child-like quality; it must be as provocative and daring as Rimbaud's poetry itself. There must be more in it than it seems – that nothing in fact is what it sets out to be... To begin with we agreed everything tawdry, tattered, splashed with mud; everything should be extremely poor, patched, darned, mended and torn again; everything should be transparent, nothing painted, nothing solid. We looked at the paintings of Klee, and certain aspects of this extraordinary painter seemed to be in the same spirit as Rimbaud...[108]

While Ashton agreed to retain the sense of innocence, he did not accept the other ideas offered by Beaton and Kirstein. The three eventually agreed to use designs inspired by Pierrot outfits and the device of a ballet within a ballet in which a troupe of Pierrots are disguising themselves as Rimbaud, as his townspeople, as his muse and as kings and queens. As the work developed, the ballet within a ballet disappeared.[109] The sets and costumes are in black and white, except in *Royauté* and *Marine*, the scenes with the king and queen, who wear the royal blue and red. Otherwise, the only other colour on stage comes from a red hat worn by the Birdcage Lady. For the townspeople, each of whom is a named character or type, the costumes are cumbersome, disguising the body with voluminous trousers and long enveloping tops. Each wears a distinctive hat, describing their occupation, and soft shoes with pom-poms on the front, matching those on their outfits. Almost all the townspeople are played by women. Men are used in *Royauté and Marine*, although the Train-bearers in these scenes are women. The costumes were criticised by some critics for being too pretty but they now look more appropriate, more successful. And, in *Being Beauteous*, the naked torsos of the men are almost contemporary in appearance.

The dance movement of the group is enhanced by the capacious outfits of the townspeople, which, through rhythmic complexity, focuses our attention on the lower body. The whole body is not outlined but disguised by these roomy clothes. There are no svelte bodies amongst these groups and even those of the two principal dancers are not clearly outlined. Sacred Love, in a below the knee tutu, initially appears somewhat cat-like with two large ears as part of her headdress and the puffed-up sleeves, enlarged with pom-poms, make her arms look slightly grotesque. Later in *Being Beauteous*, she wears a crown. Standing out from the other characters, the Poet is dressed in pin-striped tights and a blazer, the borders of which are outlined with white braid, and has pom poms for buttons.

Yet there are clearly defined bodies. The four male dancers in *Being Beauteous* are semi-naked. They wear ruffs at the neck and nothing else except tight knickers and one trouser leg (the other leg is bare). In a photograph in Vaughan's book of the four men, they gaze passively at the camera, their maleness modified. In a work in which male sexuality is central, perhaps Ashton and Beaton are making a covert statement. Unusual for the time was the absence of tights for Profane Love. She wears an asymmetrical dress adorned with a patterned sash and only one pointe shoe, which was Ashton's idea, decided on during rehearsal. Could this have been to highlight the ambiguous nature of Rimbaud's sexuality or was it a choreographic device, a self-imposed restriction?

New York City Ballet Dancers

Illuminations is a ballet made on performers whose dance style was unfamiliar to Ashton. New York City Ballet dancers had a training that was quite different from that in the Sadler's Wells Ballet and the dancers' working relationship with Balanchine even more so. He was possibly the greatest influence in the lives of most of the dancers. They strove to please him and in later years Gelsey Kirkland maintained that she loved him more than her father. Ashton, though held in affection by his dancers, had a very different relationship. For Balanchine, the classroom and the stage were one and in

company class he created the technique and style for his choreography designed to 'prepare [the dancers] to dance ballets better and more in keeping
with his aesthetic'.[110] While Ashton was not interested in training or classroom teaching, teaching was central to Balanchine's life. As Barbara
Walczak observes 'it was obvious that he would rather be teaching than doing anything else in the world'.[111] Gay Morris supports this, commenting
that Balanchine was 'an instrument maker... for his entire career he worked
at forming a more sensitive and virtuosic human instrument'.[112]

Balanchine writing in 1937 described the American spirit as 'cold, crys-
talline, luminous, hard as light'.[113] He admired this tough spirit because it
enabled performers to exhibit material without drawing attention to themselves. He wanted the dancers to show the dancing and not the dancer. And
portrayal of character was not central to his work:

> I am less interested in the portrait of any real character than in the
> choreographic idea behind the dance action. Thus the importance of the
> story itself becomes reduced to being the frame for the picture I want to
> paint. [114]

By the time Ashton arrived in 1950, Balanchine had been developing his
approach for some years. It was designed to assist and compliment the then
more athletic figures of the American dancers. He encouraged high extensions but he also demanded speed and exaggeration, 'Make it bigger, explode,
expand'.[115] He believed in 'the highest possible levels of skill and finesse,
all aimed at making real, if only briefly, the idealised beauty of the human
body.'[116] He cultivated tall, lean, even boyish-looking women. The writer R.P.
Blackmur described the female Balanchine dancers in 1958 as being a 'terri-
fying vision of proficiency' but having 'no faces and no legs that were
inhabited'.[117]

It is not known how the cast was selected, or by whom, but it is likely that
Ashton had some control. If so, he probably chose Melissa Hayden because
she had had experience outside the narrow ballet world (she had previously
danced at Radio City Music Hall). Having joined the company only a few
months before Ashton arrived, she had probably not yet acquired
Balanchine's style and had earthier qualities and more dramatic abilities
than other Balanchine dancers of the time. Lilian Moore noted that in another work, *The Duel*, performed during the 1950 season, that Hayden's
performance was dramatic, powerful and vivacious.[118] Edwin Denby, that
most perceptive of critics, observed that Hayden 'has a Lautrec edge and
vehement stab and a strange softness in her she seems to hate; a great actress
if she learns calm.'[119] Clearly Ashton perceived this Lautrecian quality when
he cast her for Profane Love.

Tanaquil LeClercq, a more sublime dancer, was at the time Balanchine's newest muse and he may well have suggested her for Sacred Love. To Ashton's eyes, LeClercq may have seemed a somewhat aloof and technically exact dancer. Her movement was bold and expansive and she covered space in a way contemporary English dancers did not. Ashton chose not to exploit her Balanchine training and did not give her movement that required attack, speed or sharp accents. Denby found that she also had a 'heavenly radiance and a lovely adagio...' as well as 'intelligence in every movement, [and] delicacy of... rhythmic attack.'[120] Ashton drew on these more serene qualities for Sacred Love.

The dancing of Balanchine's male dancers was less articulated, less vigorous than that of the women. Moore wrote that, as the Poet, Nicholas Magallanes, gave the best performance of his career. She described him as a 'neat and accomplished dancer' though rather colourless but wrote that in some scenes his dancing was 'fluid and forceful as well as technically facile'.[121] As the Dandy, Robert Barnett attracted attention; he had strong virtuoso movement with intricate beats and jumps. Barnett, who had only recently joined the company, had initially studied ballet with Irena Nijinska, whose Cecchetti style training he had enjoyed, and then with Bronislava Nijinska, who came to Irena's studio to pick those she regarded as particularly talented.[122] His earlier lessons had been in tap dancing and the effortlessness with which the Dandy's movement has to be performed with its fast, slick footwork has qualities associated with tap. And the prop, held by the Dandy, restricts his arm movement, linking the movement style to that of Nijinska.

Ashton's Choreography and Approach to the Text

Britten's music has eight poems and a one line *Fanfare* and *Interlude* and while Ashton treated each poem as a discrete element, the ballet has ten sections. Hazlewood describes the opening line in the music, the Fanfare, as the motto for the whole piece and Ashton uses it as the central motif in the ballet to highlight the Poet's changing values; moving from enjoyment of the bodily and sensual pleasures to those of the spirit.[123] The line 'J'ai seul la clef de cette parade sauvage'(I alone hold the key to this savage parade),[124] occurs three times: at the beginning, after *Marine*, and at the end of *Parade*. The Poet's movement to this line starts with a short gestural section, comprising a step forward bringing the arms to chest height and opening outwards in an inclusive gesture towards the audience. He kneels and his hands come into his chest as if in supplication. The Poet then steps forward again stretching the right arm up and as it slowly falls across the chest, the other arm frames his head. For a moment the image is frozen, captured photographically. When the gestural section occurs at the end of *Parade*, the Poet is held aloft by the Townspeople and only performs the arm gestures. Following the gestural section, the Poet performs a short section of virtuoso jumps ending, initially, in the splits. He completes the phrase cluster with a double *tour en l'air* ending lying on the floor. The second occurrence of the motif has a similar jumped section but, instead of ending in the splits, the Poet lunges to an *arabesque croisée à terre* and this time, the double *tour* ends on both knees. The third occurrence does not include the jumped section; instead the Poet simply gestures first to Sacred Love and then to Profane Love, finishing with a second gesture to Sacred Love.

Musically, the refrain is repeated exactly but as he was to do later in *Le Rossignol*, which also has three refrains, Ashton developed the movement for each phrase cluster, modifying it to suggest the changing moods or perceptions of the Poet. Dynamically, the movement does not alter. The phrases meld seamlessly into each other and the movement extends outward into the space, getting bigger in the second, jumping phrase and remaining stationary at the end. Inspired by the music and the words, the phrase refers to the mystical powers of the Poet, and the movement, initially pensive, becomes powerful and dazzling as the Poet takes control. Even in the final occurrence, he is in control. The Poet liberates himself from the grasp of the Townspeople and is free to follow Sacred Love. He has shaken off the restraints of Profane love.

Unusually for Ashton, the movement of the three main characters, the Poet, Sacred Love and Profane Love, is generally flowing, sustained and extends into the space beyond the body; it is more of a Balanchine characteristic really. In *Villes*, just after he dons a bowler hat, the Poet performs a short crisp cluster of movements which dart into the space and this is more characteristic of Ashton. Variation in dynamic is found in the short solo for the Dandy and in the choreography for the group, which frequently moves in contrast to one of the major characters. The gestures and the acting also change the dynamic. Possibly because Ashton used some of the words literally, he was less concerned with playing with the movement. Possibly too because the dancers were strange and differently trained, he could not get them to make choreographic contributions. The choreography does not depend on having actor dancers, probably because, apart from Hayden, the dancers from New York City Ballet were not renowned for their acting abilities. As Denby observes 'when one looks for miming, for acting too, one sees with surprise the company isn't performing at all'.[125] Acting is written into the movement, though it is still open to rhythmic and interpretational subtleties.

Table 2 (opposite) sets out the main dynamic elements in each section of *Illuminations*.

From this table, it appears that Ashton tied his work closely to the text of the poems but because the thoughts in the poem do not follow each other in a

Table 2

Title of Poem	Character/s	Movement	Use of poetic material
Fanfare	Poet	Movement contained within confines of body, on entrance of voice becomes sustained, flowing	Main motif: 'J'ai seul la clef de cette parade sauvage.' Not used literally
Villes	Poet, Townspeople, Dandy and Sacred Love	Townspeople: jagged and floppy Dandy: abrupt, piercing phrases; Poet: short darting, different from Dandy	Responds to words by creating bustle of town but also uses Starkie's descriptions of Rimbaud's actions in Charleville
Phrase	Poet	Gestural movement as described in the poem	Literal use of language
Antique	Poet, Sacred Love, Profane Love, duet between Poet and Profane Love	Choreography flows, movement lingers and spreads into space	Uses the poem initially for the mood and then literally for Profane Love
Royauté	Group including King and Queen	Staccato, impactive accompanied by gesture and violence	Uses the description but not the literal meaning
Marine	Poet accompanied by those in Royauté	Gesture, silent acting, turbulent, rotating movement	Literally uses tourbillons (whirlpools) and the sense of the words
Interlude	Poet with Profane Love followed by motif	Sustained with some violent gesture; main motif	Motif: 'J'ai seul la clef'
Being Beauteous	Sacred Love with four Cavaliers	Undulating, hovering, sustained	Uses some words literally: rise, swell, tremble. Also sense of the poem: the white virginal image
Parade	Group, Poet joined by Profane Love and Sacred Love	Gestural, silent acting, rough, at times crisp, at times continuous	Uses the sense literally, following the text but ends with main motif: '
[et] Départ	All	Sombre, sustained walking	Responds to the sense of the words.

logical fashion, he could not present a literal evocation of the poems. Rather, as in *A Wedding Bouquet*, he evokes the sense and imagery with an occasional literal allusion, though he also adds a number of images from Rimbaud's life.

As in the majority of Ashton ballets, the stylistic movements are limited to a small group of steps. The *rond de jambe à terre*, *pas de chat*, *petit battement* and *coupé ballonné* make their appearance and Ashton has added the beginning of a *grand rond de jambe en l'air*, the raised circular leg gesture. It begins as a circular movement but stops part of the way round in mid-air. The ballet also has a series of different rhythmic walks in which the head and hands move in different rhythms from the feet. Almost every section has something typical of Ashton's style but in order too to show his complex use of text, biography and imagery, I will highlight these by going through most sections; some in more detail than others.

Villes

I have already mentioned the recurring motif, which has much of the solo content for the Poet. But the Poet's second solo dance in *Parade* has more emphatic movement. The phrases are short, each cluster repeats three times and each ends with a pronounced extension into the space. At the start of *Villes*, the Poet picks up a bowler hat and holds it throughout this short dance, so that one of his arms is not entirely free. The moment of contact with the hat could go unnoticed but it heralds the Poet's entrance into the city, London. Starkie believes that *Villes* was written during or just after Rimbaud's and Verlaine's first visit to London in 1872. The poem shows the impact that the metropolis had on Rimbaud with its multi-cultural group- ings, its trains, suburbs, bell-towers and general noise and bustle. Rimbaud bought a top hat in London so that he might appear respectable. Starkie claims that he was 'inordinately proud of [it]. It remained for some years his symbol of riches and respectability'.[126] Delahaye, his childhood friend, also wrote that 'he loved it like an old and venerable friend...and used to smooth its silky surface with his elbow.'[127] This gesture is not in the present version but may have been in the 1950 version, since many of Starkie's observations are included in the ballet. The Dandy wears a top-hat and his presence could also be a reference to Rimbaud's London apparel. In *Villes*, Ashton alludes to other moments of Rimbaud's life. In his notes for Beaton, Ashton wrote that he would like to incorporate the following image:

> Verlaine and Rimbaud after days of the most terrible debauchery – (cov- ered with wine stains, eyes darkened from laudanum, semen dried on trousers, bodies filthy, hair wild) buying tickets for the opera – moving up the grand staircase among the jewelled ladies, the polished gentleman –

the London audiences of the time. Vaughan is critical of the duet, describing it as an over literal copulation scene between the Poet and Profane Love but while he finds the enveloping legs too literal, it is worth pointing out that it is likely that Ashton was following the poetry in two respects. In French the line is 'Ton coeur bat dans ce ventre où dort le double sexe', (the heart beats in that womb where sleeps Hermaphrodite). Profane Love's single pointe shoe hints at the poetry's reference to 'le double sexe' and possibly too to Rimbaud's relationship with Verlaine and the bisexuality of both. As the two entwine more explicitly, the words of the poem, 'Promène-toi la nuit, en mouvant doucement cette cuisse, cette second cuisse et cette jambe de gauche' (Walk at night, softly moving this thigh, this other thigh, this left leg), are echoed in the dance. Standing, pressed against each other, Profane Love, with a circular movement, raises her leg over that of the Poet, to end resting on his thigh; he then repeats her gesture with his left leg, so they are now tightly pressed together. For the dance's ending, Ashton has literally choreographed the words of the poem.

Royauté and Marine

Using the Dandy's *petits battements* as a motif, Ashton creates a version for the Herald, Drummer and Acolytes that has two taps with a pointed foot on the ground, attached to a bouncing walk. It is a reference to the earlier phrase in *Villes*, where the Dandy performs a set of three *petits battements*, which lead into a double *tour en l'air* and finish in an exaggerated pose. Ashton links the characters and, like the Dandy, the Herald and Drummer are also quite precious. The walk too recalls that in *Villes*, though there the feet in the bouncing walk move from half pointe to flat foot, whereas, in *Royauté*, the performers jump to land on a flat foot. When Ashton notes to Beaton that 'the major effect in Rimbaud is reversal', he literally takes that notion and injects it into the dance movement, just as he fragmented the dance phrases in *A Wedding Bouquet*, complementing and supporting Stein's writing. *Marine* follows without a break and the scene ends violently with the Poet usurping the crown and rejecting Profane Love, who has re-appeared to lure the Poet back into her arms. But the violence makes the scene which follows all the more sacred and serene.

Being Beauteous

Comprising a quartet of men and Sacred Love, this quintet is most closely linked with Ashton's 1965 work *Monotones*. Vaughan also sees connections with *Scènes de ballet* (1948) and *Valses nobles et sentimentales* (1947) and, although there are some, both the dynamic and pace of *Scènes* are so different that the two are difficult to compare.[132] The atmosphere is mystical, heightened by the deep blue lighting and the soft music, which has a rich harmonic texture with long phrases giving it a tranquil and lyrical feeling.[133] The densely white costumes are perhaps a reflection of the snowy background mentioned in the poem, which speaks of death:

> Des sifflements de mort et des circles de musique sourde font monter, s'élargir et trembler comme un spectre ce corps adore; (Death is all round her, and whistling, dying breaths, and circles of hollow music, cause this adored body to rise, to swell and to tremble like a spectre.)[134]

Ashton used these metaphors and adjectives for the choreography. Central to the dance is the *pas de bourrée couru*. Sacred Love enters and seems to glide across the stage forwards and backwards and in continuous turns. Perhaps Pavlova is the inspiration for this but the mood is formal, serene, peaceful and very close to that of *Monotones* and, as I mentioned earlier, *Symphonic Variations*. As in *Monotones*, the men here also have a slow grounded circular movement, a *rond de jambe à terre*. They are in a square formation and enclose Sacred Love as she *bourrées* in their midst. The supported adage section, performed generally with two men at a time appears again in the turning, frontal attitude of the later work, as does the formal use of gesture. The man offers his hand to the woman and she accepts, carefully placing her hand in his. Near the end, Sacred Love moves to each man to perform a turn ending in arabesque, linking with both *The Sleeping Beauty* and *Monotones* and just as in the latter work, the clipped ending of the phrase punctuates the smoothness of the music. The low, just-off-the-ground lifts in which the woman does little *jeté-* like walks from foot to foot anticipate *Monotones*, as do the tightly executed *entrechats*. As the woman is lifted vertically, she quickly crosses her legs forward and back in a series of *entrechats*. It is a very Ashtonian movement, both the elevation of the woman, supported by several men and the sudden agitated nature of the *entrechats*. The final section in which the woman is lifted in a split *jeté* literally presents the poem's image of a woman borne on 'light winds' (l'air léger). From the front of the stage, the poet watches but is not part of the sequence. It is as though he is hallucinating; the whole section is dream-like and a complete contrast with the previous scene.

Parade

The opening characters return here but engage more fully with the Poet. He becomes part of the action. No longer does he seem to control the events, rather he is beaten up by the other characters. Two Gendarmes attack him while the rest obliviously continue with their own dancing. Some of this looks forward to later Ashton dances, in particular *Ondine* (1958), where there is also a sinister group of pierrots, part of the Mediterranean Divertissements in Act III. They have a similar phrase of *petits jetés* as the eight in

Parade who do a small jumped *développé* (an unfolding of the leg) followed by three *petits jetés*, coupled with a semi-circular arm movement. At another moment, in *Parade*, the ensemble, arranged in two lines in front of the Poet, turns in towards him, with a raised curved arm held over their faces, and then *soutenu* out from him. In Act I Scene II of *Ondine*, the Ondines similarly obstruct the pathway of Palemon and Ondine. Ashton's tendency to re-use material in a slightly different context is significant because when he reprocesses the choreography, it looks quite different and unless we are very familiar with his work, we will not recognise it. The sound of a gunshot ends the section. Profane Love wounds the Poet and this is perhaps the closest link between Profane Love and Verlaine.[135] The Poet finally rejects Profane Love and follows Sacred Love, moving in a slow procession across the back section of the stage.

Stylistically, *Parade* is in familiar Ashton territory, evident in the quick jumps and an extended section of a kind of jumped, running movement. Running is important in Ashton dances, though it is usually used to highlight a moment of serenity as in the slow section of *Symphonic Variations* or the moment when the trio in *Monotones* run effortlessly in a large semi-circle. In *Parade* it is vigorous, even violent: as the group follows the Poet in a long procession, they start with a simulated kicking motion before performing eight jumped runs, first leaning right forward, almost horizontal and then right back. Leading from the core, the dancers are forced to move from the centre, giving the section its menacing qualities; their movements are heavy, intense and threatening. It reflects the poetry:

> O le plus violent Paradis de la grimace enragée!... Chinois, Hottentots, bohémiens, niais, hyènes, Molochs, vieilles démences, demons sinistres, ils mêlent les tours populaires, maternels avec les poses de les tendresses bestiales.

> (It is a violent Paradise of mad grimaces!... Chinese, Hottentots, gypsies, simpletons hyeneas, Molochs, old insanities, sinister demons, they alternate popular or maternal tricks with bestial poses and caresses)[136]

Response to the Ballet

Despite critics' comments to the contrary, Ashton's style is still intact: torso generated movement, a limited step vocabulary, (a few) phrases of rapid footwork and quick, uncomfortable changes of direction. Choreographically too the work is typically Ashtonian. Simple motifs are repeated, developed, made more complicated and used in different contexts and the whole, despite the fragmentary nature of the poetry and choreography, is tightly controlled.

In New York this ballet was applauded. The *New York Times* commented that Ashton had done a supremely subtle and impressive job, though 'without the slightest color of offence, with passion but with dignity'.[137] Not so the British press and particularly Richardson who wondered for whom the ballet had been intended, complaining that it could

> only be comprehensible to those who have the inclination to study the sordid existence, unhealthy mind and more frantic poems of a decadent 19th century poet, Arthur Rimbaud. The pistol shot which all but concludes the work, comes as a welcome ending to the revolting excesses of passion in which Rimbaud indulged and which Ashton prefers to stress to the detriment of the poet's more beautiful passages'.[138]

Kirstein was so incensed at a review in *The Times* that he wrote a letter complaining that 'presumably aware of the mixed beauty and grossness of Rimbaud's life and work, "our critic" could only recognise grossness on stage'.[139] In 1950, displays of sex and sexuality on stage were frowned on. Theatres were subject to censorship and it was illegal to take part in what were deemed to be homosexual acts until 1967. According to Abigail Wills, the 1950s

> saw the rise of acute public tension around homosexuality. Tabloid commentators in particular painted a picture of a hidden underworld of 'perverts' threatening the social and moral fabric of the nation.[140]

By the mid 1960s attitudes had changed and a range of what Wills calls 'permissive' legislation was brought in concerning divorce, abortion, suicide, homosexuality, censorship and capital punishment.[141] Yet in Britain, even today, the work causes controversy. In 1981, Ann Nugent found it a dated fifties piece in which the dancers were ill-used and although praising of Ashley Page, she remarks that

> [He] also triumphed in *Illuminations* – if triumph is the way to describe so unfulfilled a work where, for once, Ashton's choreography is inferior to his dancers.[142]

And an anonymous critic found it hard to believe that the work was even by Ashton.[143] Yet, many others found the work both profound and well worth mounting for the Royal Ballet, who performed it for the first time in late 1981. There were criticisms of the décor from some but not from John Percival. He wrote that the production 'does full justice to the marvellously imaginative collaboration of Ashton and Cecil Beaton'.[144] It will always remain a controversial work but analysis has helped to reveal its depths, its relationship to Ashton's other works and the fact that, despite having differently trained dancers, his style remains intact.

Conclusions: *Illuminations*

Rimbaud's life and his poetry are suffused into *Illuminations* in a way that is intriguing to unravel. What stands out in this work is its fragmentary nature but fractured differently from *A Wedding Bouquet*. In that work, the phrases, the language and sections are short, irregular without definite endings, except when the dancer exits. In *Illuminations*, the poetry is fragmented and comprises a myriad of fabulous images, placed side by side and evoking, as Ashton put it, a 'swoon of insight'.[145] In the end, what Ashton made is a succession of moving images. He does not try to explain the poems but captures their mystical ambivalence. This is why the Pierrot costumes work and are not, as Richard Buckle described them, 'too bizarre and pretty'.[146] They provide the sophisticated element while the choreography captures the untranslatable words, evoking the wonder and innocence of childhood juxtaposed with the contradictory and dream-like, hallucinatory images.

In these two works, we have seen how Ashton adapted his choreography and dance movement style to suit the music, the words and subject matter. In responding to Stein's fragmentary sentences, Ashton chopped the dances and dealt not only with the literal meaning of the words but also with the fractured sentences and short word phrases; these shaped the structure and form of his dances. There are no long solos and even the trios are but brief events scattered throughout the ballet. He also drew on stage dancing to reflect the popular dance melodies used by Berners. In *Illuminations*, Ashton used the qualities of Britten's music, the imagery and details of Rimbaud's life for his choreography. And in *A Wedding Bouquet*, I believe that there are also tacit references to Stein and Toklas's life together.

Familiar Ashton elements appear in the movement across both works. The emphasis on intricate footwork, using a small group of steps, is found in the dances of the Townspeople, the Dandy and for the Acolytes, Train-bearers, Drummer and Herald. In *A Wedding Bouquet*, intricate footwork is pervasive but with a much stronger emphasis on *épaulement*. In *Illuminations*, apart from the Dandy's dance, *épaulement* is limited and there are few quick, sudden changes of direction. It is still recognisable as Ashton's because of the short phrases and his tendency to force the torso to generate the movement.

Unusually for Ashton, his dancers played less of a role in the two works. I have no evidence that the dancers had any input into the 1937 dance but it is quite likely that they may have contributed nuances and sections of phrases. He used their individual personalities for the characters and drew on their technical capabilities. While he certainly indulged LeClercq's long flexible limbs and Hayden's acting talents, he does not seem to have drawn on the athleticism and energy of the New York dancers. Yet he was careful to make sure that Magallenes understood the poetry and vision of Rimbaud.

Where in all this is Ashton the classicist? Often seen as the conventional guardian of tradition, that Ashton is less in evidence here and this may be unsettling to those who regard him only as a maker of classical dances. Ashton was no rebel but he was not a conformer either. He was not against the *danse d'école*, far from it, but he did not use it undiluted. Whether we look at the bouncy travelling steps of the Townspeople or the playful phrases of the Wedding Guests, Ashton surprises us. We are struck by his quizzical attitude to the *danse d'école*; he plays with it affectionately, though he knew exactly what he was doing. What the analysis of these two works demonstrates is Ashton's versatility with a covert tendency to shock. They use written language as part of the choreography and are distinct from his narrative dances.

In chapter I, I outlined the complexity of style in dance and how a choreographer's style combines a number of elements which affect both the dance movement and choreography, though not all are present in every dance. In these two works, the signature steps recur, though rarely in their correct classroom form; there are also short phrases and quick changes of direction and weight. Aspects of stage dancing and of Nijinska's style are also evident, though little of Pavlova or Karsavina. Petipa's approach is glimpsed in *A Wedding Bouquet* in the divertissements section and in the Rose Adage section of *Illuminations* but not his use of steps. Absent from the works is the dancers' presence, though in *A Wedding Bouquet*, the personality of the original dancers is conspicuous. We can see too that material which appears again in different contexts is an important feature of Ashton's dances. It is not so much that he recycles the movement, rather he creates a dialogue with his own dances and we see it differently as a result. Sometimes this is a way of alerting us to a similar feature of a character or situation and sometimes it is there as a motif, or even as a satirical reference. These stylistic features recur throughout his work and his reprocessing of material appears in different contexts, making it look unfamiliar. They are found in his other works and continue to be a major focus of the chapters which follow.

1. Ashton was part of a fashionable, artistic set during the 1930s, see Kavanagh's biography.

2. Dickinson, (2008) 17.

3. Stein had a house in that region and it is thought Berners and Stein used the area as a background to the work.

4. Stein collaborated with Virgil Thomson on this and the production, which opened in New York had choreography by Frederick Ashton.

5. Kavanagh, Julie (1996) 152.

6. Haskell, Arnold (1937) *The Bystander*, June 2, 460.

7. This company became the Sadler's Wells Ballet in 1940 and The Royal Ballet in 1956

8. Stein (1874-1946) Berners (1883-1950) Ashton (1904-1988).

9. The libretto for *The Triumph of Neptune* was by Sacheverell Sitwell and choreography by George Balanchine.

10. Thomson, Virgil (1967) *Virgil Thomson*, London: Weidenfeld and Nicholson, 231-247

11. Dydo (2003) 12.

12. She did not, strictly speaking, collaborate with Ashton and Berners, since the play was written before the ballet but she accepted the cuts and changes made by Berners and, probably, Constant Lambert.

13. Kavanagh, 218.

14. Bay-Cheng, Sarah (2004) *Mama Dada: Gertrude Stein's Avant-Garde Theatre*, New York and London: Routledge, 2-3.

15. Bey-Cheng, 4.

16. Amory, Mark (1918) *Lord Berners: the Last Eccentric*, London: Chatto & Windus, 104-107.

17. Gifford, Mary (2007) *Lord Berners: Aspects of a Biography*, Unpublished PhD Thesis, Kings College, University of London, 152.

18. Jean-Aubry, Georges (April 1919) *The Musical Quarterly*, 5, no.2, 210-211, quoted in Gifford.

19. See Gifford, 157-158.

20. Quoted in Gifford (2008) 123.

21. Ibid.

22. See Dickinson, Peter (2008).

23. Dickinson Peter (2008) *Lord Berners: Composer Writer Painter*, Woodbridge: The Boydell Press, 18.

24. Stein, Gertrude (1949) *Last Operas and Plays*, New York: Rinehart & Company.

25. Quoted in Bay-Cheng, 49.

26. James Joyce *Ulysses* (1922) fragments the narrative as does Virginia Woolf in *Mrs Dalloway* (1925). In the latter, time is not linear and the characters move forward and backwards in time.

27. Stein, Gertrude (1935) 'Portraits and Repetition', in *Lectures in America*, New York: Random House, 165-208,

28. Dydo, Ulla (2003) *The Language that Rises*, Illinois: Northwestern University Press.

29. Dydo, 23.

30. Dydo, 16.

31. Dydo, 19.

32. Dydo, 19.

33. Interview, June 2008.

34. In France, there are strict rules of inheritance. Children cannot be disenfranchised and in the absence of children, close relative have claims on a substantial section of a property.

35. Amory, Mark (1998) *Lord Berners: The Last Eccentric*, London: Chatto and Windus, 164.

36. Letters in Berners Archive now in British Library.

37. Letter 18th July 1936 from Berners to Stein. Berners Archive.

38. Jones, Bryony (2003) *The Music of Lord Berners (1883-1950) 'The Versatile Peer'*, Aldershot, Hampshire: Ashgate, 95.

39. Jones, Bryony (2003) 93.

40. Ibid, 95.

41. Undated letter from Berners to Stein but probably written before 17th of March 1936. Berners Archive.

42. Berners in Amory (1998) 164.

43. Letter written to Stein from Berners on 17th March 1937, Berners Archive.

44. Quoted in Amory, 167.

45. Jones, Bryony (2003) 93.

46. This and the previous quote are taken from Flaubert, Gustave (1856-7/1981) *Madame Bovary*, trans. Alan Russell, London: Penguin Books, 39.

47. In July 1988, in an interview with some members of The Royal Ballet, de Valois makes a long plea for the teaching of all 23 *pas de bourrée*, because knowledge of them gives rise to incredible floor patterns of the feet. (Interview in the archives of The Royal Ballet).

48. There are two different versions of this. In the 1965 version she performs a quick *bourrée* movement before the eight *ronds de jambs*, while later this is omitted.

49. I have been unable to find an exact translation of this phrase but it seems to mean someone who is sophisticated, unaffected by the rest of the world. Letter from Berners to Stein, 17th March 1936 in the collection of the Berners Trust.

50. Strictly speaking the *chassé* is a chasing movement with the back foot pushing the front one forward but it is also used to describe a sliding movement.

51. Interview with Ninette de Valois , July 1988, in collection of the archives of the Royal Ballet.

52. See below for Jennings reference.

53. See the Ashton chapters in Jordan, Stephanie (2000) *Moving Music*, London: Dance Books and (2007) *Stravinsky Dances: Re-Visions Across a Century*, Alton: Dance Books.

54. It is difficult to hear how many times the words are repeated in the choral version as the sound tails off at the end.

55. Vaughan, David (1977) 13.

56. Interview with the author June 10th 2008.

57. Picarda, Pierre (1938) 'The Status of French Women in France', *Transactions of Grotius Society*, 24, 71-79.

58. Vorhaus, John (1994) *The Comic Toolbox*, Los Angeles: Silman–James Press, 42.

59. These are all small, quick jumps, either from one to two feet or from two to one or two to two as in the case of the *glissade*.

60. Sibthorp, H. S. (1941?) *The Vic-Wells Ballet 1931-1940*, unpublished manuscript in Theatre Museum, Victorian and Albert Museum.

61. Haskell, Arnold and Philip, J.S. Richardson (1932, facsimile reprint 2010) *Who's*

Who in Dancing 1932, London: The Noverre Press. It was edited by Haskell and Richardson and comprised a list of 'the leading men and women in the world of dancing'. This invaluable book summarises the contemporary state of dance and ballet in Britain, the latter, still referred to as operatic dancing.

62. An examination of the syllabuses of Enrico Cecchetti and the Royal Academy of Dancing testifies to this.

63. It seems from Berners' letters to Stein that the costumes were conceived before Berners met with Ashton but presumably too Ashton agreed to the long skirts and used them to advantage.

64. Sorley Walker, Kathrine (1996/7) 'A Wedding Bouquet', *Dance Now*, 6, no.1, 76-81

65. Quoted in Sorley Walker, 78.

66. Woodcock, Sarah (1993) 'Michael Somes', in Bremser, Martha, ed. *International Dictionary of Ballet*, Detroit, London, Washington: St James Press, 1322-1324.

67. Interview with Pamela May 1999.

68. Clarke Mary (1969) 'The First Wedding Bouquet', *Dancing Times*, November, 69.

69. Bradley, Lionel (1937) *Ballet Bulletin*, in the archives of the Theatre Museum, Victoria and Albert Museum, London.

70. Anon. (1937) *The Bystander* May 12, 263.

71. Haskell, Arnold (1937) *The Bystander*, June 2, 460.

72. Haskell, Arnold (1937) 'Balletomane's Log Book', *Dancing Times*, no. 321, June, 280, 281, 287.

73. Sibthorpe, H.S. (1941?) *The Vic-Wells Ballet (1931-1940)*, Unpublished manuscript in the Theatre Museum Victoria and Albert Museum, South Kensington London.

74. M. J. (James Monahan?) (1937) 'Ballet at Sadler's Wells', *The Manchester Guardian*, Thursday 29th April, 12.

75. Haskell, Arnold (1937) 'A New Choral Ballet', *The Daily Telegraph*', Wednesday 28th April, 12.

76. Haskell, Arnold (1937) *The Bystander*, June 2, 460.

77. Richardson, P.J.S. (1937) 'The Sitter Out', *Dancing Times*, no.321, June, 275

78. Monahan, James (1965) 'Dividends of Nostalgia', *Dancing Times*, LV, no. 652, January, 177-179.

79. Mackrell, Judith (2004) 'Royal Ballet Triple Bill', *The Guardian*, 25th October (no page numbers available).

80. Clarke, Mary (2004) 'Royal Ballet', *Dancing Times*, 95, no. 1132, December, 51, 53

81. Jennings, Luke (2004/05) 'They Must Be Wedded', *Dance Now*13, no. 4 Winter, 20-23.

82. Ashton in Crisp in Cohen (1974) 'Frederick Ashton: A Conversation', in Cohen, Selma Jeanne *Dance as a Theatre Art*, London: Dance Books, 169-173.

83. Vaughan (1977) 239.

84. Kavanagh, Julie (1996) 375.

85. Robb, Graham (2001) *Rimbaud*, London: Picador Books, 79-80.

86. Starkie, 239.

87. Starkie, 232.

88. quoted in Starkie, 234.

89. Starkie, 95.

90. Quoted in Starkie, 237.

91. Palmer, Christopher (1984) 'Embalmer of midnight' The Orchestral Song-Cycles', in Palmer, Christopher ed. *The Britten Companion*, London: Faber and Faber, 308-328.

92. Mitchell, Donald (1981) *Britten & Auden in the Thirties: The Year 1936*, London: Faber and Faber, 115.

93. Palmer, 311.

94. Mitchell, Donald, 87.

95. Sidnall, Michael (1984) *Dances of Death: The Group Theatre of London in the Thirties*, London: Faber & Faber.

96. Porter, Peter (1984) 'Composer and Poet', in Palmer, Christopher ed. *The Britten Companion*, London: Faber and Faber, 271-285.

97. Mentioned in BBC Radio 3 programme, *Discovering Music*, 6th May 2006.

98. BBC Radio 3 programme, *Discovering Music*, 6th May 2006.

99. Kavanagh, 375.

100. Kavanagh, 23.

101. See my article , Morris, Geraldine (2008) 'Visionary Dances: Ashton's Ballets of the Second World War', *Dance Research*, 26, no.2, 168-188.

102. Unpublished and undated transcript of a letter in the Ashton library.

103. Ibid.

104. Starkie, 234.

105. Unpublished and undated transcript of a letter in the Ashton library.

106. Ibid.

107. Beaton, Cecil (1951) *Ballet*, London: Wingate, 70.

108. Beaton, Cecil (1950) *Vogue*, no title and no page numbers.

109. Beaton, 73.

110. Shorer, Suki (1999) 'Balanchine Technique', *Ballet Review*, 27, no. 3, Fall, 11-38, 13.

111. Walczak, Barbara and Una Kai (2008) *Balanchine the Teacher*, Florida: University Press of Florida 9.

112. Morris, Gay (2005) 'Balanchine's Bodies', *Body & Society*, 11, no. 4, 19-44.

113. Balanchine, George (1937) 'Ballet Goes Native', *Dance*, December, 13.

114. Balanchine, George (1992) 'Marginal Notes on the Dance', in Sorell, Walter ed. *The Dance Has Many Faces*, Chicago: Cappella Books, 41.

115. Walczak and Kai (2008) 13.

116. Shorer (1999) 14.

117. Blackmuir, R.P. (1958/1983) 'The Swan in Zurich', in Copeland, Roger and Marshall Cohen eds. *What is Dance?*, Oxford: Oxford University Press, 354-361.

118. Moore, Lilian (1950) 'Ashton's New Ballet', *Dancing Times*, no. 475, April, 410-411.

119. Denby, Edwin (1986) 'A letter on New York City's Ballet', in *Dance Writings*, London: Dance Books, 426.

120. Ibid.

121. Moore, Lilian.

122. Interview (2007) with Pamela Gaye online at www.ballet.co.uk/magazines/ yr_07/aug07/interview_robert_barnett.htm

123. Hazlewood, Charles (6th May 2006) 'Discovering Music', BBC Radio 3 programme.

124. Programme, Royal Opera House Covent Garden, 1st May 1996, *Illuminations*, translated by Helen Rootham *Prose Poems for Les Illuminations of Arthur Rimbaud*,

London: Faber and Faber, no page numbers available.

125. Denby, Edwin.

126. Starkie, 252.

127. Ibid.

128. Quoted from a letter or notes Ashton made for Beaumont and found in Ashton's library after his death. Library is now in The Royal Ballet School.

129. Starkie, 186.

130. Vaughan, 430-432.

131. See the youthful photograph of McBride and Tanaquil Le Clercq in 'Remembering Tanaquil Le Clercq' *Ballet Review*, 29, no.2, 35-66.

132. *Valses* is not available for viewing at the moment.

133. Evans, Peter (1996) 'A Unique Sound World', Programme *The Royal Ballet*, May, no page numbers are given.

134. Rootham, Helen (translator) from *Prose Poems for Les illuminations of Arthur Rimbaud*, London: Faber and Faber. Taken from Programme *The Royal Ballet*, 1st May 1996, no page numbers given.

135. The relationship between Verlaine and Rimbaud ended when Verlaine shot Rimbaud in the arm, wounding him and resulting in Verlaine spending some time in prison.

136. Ibid.

137. Quoted in Vaughan, David (1977) 243.

138. Richardson, P.J.S. (1950) 'Sitter Out', *Dancing Times*, September, no. 480, 724.

139. Quoted in Percival, John (1981) 'Sir Frederick Ashton', *The Times*, 28th November, no page numbers available.

140. Wills, Abigail (2005) 'Delinquincy, Masculinity and Citizenship in England 1950-1970', *Past &Present*, no. 187, May, 157-185.

141. Wills (2005), 177.

142. Nugent Ann (1981) 'Faun makes an Impact', *The Stage*, 17th December, no page numbers available.

143. Anon (1982) 'Retrospective', *Illustrated London News*, February, no page numbers available.

144. Percival, John (1981) 'Illuminations', *The Times*, 5th December, no page numbers available.

145. Ashton notes to Beaton (1950?).

146. Richard Buckle (25/7/50) 'Ballet', *Observer*, no page numbers available.

Chapter 4
Non-narrative Ballets:
1950s Decorum and the Swinging 60s

Writing about what inspired his choreography Balanchine observed that his

> Imagination is guided by the human material, by the dancers' personalities. I see the basic elements of the dance in its aesthetic manifestations, that is in the beauty of movement, in the unfolding of rhythmical patterns, and not in their possible meanings.[1]

Ashton too was guided by his dancers' personalities and nowhere is this more evident than in the two ballets I explore in this chapter. Neither has literary references, rather they depend on solving balletic problems. This, at least, is how Ashton understood choreography.[2] As he so frequently stated, his ballets were about dance not about storytelling.

In the years between 1956 and 1968, Ashton made fifteen works, of which nine were non-narrative, either structured according to a notional theme or guided by the music. It is these works, I now focus on, looking at two utterly different dances, *Birthday Offering* (1956) and *Jazz Calendar* (1968). These might be thought of as unusual choices in view of the fact that some of his most lauded works are in this genre; *Symphonic Variations* (1946), *Scènes de ballet* (1948) and *Monotones* (1965) not to mention *Façade* (1931), *Les rendezvous* (1933) and *Les patineurs* (1937). Several of those works have been discussed in depth by Jordan and Macaulay, amongst others, yet both *Birthday Offering* and *Jazz Calendar* are frequently overlooked; the former was regarded as a show piece for the Sadler's Wells Ballet and the latter as the attempt of an ageing man to embrace 1960s swinging London.[3]

Birthday Offering has proved to be more than a showcase. As Vaughan points out, it is Ashton's approach not only to classical dance but also to Petipa.[4] Choreographically it draws on the latter but it is the particular use of the *danse d'école* that is central to the dances and this is different from that of Petipa. He took inspiration for the selection of movement and arrangement of the dances from his dancers but elements from other sources can also be found in the work. I want to reveal the range and variety of his dance movement style and the effect his dancers had on it and this work provides an ideal example. While some aspects are particular to this work, others demonstrate how he re-fashioned material in ingenious and inventive ways. He takes us on a journey through the *danse d'école* showing us what he can do with it; it's as if he is saying 'you think there is only one way of doing a *rond de jambe* but let me show you what can be done'. Equally, the ballet demonstrates the historical dance style of both the company and its dancers, raising issues for its performance today.

Though seen as a light, unimportant work, *Jazz Calendar* was still performed until the 1990s. Despite a lack of recent performances, the work needs a fuller discussion than it has hitherto received. Its décor by Derek Jarman has hardly been touched on, either in the dance or fine art press and its dance movement was dismissed by Vaughan as inconsiderable. While Vaughan may be right in some respects, analysis of the work indicates that it is well worth revisiting. Intriguingly too, Vaughan suggests that it may well have elements of the revue numbers Ashton made in the 1930s and so can give us a glimpse of how these works might have looked.[5] Ashton linked it with *Façade* and *A Wedding Bouquet*. In both, there are aspects of 1930s stage dancing buried within the *danse d'école*. And in *Jazz Calendar* the costumes and set also have a distinctive element of the 1920s and 1930s. Little has been written about the score, by Richard Rodney Bennett, which Vaughan believes dates the ballet but in retrospect, this criticism is somewhat unwarranted. In the second half of the chapter, I discuss the work and consider the idea that *Jazz Calendar* is more about the 'Bright Young Things' than Swinging London.

Analysing *Jazz Calendar* requires a different approach from that used in *Birthday Offering* because as well as examining the dance and dancers' styles, I focus in some depth on the contribution of Jarman. Rodney Bennett's involvement in the work is more tenuous, since the music had already been written in 1964 before the dance was conceived. In my discussions of the works I have allowed each ballet to dictate the nature of the investigation and, unlike the two works in the previous chapter, I spend less time here on the combined contributors. The main purpose of course is to highlight the stylistic threads that are common to all Ashton ballets and, which, despite the different appearance of the two works, run through both. And, the design choices contribute substantially to the style. Sophistication is central to Ashton's dances and both of these works have it in equal measure.

Birthday Offering

The work was choreographed in 1956 to celebrate the 25th birthday of the Sadler's Wells Ballet (soon to become the Royal Ballet). The critic A. V. Coton, though not always praising of Ashton, was an admirer of non-narrative works, particularly this one, which he described as 'abstract dance pictorialism' and he was convinced that choreography should abandon the convention of 'scoring ballet to story'.[6] The ballet showcases the talents of the ballerinas of the Sadler's Wells Ballet and comprises some group dances, seven solo variations, a duet and a dance for the men.

It does not have the psychological intrigue of MacMillan's *Noctambules*, nor the edgy brilliance of Balanchine's *Allegro Brillante*, both of which were premiered on 1 March, two months before *Birthday Offering*. But then we do not go to Ashton for those qualities and his refusal to tell complex stories in dance or to present flashy technical treats can make revivals of his works difficult. His style is fragile, easily lost and nowhere more so than in a ballet like this one. It was made for and depended on the particularities of the seven dancers: Elaine Fifield, Rowena Jackson, Svetlana Beriosova, Nadia Nerina, Violetta Elvin, Beryl Grey and Margot Fonteyn. Their variations are still a formidable challenge to the dancer, even those as capable as today's. To perform the dances in the spirit in which they were created, the dancers need to know that they are performing Ashton's dance movement and not its classroom version and that the dance style of the original work is also embedded in the dances. By far the most important collaborators were the dancers. Their dancing deserves an extensive exploration, since beyond praising their talents, little has been written about the distinctive dance style of each.

Design

The ballet's designer André Levasseur was a member of the haute couture house of Dior during Dior's lifetime. Dior rose to fame in 1947 when he introduced the 'New Look', a style of dress which demanded calf-length skirts and swathes of material and his couture became a synonym for glamour. The association of Dior with the Sadler's Well Ballet reinforced the image of a company which was both sophisticated and fashionable. Levasseur worked again with Ashton in 1958 on *La valse* and both sets of costumes have an aura of sophistication. The shape of the dresses in *La valse* was distinctly reminiscent of Dior's sensational 'New Look', while the elaborate patterns on the ball gown for Princess Grace of Monaco owe something to his costumes for *Birthday* Offering. The effect of using Levasseur was to place *Birthday Offering* in the world of celebrity culture which at that time embraced high society. Thus Ashton achieved his ambition to work with couture fashion. For his first ballet, *A Tragedy of Fashion* (1926), his preferred designer was the ultra fashionable and chic Coco Chanel who had designed the costumes for Nijinska's *Le train bleu* (1924). But for many reasons, not least cost, he was dissuaded from this by Rambert.[7]

Tempo

The conductor Robert Irving, who also arranged the music, had already worked with Ashton on both *Picnic at Tintagel* (1952), for which he chose the score, and *Sylvia* (1952), where he re-arranged some of Léo Delibes' music. In *Birthday Offering*, Irving used music by the Russian composer Alexander Glazunov. He took five of the variations from *The Seasons* (1900) while the remaining two and the duet were from Glazunov's *Scènes de ballet* (1894) and *Ruses d'Amour* (1900).

Irving had a specific approach to music and to conducting for ballet. He believed that, in general, the dancer should follow the conductor, encouraging them not to lag behind the music and frequently taking them just out of their comfort zones. While sympathetic to the dancer, he was also careful to preserve the integrity of the music.[12] In performances of *Birthday Offering*, up to the 1970s, the tempi were brisker than those of later performances where some solos are as much as thirty seconds longer. This has implications for the movement and style as well as for the music. In both Fonteyn's dance and that for Beriosova, the tempo today is so slow that the dances begin to lose meaning. Fonteyn's is twenty-nine seconds slower and, in a dance comprising mainly small footwork and beaten jumps, the sluggish tempo places emphasis on closing positions, causing the dancer to falter and the jumps to appear leaden. The funereal tempo of Beriosova's variation, thirty one seconds longer, causes the dancer to wobble and stagger through what is usually a cool, controlled dance. Such a lack of regard for the choreographer, since it is the dances which suffer, raises issues about the role of the dancer and her dance knowledge and perhaps too that of the repetiteur.

Choreographic intention is significant here and in this particular work, both the talents of the original dancers and the speed at which the music was played seem to be integral to the style. The desire to favour position over action, the prevailing aesthetic of today's dancers, can harm these dances. In this work particularly, it seems choreographic style is central to the meaning as the discussion which follows will highlight.

Entrance and Men's Dances

When making the dances for *Cinderella* (1948) Ashton mentioned that '[he] always return[ed] to Petipa over everything'.[8] In *Birthday Offering*, he does so for the compositional elements. Clearly there are links with the structure of the Fairies' ensemble in the prologue of *The Sleeping Beauty*, which contains a waltz, adage, variations, male dance and finale. *Birthday Offering* is also divided into five sections: entrance; variations; men's dance; duet and finale. Ashton added a duet and arranges the couples quite differently from those in *Beauty*.[9] While the Fairies assemble in straight lines and gather in circles around the Lilac Fairy, in *Birthday Offering* the dancers have more complex patterns.

Stepping and waltzing in an expansive semi-circle, the seven couples enter from upstage left but as they form across the front of the stage, the groups break to make two lines, interchanging with each other forward and back. Like a flock of birds, the ensemble flows and gathers, scatters and mingles, before repeating the opening circular waltz phrase. This opening is brisk and

the slower, adage section which follows, although beginning with prom-
enading balances in attitude, mainly comprises high lifts interspersed with
turns. As in the Prologue of *The Sleeping Beauty*, Ashton organises his dancers in a half moon shape with Fonteyn, golden clad, shimmering and
sun-like, displayed in the centre. Both choreographers use the group sym-
metrically in opposite pairs who mirror each other, although Petipa uses six
couples to Ashton's seven. Whereas the Fairies' lifts progress from high lifts
for the upstage couples to *arabesques* for the centre couples and low reclining
poses for the couples at the front, Ashton plays with this. His high lifts begin
with the front couples, move to those in the middle and then both front and
back pairs perform them together.

Paradoxically, Ashton's adages are not slow and although they give the
impression of a continuous flow of movement, they are punctured by sudden
stops. For instance, with the couples in a long diagonal, the women perform
a supported double *pirouette* into a swift low, briefly held *arabesque* and as
they finish, the end couple runs to the start. As the phrase is repeated, each
in turn dashes to the top of the diagonal, performing the *pirouette* phrase as
they move backwards down the diagonal. The sequence creates an impression of flow but the sudden stops in *arabesques* add definition.

Ashton's duets tend to be brisk, with phrases that move without breaks in
between. They frequently have moments when the man and woman separate, each performing short variations and this entrance also separates the
dancers along gender lines. While the men are given more conventional,
identifiable steps, the women in their group movement have steps which
deviate from the *danse d'ecole*. For example, a series of little stuttering steps is
interspersed with parallel runs forward on pointe. Three women advance
forward while the other four travel backwards, moving upstage. Rarely do all
seven perform the same phrases together and this adds to the impression that
the dancers are like flocks of birds, assembling and dispersing before joining
again with the men to perform in unison.

This whole opening section ends with a long line across the front of the
stage in which the dancers change partners, moving back and forth before
making a final reference to Petipa. Like Aurora in Act III at the end of her pas
de deux, the dancers, in a staggered group, *bourrée couru* forward and perform rapid turns, repeating this before ending in a line across the front of the
stage. These allusions are tantalising. The choreography is not the same as
The Sleeping Beauty but the links are there.

The men's dance, which comes after the women's solo variations (discussed in the next section), picks up on the staggered patterns of the opening
section. From a long line up stage, they travel in threes and fours backwards
and forwards, in and out before settling in two triangles, the apexes of which
point to the central, principal male. Ashton then creates a whirling stage:

while the three middle men perform a hopping turn *à la seconde*, the four outside men do the same turn in *attitude devant*. Step phrases from the *danse d'école* form the main movement but inserted into the dance is a typical Ashton invention. Making a deep sideways lunge, they follow almost immediately with a slide, drawing the free leg upwards to fifth on half-pointe. It is a bit like a sideways *chassé* in reverse.

The dance is given interest through the moving patterns, though the heavy, solid movement of the men is typically gender specific. But Ashton was working within what Ramsay Burt describes as the 'constraining obligations of tradition'.[10] He was not free to depict men as other than aggressively heterosexual, though he had already choreographed a male, male duet in *Façade* and later a second one crops up the 'Nimrod' section of *Enigma Variations*. But the dance movement in *Birthday Offering* is not really Ashton's male dance style, although the ways in which the dancers are used and the composition puts an Ashton stamp on the dance. The more lyrical, undulating dance movement he made later for Dowell broke new ground and is more stylistically Ashton.[11]

The Seven Variations

From a social perspective, *Birthday Offering* reflects the hierarchies that existed both within the company and the 1950s in Britain. The country still retained some of the class structures of the pre war era and this was particularly evident in the ballet world; there the structures had been inherited from Imperial Russia. In 1956, Fonteyn was at her peak and the choreography of *Birthday Offering* reflects not only her privileged position and exacting technical ability but also that of the other dancers.

As Hylda Zinkin, a former member of the company, remembered, Fonteyn was 'Amazing, wonderful, perfect, she wasn't really a person, more a creature'. Zinkin remarked that Fonteyn was perfection from any angle and that when she was on stage, no one else existed.[13] This was the aura surrounding Fonteyn at the time and to some extent it rubbed off on the other principal dancers. They were remote creatures who did not mix with the corps de ballet. According to Zinkin, '[she] didn't know them at all, they were very much apart'.

To epitomise the style of the Sadler's Wells Ballet, Ashton chose seven women, only two, Fonteyn and Grey, had been in the company longer than ten years. Of the others, four joined in 1946 and one, Beriosova, in 1952. Both Beriosova and Elvin were Russian trained: Beriosova in the style of the Imperial Russian ballet and Elvin in that of the Soviet system. Fifield, Jackson and Nerina came from Commonwealth countries: Australia, New Zealand and South Africa respectively. Fifield and Jackson had the contemporary style of the RAD as their training, while Nerina had a background in Cecchetti. None spent more than a year at the Sadler's Wells Ballet School and neither of the Russians spent any time at all there. If the style that emerged in the company in 1956 had a homogeneous element, it must have been the shared choreographic and professional experience, rather than a shared training.

Another important contributor to the dance style was Vera Volkova. Her involvement cannot be overlooked and, though her relationship with the Wells was complex, it needs some discussion, more particularly when reflecting on Fonteyn's variation. According to Volkova, the RAD training was too precise and confining, as was the Cecchetti System, both of which were taught at the Sadler's Wells School alongside the methods of other teachers. Volkova not only disagreed with the way in which the students were taught there but also with the methods of de Valois and Peggy Van Praagh. English dancers, she insisted, needed more fluidity and to be given opportunities to create nuances of dynamic.[14]

Between 1946 and 1956, the repertoire was dominated by Ashton works; he created fourteen new works in this period. Although nineteenth-century ballets were an important part of the repertoire and, despite a desire by de Valois to introduce other contemporary choreographers, the dance style was influenced more by Ashton than anyone else and probably contributed most to the bodily aesthetic of the era.[15]

Elaine Fifield (1930-1999): First Variation

In her RAD examinations Fifield received the highest grades ever given in Australia, achieving the Solo Seal at the age of fourteen.[16] Trained in the Frances Scully School and with Leon Kellaway, she won a RAD scholarship in 1945 to study at the Sadler's Wells Ballet School, where she spent a year before entering the Sadler's Wells Theatre Ballet in 1947.[17] Her skills were clearly shaped by the RAD syllabus, which by then had become a slightly dry system of training, encouraging students to acquire knowledge of the *danse d'école* but allowing them little spontaneity.[18] Examinations had begun in Australia in 1931, so when Fifield began training, the system was well established. During Fifield's year at the school, it is likely that she was taught by Ailne Phillips and Ursula Moreton. Fifield also had lessons with Olga Preobrajenskaya in Paris and this may well have modified some of the inflexibility of the RAD training. Whether Fifield attended Volkova's classes too is not clear but in 1948, after a long tour, the Sadlers' Wells Theatre Ballet had a series of guest teachers, one of whom was Volkova, so Fifield must have encountered her then.[19] Volkova's classes would certainly have encouraged and strengthened her expressive feet and arms, for which Fifield was subse-

Elaine Fifield. © Roger Wood, Royal Opera House Archives.

Ashton's signature pose.

quently applauded. Her varied training was clearly beneficial, for she became known not only for her technical assurance but also for her sensitive phrasing.[20]

The combination of beautiful feet with a talent for extravagant turns and an easy engagement with quick *batterie* meant that Fifield had just the right qualities to perform Ashton's dance style. In her first years in the Sadler's Wells Theatre Ballet, she performed the polka from *Façade* and the lead in *Les rendezvous*. In 1947, Ashton created a role for her in his new work *Valses nobles et sentimentales* and in 1955 the title role in *Madame Chrysanthème*.

Only two publicly available films of Fifield's dancing exist. In *Steps of the Ballet*, a documentary film made by the British Council in 1948, she is shown aged eighteen as a competent dancer but little in the film suggests she would become more than a proficient corps de ballet member. Fifield is also seen performing Summer in Ashton's *Cinderella* in a film made for American television in 1957. Regrettably, in the solo variations, the Seasons are shown with a negative background and her dancing is submerged in mist. Nevertheless, it is astonishing that she was chosen to dance this variation as it is not a mere virtuoso display of steps but a languorous, sensual expression of heat, more often danced by a tall, willowy dancer and Fifield was tiny. It says much about her range that Ashton chose her to dance Summer. Originally made for Elvin, the dance is leisurely and the movement expansive. Fifield's performance is brisk but her upper body has all the liquid qualities that the dance demands. Technically, she can do anything and in the phrase comprising a double turn ending in a step into *arabesque*, she gives it speed, putting a sharp emphasis on the step to *arabesque*, though without disturbing the dominant quality of the dance. Strangely, she never performed the title role in *Cinderella*. By all accounts, it would have played to her strengths, since she was a dancer with an 'easy gift of speed'.[21] Despite the fact that Ashton clearly appreciated her dance style, she left the Royal Ballet on a whim in 1957 and never fulfilled her potential.

Following her Swanhilda in *Coppélia*, one newspaper claimed that she was 'A Pavlova', while *The Times* enthused about her neatness and musicality.[22] This perfectly placed, technically at ease dancer was noticed early on in the dance press but the most telling tribute comes from Joan Lawson. She found Fifield's performance to be 'an exquisite creation, so finely etched and butterfly-like in its lightness that each movement seems to break away from its context'.[23] Ashton exploited all of these features in her *Birthday Offering* variation. It is a dance which owes more to Pavlova than do any of the others. Films of Pavlova, particularly in dances like *The Fairy Doll*, shows a butterfly-like quality, a dancer who whizzed lightly around the stage in fast, yet glidingly smooth, *bourrée couru*. Her wit and sophistication were noted by H.T. Parker who mentioned that the impression and the emotion is of the airy lightness of the movement, the blending of each one of its parts into a single lovely flash. Her technique has impalpability; it is like air in motion; it is as fluid as water; as swift as fire.[24]

He could have been discussing Fifield. Fifield's exceptional quality of movement put her in a special category and she clearly had some of Pavlova's characteristics.

Ashton frequently mentioned the marvellous way Pavlova had of highlighting her beautiful feet. He showed dancers the 'tricks that [she] had used to show them off' and these are evident in Fifield's dance in *Birthday Offering*.[25] Dressed in palest grey, Fifield is on pointe throughout much of the dance, so the movement seems fragile, even delicate. As she flicks or beats the foot, she has to lean forward, drawing the audience's attention to her highly arched, articulate feet.

Choreographed to *Marionettes* from *Scènes de ballet*, this music is light and tinkling. The dancer begins centre stage and travels forward making this elegant, foot flicking action, moving from one foot to the other. Then, as if changing her mind, she retreats, travelling up stage, in a series of *posés retirés* and quick *petits battements*, performed with a deep bend of the upper body. It heralds a slight change in dynamic, though this is not suggested in the music. Ashton then introduces a phrase that reappears later in Lise's first dance in *La fille mal gardée* (1960): a turning *saut de basque* followed by a low *relevé* to second and a quick snap of the leg back to a low *retiré* with a flick of the head; the arms remain low. Interspersed with turns, the next phrase evokes a similar one in *Les rendezvous* where it is performed by the pas de trois woman. A clipped jump (*pas de chat*) on one side is followed by a turn, one way and then the other way, ending with a third turn. Few dancers can master the crisp, sprightly nature of the phrase because it demands quick alterations of weight and direction. The final section of the dance comprises a formidable collection of turns first in *attitude* then a quick whipped turn, then a *pirouette*. The dance ends with a pose that Ashton frequently used, notably for the Blue Skater in *Les patineurs* (1937) and for Puck in *The Dream* (1963). With elbows bent and palms upturned, the dancer looks quizzically at the audience; 'it's easy, no trouble at all'.

Despite the difficult though unspectacular turns at the end, there is nothing showy in this dance. It is made up of repeated phrases generally in groups of two and three, most of which draw attention to the intricate, ornate footwork. The steps are frequently clipped, as in the *pas de chat* phrase, and the ability to alternate quickly from one side to the other is paramount. Ashton chooses little beaten movements (*petits battements*), little runs and *jetés* all on pointe and there are hardly any jumps. The space around the body is disturbed, but only a little, as much of the arm movement is kept close to the body. It is a typical Ashton dance with movement chosen from a small group of steps, many of which would be described as linking steps. None of these have flamboyant qualities but are juxtaposed in such a way as to create motion in the whole body. The whole dance is suffused with the qualities described by Parker above, 'air in motion; fluid as water and swift as fire'. Nowhere else in this work does Ashton stamp his Pavolva image more forcefully than in this variation.

Kavanagh dismisses Fifield somewhat by suggesting that the dance highlights her 'rather vacant prettiness and mechanical precision...'.[26] This is what the dance can become if the Pavlova references are misunderstood. The overriding motif is qualitative: attention to shading, and to contrast, between elegant and sparkling, are central to its presentation. Apart from a performance by Antoinette Sibley in 1962, few dancers seem to understand or are able to perform this intricate dance with a Pavlova-like quality. Sibley gets the wit and humanity and presumably so did Fifield. In Sibley's performance the dance lasts for 1.28 minutes and later performances of the dance decrease the speed by eleven seconds, placing more emphasis on static moments. It is one of those Ashton dances that if misinterpreted, can become almost trivial.

Rowena Jackson (1926-)

Rowena Jackson who danced the second solo was dressed in scarlet and as the colour intimates, she was a vastly different dancer from Fifield. Trained in New Zealand, Jackson won a RAD scholarship to study at the Sadler's Wells Ballet School in 1946 and, later that year, the RAD's Adeline Genée gold medal before joining the Covent Garden-based company in November 1946. She was known for her exuberance, her astonishing speed and, particularly for her ability to perform *fouettés* without moving off the spot.[27] The film of Jackson dancing the *Bluebird* pas de deux and variations with Brian Shaw in 1955 shows that her technical ease and speed of execution is formidable. She seems to find the dancing effortless.

Apart from *Birthday Offering*, Ashton made very little for her. Jackson was one of the three soloists in *Variations on a Theme by Purcell* (1955) and had a short variation in *Homage to the Queen* (1953). She was also renowned for her Blue Girl in *Les patineurs* and for her performances of the Ballerina in *Scènes de ballet*. When she first performed the latter role in 1952, Richardson commented on her speed, precision and nice timing, adding that she had a fine understanding of line and could recognise the value of *épaulement*.[28] Yet, she never managed to acquit herself in the major roles. Following Jackson's performance as Aurora in *The Sleeping Beauty*, Clarke observed that although the performance was sound, it was a 'copy book one: all the rules had been carefully learned, but there was no warmth of feeling to bring the ballet alive'.[29]

In *Birthday Offering*, Jackson's solo lasts only 52 seconds. It is a fast, high-spirited, yet sophisticated dance, performed to *Le givre* (frost), that captures her sheer delight in dancing. Despite her fabulous capacity for turning, Ashton restricted himself to a few swift spins; conventional *pirouettes*, with an unconventional ending, and a string of *chaînés*. Instead he chose to show off her speed and facility for quick, sudden changes of direction.

As if blown from some tropical storm, the dancer enters the stage in a rapid *bourrée couru* travelling backwards from stage right. Quick *ronds de jambes en l'air* into *écarté*, a Cecchetti phrase, are performed before she again hastens, in a backwards-travelling diagonal, upstage. These sharp diagonals are followed by a semi-circular swirl before the dancer pierces the space again, moving towards the downstage wing. This floor pattern is repeated four more times, after which the dancer advances down a final diagonal to finish just beyond the centre. The speed is breathtaking and the dancer is continually thrown into off-balance moments. She moves in ever widening circles which become more frenetic as the dance progresses. Other major characteristics of the dance are the sudden twists and turns and changes of direction, it is as if the dancer cannot make up her mind. The floor paths turn sharply from one way to the other, requiring quick thinking and real technical command.

One particular movement cluster, a typical Ashton phrase, though sharp and jagged, shows how contrasting designs are used to draw attention to the upper body and increase the perception of motion even when there is limited travelling. By an ingenious use of rhythm and design, the audience's eyes are drawn to the abrupt, precise, halts in the phrase. The movement in the cluster does not stop but each section ends in a strongly accented body design, forcing the dancer to form a clear body shape at a pace which is less than comfortable.

A *retiré derrière* on a bent leg is followed by a quick hop into an open *arabesque* on *pointe*; the *retiré* phrase is repeated but this time, with the upper body bent over the working leg and the phrase ends with a *bourrée couru* in fifth moving rapidly backwards (see drawing).

There are no pauses. Each section of this highly complex cluster has a contrast between the upper and lower body: the first and third have diamond shaped legs with a curved upper body; in the second the body is star shaped while the fourth is curved, given sharpness by the vigorous motion of the *bourrée couru*. Because these actions are much faster than is generally found in the classroom, the torso has highly exaggerated bends and the limbs are spiky. The whole cluster is highly concentrated, with each body part moving simultaneously: head, arms, legs, feet and torso.

It is a typical Ashton moment: no virtuoso steps but the speed and compacted nature of the movement creates its own challenge.

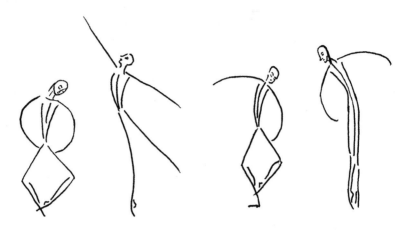

The phrase has links with one in the Hostess' dance in *Les biches* where she performs eight continuous *entrechats six* followed by a *demi-contretemps* to each side and a *glissade, assemblé*. It is packed with steps and movement; the elbows are bent and the shoulders change with each step. The torso, limbs and head also change with each movement, but whereas the Hostess' phrase is perceived as fluid and easily accomplished because of the lack of body design, Ashton's phrase looks harder to achieve and more spectacular. In Jackson's dance, this moment is a key Ashton phrase; it illustrates his concern with body design and with sparkling, sharp dynamic.

It is a virtuoso dance without virtuoso steps. These were not of much interest to Ashton; amassing mere inventories of steps was not his aim. Instead, he makes the dancer move and travel in all directions, as though emitting sparks. The contrast with the preceding dance is powerful; the one light and air blown, the next fast and glittering. Of subsequent performers, Georgina Parkinson had some similar qualities to Jackson and when she danced it, the variation retained many of the characteristics for which Jackson was famous.

Svetlana Beriosova (1932-1998)

Like the variations for the Fairies in *The Sleeping Beauty*, the dances in *Birthday Offering* are arranged to complement each other. So Fifield's stylish dance is followed by Jackson's whirlwind. The cool green elegance of Beriosova's dance is next. Later, when she danced the duet, her variation came last, disrupting this carefully arranged pattern.

Beriosova trained in New York with Ludmilla Schollar and Anatole Vilzak, both of whom had been schooled in the Imperial Russian Ballet style and danced with Diaghilev's Ballets Russes. Schollar had been one of the two women in Nijinsky's *Jeux* (1913) and she was also a favourite dancer of Fokine's. In later years, she became renowned for her knowledge and teaching of repertory. Schollar had also worked closely with Nijinska, and Beriosova's understanding of Nijinska's style must have been absorbed from Schollar. This might well have influenced Nijinska when she chose Beriosova to dance The Hostess in *Les biches* for the Royal Ballet revival in 1964. Vilzak, a pupil of Fokine, had been one of the three men in Nijinska's *Les biches*. He was celebrated for his eloquent sense of line and ability to communicate lyricism.[30] Little has been written about what Schollar and Vilzak taught, though one dancer remembered fast footwork and elegant *port de bras*. Like other dancers of this era, Beriosova had an eclectic training, since she also worked with Preobrajenska and Volkova.[31] After two years spent with the Metropolitan Ballet, she was asked by de Valois to join the Sadler's Wells Theatre Ballet in 1950, moving to the Sadler's Well Ballet (at Covent Garden) in 1952.

Her style was reserved and serene; to the anonymous writer in *Ballet* what Beriosova 'may lose in brilliance and immediate audience-appeal... she amply gains in smoothness, musicality and nobility.[32] Smooth, musical and noble exactly describes her variation in *Birthday Offering*. Tellingly Ashton chose *La glace* for this variation. Yet Beriosova was far from icy and the music is smooth and leisurely, helped by the warm, rich sounds of the violas and smooth, creamy tone of the clarinets.

Divided into three parts, the dance moves back and forth in a stately diagonal from stage left to downstage centre and straight upstage before a rush forward to finish just off centre stage. Each part ends in a flurry of movement and these sudden eruptions prevent this stately dance from being boring. Ashton used ballet steps for their dynamic qualities and, despite the lyrical musical sound, he rarely stayed with a single effort cluster throughout a dance. Just as Beliaev, after a slow, sustained opening, has a sudden bout of restless *entrechats* in *A Month in the Country*, so Beriosova has slow enveloping movements which eventually disperse into a flurry of quick, crisp footwork, ending in a firm, closed position. Typically, Ashton does not allow us to indulge in the luxurious movements, thwarting our expectations by introducing these swift flurries.

In the first part, the phrase of *entrechats* and quick *relevés* comes as a surprise after the opening leisurely *rond de jambe à terre* and *relevé enveloppé* movement, in which the working leg is raised to the side and gradually drawn into the knee of the supporting leg. It is a ballet movement which can be sharp or, as danced by Beriosova, gracefully indolent. A film of her dancing the solo still exists, so we can be confident that this is how she moved. In spite of the reduced dynamic which film produces, the recording accords with my own memory of watching Beriosova performing the solo.

Her second section comprises a short step into *arabesque*, followed by two *retirés* moving upstage and then a long indulgent lunge into an extended fourth; this phrase is repeated. The cluster finishes with a sudden explosion of sharp, little *sissonnes*, each closing abruptly, before the phrase is completed by a quick rise on pointe to *attitude*.[33] Section three has one of Ashton's favourite movements: the deeply curving *coupé renversé*. It continues into a turning twiddle on pointe and is repeated. The dancer then travels back upstage in a series of sharp *posés retirés* softened by slow moving arms which move upwards over the head to frame the upper body, drawing our attention upwards. Ending in a quick curtsey and Ashton's signature pose, already seen in Fifield's variation, the dance shows us Beriosova's luscious technique and ability to move expansively.[34] Yet the quick sharp interjections at the end of each phrase cluster also demonstrate her rapid, clean footwork.

In later ballets, *Persephone* (1961) and *Les biches*, these talents were again showcased. Persephone too has these sudden, sharp moments, interspersed with languorous *arabesques*, and the dance for the Hostess is laden with quick sparkling jumps, interrupted by more laid-back moments. Although Beriosova did not have a particularly spectacular jump, she was a relatively tall woman and could cover the stage in just a few movements.

In this seemingly simple dance in *Birthday Offering*, Ashton draws on Beriosova's elegance and composed appearance. She never seems to be in a hurry, yet the dance, lasting 1.06 minutes, demands a degree of speed. In the more languid sections, the movement flows while body design is highlighted in the faster sections. The dance is brief and the dancer has to move both continuously and quite quickly.

There are no impressive steps in this dance and some have suggested that it failed to do justice to Beriosova's abilities. Yet she never sentimentalised the dance or made concessions to the luscious music. In films of later dancers, several misunderstand the music and not only slow it down but fail to understand the upbeat opening. Beriosova's performance not only demonstrates her acute musical understanding but also her approach to dynamic contrast. As performed by Beriosova, the dance starts on the upbeat, so the *relevé envellopé* is performed on the downbeat or first beat of the bar. As Jordan points out this is typical of Ashton's use of music and contributes to a more lyrical style.[35] It also gives a quirkiness to the dance preventing the performer from over-indulgence in the even rhythms of the music. Besides, Beriosova's sophisticated presentation of the contrasts between the lusciousness of the *envellopé*, *épaulement* and *renversé* sections and the sharper dynamic of the jumps is also missing from later dancers' portrayals. It is these interesting touches which make the dance special and dancers ignore them at their peril. As with the two previous dances, it is the qualitative elements, the contrasting light and shade, which form the dominating motif.

Nadia Nerina (1927-2008)

Nerina was the only dancer whose formative training was in the Cecchetti method. Her initial training at a local school in South Africa seems to have been rule-bound and informed only by the syllabus. On arriving in London in late 1945, she joined Rambert's school at the Mercury Theatre, where the teaching was again based on Cecchetti but differently so. In an interview, Nerina recollected that 'The Mercury was professional, so it wasn't Cecchetti as I'd been brought up on it. Professional classes aren't academic in the same way as sticking to a syllabus.'[36] Despite her strong Cecchetti background, she seems to have blended easily into the Sadler's Wells Ballet, joining the Sadler's Wells Theatre ballet in late 1946 and the Covent Garden company in 1947.

Her training may have shaped her 'precise footwork' but it also enhanced her elevation, which Clarke found unique in the Royal Ballet.[37] A great technician with a reputation for exuberance is how Nerina was often described and these qualities are seen in ballets like *Coppélia* and *La fille mal gardée*, in which she performed Swanhilda and Lise. Yet, as Clarke observed, she was not much acclaimed for her ability to 'touch the heart', although her Giselle was well respected.[38] And Nerina was not merely a technician; she believed that mastery of technique could serve as a fine resource. Writing for the *Ballet Annual* she observed that:

> Transmitting commands through to the various parts of one's body should be an inner conscious pleasure and satisfaction. Through this inner awareness, movement gains a fluidity and poise and harmony within the music. Ultimately there is a complete and serene unity between thought and movement.[39]

Despite her comments about the music, Nerina was not acclaimed for her musicality. Unlike Fonteyn, she rarely played with the musical phrase and, in her *Birthday Offering* dance, there is little of the subtle interplay between the music and the movement that was found in Beriosova's dance.

But Ashton loved risk-takers and Nerina was quite fearless when it came to performing high lifts or difficult movements. She also loved challenge, as the following quote from an obituary in the *Daily Telegraph* indicates:

> Renowned as the best technician at Covent Garden in the 1950s and 1960s she impressed and humbled Rudolf Nureyev when he attempted to show off in a performance of *Giselle* with a series of 16 entrechats six... Performing *Swan Lake* a few nights later, with Nureyev watching from the

stalls, Nadia Nerina doubled his feat to 32 – an unheard-of achievement for a female dancer – and a furious Nureyev stormed out of the performance.[40]

In addition to her variation in *Birthday Offering*, Ashton made five important roles for Nerina: Lise in *La fille mal gardée*, Spring in *Cinderella* (1948), Queen of the Earth in *Homage to the Queen* (1953), a soloist in *Variations on a Theme by Purcell* (1955) and the Beloved in *The Beloved* (1956).

Ashton exploited her buoyant jump, strong pointes and ability to turn but he also used her courage, giving her some of the most challenging combinations he ever created. The dance movement in Spring (*Cinderella*) requires rapid changes of direction and extensive use of *épaulement*. The dynamics are clipped; so clear, well formed footwork is needed with a corresponding precision of the arms and head. The movement seems to be shooting out in all directions; the arms and legs spray virtual lines upwards and outwards at the end of almost every movement. Ashton asked Nerina what Spring meant to her. 'Buds bursting' was her reply and he achieved this by making us conscious of the virtual lines coming from the short bouts of movement which explode in the space.[41] This variation needed a light jump and strong feet, something that her training may well have supported. Despite Nerina's small stature, her dance style is expansive. She could cover large areas of floor space with a single leap and her use of the kinesphere too is extensive, appearing to stretch almost beyond her limits.

Nerina's flamboyant jump is the focus of this variation in *Birthday Offering*. Dressed in bright acid lemon, the dancer bursts on to the stage. The effect of this is thrilling and the contrast between it and the previous cool green of Beriosova's dance dramatic. Ashton chose *La grêle* (hail) for Nerina. She moves throughout like a short sharp shower of hail, sweeping back and forth across the stage. Like the Spring variation, the movements shoot virtual lines into the space, though the dynamic is stronger here and her limbs pierce the space with sharp laser-like movements. Lasting only fifty five seconds, the dance has five clear sections, all airborne. The first opens with a phrase of two travelling *saut de chat*, a jump in which both legs are bent in a low *attitude* behind, into a pose and then, typically, Ashton reverses the phrase, so that the dancer now jumps with the legs thrusting forward and ends with a soaring *arabesque*. Throughout, the dancer darts over and back across the stage and this phrase cluster ends with a series of sharp pointing movements in which the foot shoots forward and back like an arrow. These brisk phrases are made more active because the upper body and arms also bend forward and back, replicating the incisive thrusts of the feet. In one short group of phrases, Ashton establishes the dancer's exuberance and athleticism.

Nerina's enjoyment of jumping is displayed, particularly in the second section which combines a reversed *fouetté* jump with big *jetés*. In the former, the body sharply changes direction led by the raised leg but, in this dance, instead of turning away from the leg, as in the classroom version, the dancer turns towards it, so the leg ends in front of the body. The phrase is completed by a swish of the raised leg backwards to a jumped arabesque and is followed by big *jetés*, where the dancer propels herself from side to side dashing across the stage, as though blown by wind. Ashton used the first part of this phrase again in *La fille mal gardée*, though with two consecutive reversed *fouetté* jumps. It happens near the end of the major ribbon duet in the second act, where Lise enters doing a combination of big *jetés* and reversed *fouetté* jumps. This is one example of Ashton inventing movements based on the *danse d'école* but which in their combinations, reversals and use of the upper body, stray significantly from the orthodox versions.

What is interesting in the film version of Nerina dancing in her solo from *Birthday Offering* is her approach to elevation, which contrasts with that of today's dancers. She makes a pronounced impulse at the start of the movement stressing the upward action. In general, today's dancers have a wider split jump in which the impact comes at the end. It is a different aesthetic and means that buoyancy is absent and the ending shape emphasised. The effect of Nerina's approach is to create a perception of effortless and abandoned movement. This is helped by the way in which she throws rather than places her limbs in the space. Ashton used these qualities to advantage to invent new movements like the reverse *fouetté* jump.

The short group of phrases in the third section is more contained, the only contained section of the dance, but even here the movement travels and includes a very quick *rond de jambe à terre*, a signature step.[42] The dance ends with a series of sliding phrases which pull the dancer upstage before she darts down a diagonal in a series of *petit jeté en tournant*. She ends abruptly in a raised *arabesque*, almost as though she has no time to stop.

Many of Ashton's signature steps are present: the *rond de jambe à terre*, *petit jeté en tournant* and little *pas de chat*. Typical too of Ashton's style is the full use of the upper body: whether the dancer is sliding or dragging backwards or performing the quick beaten steps of the more contained phrase, her upper body bends right forward over the working leg or forward and back in the case of the latter. It is a fast, furious and energetic dance.

Nerina's exuberance is what Ashton chose to focus on and it is the only one of the seven variations to have almost non stop elevation. Apart from in *Sylvia* (1952), Ashton did not often require his female dancers to perform big, expansive jumps and it is testament to Nerina that they are dominant here. Buoyancy is the noun that most obviously describes this dance and is also the dominating motif.

Violetta Elvin (1925-)

Arriving from Moscow in 1946 as Violetta Prokhorova, Elvin was the first Soviet trained dancer to enter the Sadler's Wells Ballet. An exact contemporary of the Bolshoi ballerina, Maya Plisetskaya, Elvin trained with Elizaveta Gerdt, a highly regarded Soviet official, who was one of the senior teachers at the Bolshoi Academy. According to Plisetskaya, Gerdt was not an accomplished teacher, having no understanding of ballet and even less about how to teach it.[43] There was a suggestion that Agrippina Vaganova also trained Elvin, but Vaganova only taught in Moscow between 1943 and 1944, and Elvin graduated from the Academy in 1942. Because the Bolshoi was evacuated from Moscow during World War II, records are patchy and it is difficult to guage the accuracy of this information. It is more likely that the major influence on her was Volkova, with whom she worked on her arrival in London. And it was Volkova who helped to hone and refine her technique.

The technical, Soviet aesthetic of the late 1930s and early 1940s can be gleaned from snippets of film showing Marina Semyonova dancing and teaching. Semyonova was the leading ballerina of the time and, according to Plisetskaya, her approach to dance dominated the aesthetic of the period.[44] The films show a dancer with a fluid upper body, supple back and undulating movement. Semyonova was the first dancer to have been fully trained by Vaganova, whose principles are so clearly evident in her movement and Elvin, it seems, had absorbed some of these qualities, though not their dogmatism. Percival describes her dancing as having

> a certain roundness in her movement; a way with music; some special grace about the carriage of head, shoulders, arms; a magnetic gift for conveying drama in the movement.[45]

Ashton admired her dancing and created several roles for her. The first was Summer in *Cinderella*. Starting with luxurious arm movements, the dance alternates between swift crisp phrases and slower more languorous ones. The second role Ashton made for her, Lykanion in *Daphnis and Chloe*, is discussed briefly in Chapter V. The other leading Ashton role she created was Queen of the Waters in *Homage to the Queen* (1953), which Vaughan describes as

> exploit[ing] Elvin's beautifully sinuous arms and body to the full and convey[ing] the falling of cool running water by... soft *bourrées, pirouettes, temps levés* and lovely *port de bras*.[46]

In his choreography for her, it seems that Ashton concentrated on her more sensual upper body and this is exactly what the variation in *Birthday Offering* exploits. Percival observes that her solo has been the most difficult to cast in subsequent revivals, not for what is in it but for what is not in it. The other six ballerinas at the première were all given steps, often highly demanding ones, that showed their particular strengths; Elvin's solo was the simplest technically because Ashton knew that he needed only to give her quiet, gentle movement that flowed and eddied with the music.[47] In one sense Percival is right, the solo does not seem to have difficult steps but this is the voice of a non-dancer speaking. It is not the steps that are problematic, steps in themselves rarely are, but it is the way in which they are combined and this is why and how Ashton's dances are often so difficult to dance. Elvin's variation is no exception. As in the other variations, this has Ashton signature steps, which are exploited to create texture in a dance which could otherwise seem bland.

Musically and physically *La neige* is meltingly soft and lasts just just 63 seconds, though in later performances, this has increased to 69. She is the calm after Nerina's hail storm. The dance seems shorter than Nerina's and this may be because it has only three phrase groupings. The dancer enters to the music and takes a pose in which the upper body is turned to stage left and the arms clasped above the head, but framing the face, as though Ashton were presenting a portrait. Her opening phrase comprises a quick parallel *bourrée couru* moving forward, a step on pointe to a low *arabesque*, three waltzing steps into a further *arabesque*, then a picked up *pas de bourrée*, ending with a quick double *rond de jambe en l'air*. The phrase is then repeated. Ashton's signature *rond de jambe* and *pas de bourrée* are there but danced according to the classroom rules and yet they come as a surprise at the end of this meltingly soft phrase. Interest is added to the waltz steps by changes of direction and by a sweeping use of the upper body. The dancer waltzes back and low, forward and high, and sideways, high, facing upstage. Movements follow each other without a break, preventing the dancer from catching her breath. It appears languid and slow, yet when I tried this myself, I realised just how much movement and speed the two phrases require and the phrase which follows adds to the demands. Comprising a *grand battement* sideways with the supporting leg rising on pointe, followed by a whipping turn to *attitude*, the phrase is repeated three times. This on-going, continuous quality increases the perception of fluidity and makes the dance seem calm and unhurried. At no time does the dancer appear rushed and the slow turns at the end intensify this feeling. In this final phrase, the dancer makes her way down the diagonal in a series of controlled *chaînes*, continuous turns which are usually done quickly but here are slower and more fluid. The arms, instead of being rounded and close to the body, like a spinning top, rise gradually out and up and this slows down the turn.

In contrast to that in the previous dance, the stage space is confined as the dancer moves forward and back and side to side. Turning back on herself in the two *arabesques* which complete the third phrase, she moves from side to side in short diagonals. Ashton's use of stage space is often intricate and this is evident in all of these dances so far; yet it is at its most confined in this dance. Interestingly, Ashton does not give this ex-Bolshoi dancer the expansive travelling movements, common to Bolshoi choreography. Instead, the arms amplify the space around the body and the torso has sweeping bends; it seems as though she quite literally gobbles space but it is the space around the body and not the stage space. Because the tempo of this dance seems measured, the restless, confined use of stage space is not apparent. It is typical of Ashton's style though. He rarely used long diagonals and phrases which follow each other in a straight line.

Ashton and Levasseur chose the colours carefully for each dancer and it seems that the the rich luxuriousness of the deep imperial purple matched both Elvin's personality and dance qualities. Elvin retired a few months after the première of *Birthday Offering* and as Percival puts it

> she left something of herself behind: a new colour in Ashton's palette, a different example for the rising generation to follow in the classics, a group of wonderful roles for her successors, and vivid memories in the hearts and minds of many spectators.[48]

Beryl Grey (1927-)

As the only female dancer to have been trained almost solely in the Sadler's Wells school, Grey was unique in *Birthday Offering*. Characterised by a clear, precise technique, she had an easy command of the technical vocabulary, evident in films of her dancing *Swan Lake* in Russia in 1957, and a breadth of line that was much admired.

Grey was not an Ashton dancer. He created few roles for her and of these only one could be seen as major, that of the Duessa in *The Quest* (1943). It was made for Grey when she was just fifteen. She also created Winter in *Cinderella*, Countess Kitty in *Les Sirènes* (1946), Ashton's last collaboration with Berners, and Fire in *Homage to the Queen* which Richardson described as giving an 'impression of dangerous beauty by the use of swiftly changing *épaulements* and brief *élancé* movements'.[49] What can sometimes be forgotten in accounts of Grey's achievements is that Ashton also made the Aurora variation in Act II of *The Sleeping Beauty* for her in 1952, a solo which is still in the Royal Ballet version. According to Vaughan, Ashton based the variation on Elvin's memories of the Bolshoi version but it was Grey who first danced it.

While Grey was a popular dancer, not everyone agreed about her talents. When she left the Royal Ballet in 1957, Arthur Franks wrote that she was:

A dancer of magnificent ease and assurance with breadth of movement, beauty of phrasing and true simplicity of style, her personality is warm and generous; when she is on the stage she 'gives'. She is not, however, a very subtle actress and not well suited to roles which require fantasy or delicate nuances of feeling. She is not, in short the kind of dancer likely to appeal to the Royal Ballet's chief choreographer and she has received very few new roles from Ashton.[50]

Ashton's hesitation in working with her is to some extent evident in her dance in *Birthday Offering*. Following on Elvin's dance it could, if danced by an unaccomplished dancer, seem awkward after the sumptuousness of the previous number. But analysis shows that it is a complex piece of choreography with some of the hallmarks of Ashton's style, though perhaps not as remarkable as the other variations. It was choreographed to *L'été* but has none of the languor of the Summer variation in *Cinderella* and lasts 1.12 minutes.

Dressed in ice blue, the dancer enters running in parallel on pointe, making a small circle. This fluttering opening run introduces one aspect of the dance: a tremulous, almost diffident, dynamic, suggesting delicacy and intricate movement. What follows challenges this impression, although occasionally the dancer's arm and wrist movement retain this nervous quality. It is as if Ashton wanted to exploit the smaller, sparkling actions, which are not usually associated with a tall woman.

The opening group of phrases starts with a motif referencing the beginning of the woman's solo in *Les rendezvous*: a double turn in *attitude* goes straight into a double turn *en dehors* and ends with a swivel on two feet from a fourth position. The upper body makes a sharp twist from back to front for the final part and the phrase ends in an abrupt fifth position. Grey had danced the lead in *Les rendezvous* (1933) a role originally made for Alicia Markova. I could find no account of Grey's dancing in this role but I assume it was impressive, for Ashton to evoke it here. The phrase cluster is quite dazzling, even humorous in *Les rendezvous* but because the music has a more sustained quality, it is less striking in *Birthday Offering*.

The remarkable thing about this dance is the economy of means by which it is achieved. The two principal motifs are confined to turns of every sort and a forwards unfurling of the working leg, interspersed with *arabesques*. Turning dominates and this fluctuates between *pirouettes* from two feet to single foot turns and turns which unfold into low extensions of the leg. Turns are first established in the opening cluster and the ending of the cluster has turns again but with the leg unfolding in front at the end of each turn. Various kinds of *arabesques*, either performed with a deep forward bend or more upright with the leg unfolding backwards, follow. Are these to draw the audience's attention to Grey's sumptuous line, or simply to create a respite between the turns? *Pirouettes* are present again in the next phrase, but now the dancer finishes each one on one leg with the working foot crossed over. Her toe rests on the ground, testing the dancer's balance. More unfolding and turning occurs in the next series of phrase groups and then *arabesques* return again. After a series of sustained *relevés* with the working leg unfolding in front, the dance ends abruptly with a double turn into a turning jump and further sustained turn into a pose with the arms up. In contrast to Elvin's pose which ends on the floor, Grey's is standing but the arms are similar in both.

This is a dance which teases. It seems unhurried and sustained but that is caused by the smooth runs on pointe, the steady, measured turns and the long phrase clusters. Actually the dancer has to move continually and be able to make rapid alterations in weight and direction. The movements follow each other without a break; there is little time to catch a breath, except at the end of the long phrases. The languorous *arabesques* appear too to give a sense of effortlessness. Unusual choreography for the arms and wrists is a feature of Ashton's style and in this dance, the arms make winding movements around the body but extended away from the torso. The arms become a feature throughout the dance: with curling wrist movements during the chain of turns, softening rounded arms for the *arabesques*, exaggerated fifth positions, with the torso leaning forward and arms which cross the body at the end of the double *posé* turns.

Interestingly, this dance is now frequently performed by shorter dancers renowned for their technical ease, so it was a curious dance for a tall woman like Grey. Since there are few records of Grey's dancing, this testifies to her extraordinary technical abilities, though without making her appear to be merely a technician.

Ashton made dances that look deceptively simple and the relaxed, easy quality of this dance does just this. The cold ice blue of Grey's costume was an unusual choice but it gives an impression of cool, masking the dance's difficult technique. It is not an easy dance to classify and, of all the dances, it seems to have less personality than the others. In it Ashton reminds us of another ballet in which Grey danced but he seems to have been at a bit of a loss when it came to articulating her personality and major characteristics, beyond technical competence.

Margot Fonteyn (1919-1991)
The final variation was for Fonteyn, then the undisputed queen of the Sadler's Wells Ballet.[51] Her training was an eclectic mixture, comprising fancy dancing, RAD and Imperial Russian ballet. She began her serious

Margot Fonteyn. © Roger Wood, Royal Opera House Archives.

Fonteyn's pose is the epitome of the 1950s perfect arabesque. But in comparison to those on page 46, the arm positions and upper back are quite different.

training in China before moving to London to study at the Sadler's Wells Ballet School at the age of fourteen in 1933.

A major influence on Fonteyn's dancing were the classes she took with Volkova, whom she first met in China but had not studied with there. It is difficult to determine from Alexander Meinert's biography of Volkova and other writings about her, exactly when Fonteyn started attending Volkova's classes in her West Street studios.[52] What is evident though is that Fonteyn was there between 1942 and 1949, as was Ashton after 1945.[53] Volkova admired Ashton's work and it was through her influence in Denmark that he choreographed his *Romeo and Juliet* (1955) there.[54] She is given no more than a cursory reference in histories of the Royal Ballet, yet, evidence from Meinertz's biography indicates that Volkova had a major impact not only on Fonteyn's style and whole approach to performing but also on several of the Sadler's Wells dancers.

Her teaching encompassed a mixture of Vaganova, since Volkova had studied with her, and Russian teachers she encountered in Paris when she first came to Europe, such as Olga Preobrajenskaya and Lubov Egorova. According to Meinertz, 'Preobrajenskaya did not use *épaulement* or exercises for the torso during her classes; her focus was primarily on the legs and lower part of the body'.[55] Volkova preferred Egorova's classes, perhaps because they reminded her of those of her old Russian teacher, Maria Romanova. As an old-style teacher, Egorova remained seated throughout the class until the adage which was more of a performance than an exercise.[56] Volkova described it as dancing:

> Every step had *épaulement*; Egorova's emotive choreography covered the whole room, searching, striving and longing for something intangible. It was *plastique*, sculptural, and ended with a pose of supplication, like a prayer.[57]

How and what Volkova taught in West Street is not wholly clear and much more in-depth analysis is needed to understand a teacher's contribution.[58] When Volkova first arrived, she found the British dancers beautifully trained but lacking in quality in the upper body. 'I had to... add harmony of arms and shoulders to release them a bit emotionally.'[59] But she also strengthened the whole body, including the dancers' feet.

What Volkova communicated above all was the joy of dancing. Tommy Linden, who danced in West End musicals, put the point succinctly:

> I knew there was a reason why I wanted to dance, but the goal – to be able to express the entire register of human feelings with one's body and in movement had never been formulated in classes. This I found with Vera, all in one parcel containing technique and style and the lot.[60]

Pamela May makes clear just how individual her classes were. She not only understood everyone's needs but also helped them with their specific problems.

> She always came and watched performances... She didn't teach us the same things, she would change things and steps if something looked better on me. Some things suited Margot better, some things suited me better.[61]

Although forbidden by de Valois to attend Volkova's classes, Fonteyn and many other dancers from the Sadler's Wells Ballet ignored this order. For three years during the 1940s Volkova had taught at the Sadler's Wells school but when requested by de Valois to close her West Street studio, she refused and de Valois sacked her. Because of this and the dancers' refusal to abandon Volkova, relations between de Valois and Volkova were strained. Many of the dancers preferred Volkova's approach to that of de Valois and the latter probably sensed this but was powerless to prevent them from attending the West Street studio.

Using technique as a vehicle and not as a means to an end, seems to have been the main characteristic of Volkova's approach and Fonteyn fully absorbed this. Volkova also worked privately with Fonteyn on her roles. Most of the critics applauded this and found her influence on Fonteyn to be exceptional. I can only assume that it was Volkova's effect on Fonteyn that helped, in part, to propel her into stardom, particularly evident when the company opened at the Royal Opera House in 1946 and again in the USA in 1949. Fonteyn's variation in *Birthday Offering* owes something to Volkova's coaching. It is one of the first Ashton made for her in which the focus is more on her footwork than the upper body. Film of Fonteyn during the 1950s, particularly a short extract of her in *Daphnis and Chloe* (1951), reveals real joyfulness and, in addition, her dancing has a degree of elegance and formality that epitomised the decorum of the 1950s. This is because, as William Chappell puts it, she was no 'showman', giving performances that were as unmannered as they were academically pure.[62] Although Ashton's steps are rarely 'academically pure'!

It was no secret that Fonteyn had problematic feet and I believe that because of this, in his earlier works, Ashton had focused more on her graceful upper body and expressive eyes. By the 1950s, with the benefit of Volkova's training and education, Fonteyn's feet had improved and her upper body had become even more expressive. It may be because of this that the solo Ashton made for Fonteyn in *Birthday Offering* has a strong focus on feet through using intricate beaten steps. When working on the dance, Ashton apparently, and perhaps somewhat wickedly, stated that he was going to force the audience 'to look at Margot's feet'.[63] Indeed, the opening and closing diagonals with their elaborate beats and quick footwork do just this, by drawing our eyes downwards.

As a variation for Fonteyn it is remarkable. It is a playful dance comprising teasing footwork with a relaxed upper body: the feet make elaborate patterns, while the arms change only occasionally. The solo has links with the kind of dances Ashton made for her between 1948 and 1956, particularly in *Scènes de ballet* and *Sylvia* where precision and intricate foot work are a feature of both, though our eyes are not encouraged to observe the feet. In *Birthday Offering*, Fonteyn dances to *Ruses d'Amour*, which begins with the solo violin, a typical instrument for nineteenth century female, ballerina, solos. Because of the music's polka rhythm and the variation's meticulous footwork, the dance reminds me of variations in *The Sleeping Beauty* Act III, in particular, Aurora's variation, which is characterised by the clear-cut precision of the feet to pizzicato strings.

The opening series of phrases consist of a little jump (*pas de chat*) into a *pas de bourrée à cinq pas* followed by three steps on pointe into a low pose. This is repeated twice more and the final phrase of the cluster has only two steps: a beaten jump with a tap of the foot behind, repeated twice. The focus is now transferred to the upper body. For in the next phrase cluster, the opening series is reversed with the *pas de bourrée*, replaced by a version of the polka step. The cluster is completed by a final phrase consisting of a series of recurring poses, travelling right across the stage to stage left. As well as shifting its focus, the dance also moves between formal ballet steps and folk dance; in the polka step, the hand is placed on the hip, giving it an unexpected air of informality. Ashton has taken a rhythmic phrase the *pas de bourrée à cinq pas* and added little single stepping movements in the opening cluster of the dance; in the second phrase cluster, he uses the polka step, performed on pointe, and follows it with a small jump into an articulated *pas de bourrée*, which ends with a pose in a closed position on pointe with the torso leaning forward.

The middle section of the dance has a sweeping travelling *pas de bourrée* into a large jump followed by poses in a low *retiré* position on pointe which are repeated. The final diagonal group of phrases comprises an assortment of small beaten jumps, following a circular pattern, uninterrupted by poses. This variation gives the impression of a dancer with an easy command of intricate beats and footwork. It is a short witty dance, made more playful by the juxtaposition of flurries of dance with sudden poses. But of course it depends on who is dancing and how much she chooses to emphasise these features. As there is no film of Fonteyn performing this dance in 1956, I cannot assume that she drew attention to its wit, although evidence from her performances of other dances suggests she would. Even though much of Ashton's choreography depended on short bursts of continuous dance phrases, he also liked to draw attention to a pose. In this variation in *Birthday Offering*, the held poses are as significant as the intricate beaten steps. It is an interesting dance because it shows Fonteyn as being not only a highly accomplished dancer but also one whose mastery of the technical values of the era was supreme, even if at first glance, it does not appear as a virtuoso dance.

Fonteyn's solo is a masterpiece of variations on the theme of the *pas de bourrée*, enhanced by its coupling with little quivering beats. In the lower body the spatial paths are complicated, drawing scribbles around the lower limbs, while the upper body is more demonstrative, with the arms making broader paths and lines around the torso. And this confuses us; the ease of the upper body is in direct contrast with that of the lower, particularly in the opening and closing diagonals, where the feet are working fast and furiously.

What is it about Ashton's powers of invention that leave us so in awe? Is it his ability, like Jane Austen's, to take a very small square of ivory and etch seemingly endless variations on a singular theme? Or is it the appropriateness of his choice of movement for his dancers? Interacting with Petipa was only half of what Ashton was doing in *Birthday Offering*, the other was presenting the ballerinas of Sadler's Wells and, as prima ballerina, Margot Fonteyn. There are no showy steps, high extensions, ferocious balances or spinning turns here, only variations on the *pas de bourrée* and the *brisé volé*. This is very different from Balanchine's tribute to Petipa and his muse Suzanne Farrell in *Diamonds* (1968), where, amongst other things, the woman's variation has hard-edged, spectacular balances, high extensions and multiple turns.

Conclusion

The seven variations show real dancing, not technical display, and the dance movement of these seven solos embodies both Ashton's dance style and that of the contemporary Sadler's Wells Ballet. Key to this style is the training and even if these dancers had been trained by different teachers, they seem to have been adaptable enough to embrace Ashton's stylistic demands. Despite the range of training, it is apparent that the dancers had enough similarity in their attitude to the dance movement to create a coherent style. Company classes, the effect of the repertoire on their dancing, and the fact that Ashton was always present, also created similarities in style.

These dances do not have breathtaking athleticism but a kind of decorum and restraint. In place of athleticism is dense footwork that compels the dancer rapidly to change weight and direction. Phrases that start facing downstage end up facing the back, as in Jackson's variation, and turns do not simply end but require the dancer immediately to turn in the opposite direction, as in those of Fifield and Grey. The dances are also rhythmically complex, not just in terms of the music but also the movement. Stress is placed on some actions, diminishing others, and there are often abrupt changes in dynamic from one movement to another.[64] Not only does this force the dancer to anticipate future phrases, beyond the one she is dancing, but it also gives scope for interpretation. Dancers can play with the phrasing by emphasising their strengths.

The dances do not gobble space as do those of the Soviet choreographers, rather they revel in the intricate stage patterns that move restlessly backwards, sideways, forwards as in Elvin's dance and Fonteyn's. Nerina's variation travels most but she dashes back and forth rather than swallow up the space in one long diagonal. Pauses are few and only after quite protracted phrases do the dancers present a pose or body design.

What makes these dances special is the way Ashton makes unexpected links between steps. Who would have expected the series of body designs comprising little *pliés* in a low *retiré* into a quick *relevé* into *arabesque* that occur in Jackson's dance? They are rapid but create sharp, sparkling images. Ashton's dances appear elegant, unspectacular even but as Denby put it:

> The steps do not look like school steps (though they are as a matter of fact correct); they are like discoveries, like something you do not know you can do with the deceptive air of being incorrect and accidental that romantic poetry has. But how expressive, how true to human feeling the dances are.[65]

Denby captures what is important about these ballets, though I disagree with him about the correctness of the 'school steps'. Ashton never treated the dancers as bodies but as fully human people and *Birthday Offering* fully justifies Denby's observations. Arlene Croce once described the variations as

> chattering on outrageously [with] sudden stops and changes of direction, flowery port de bras, many little appurtenances to style that another choreographer might edit out.[66]

But what is most striking about these dances is both the elegance and complexity of the footwork, with a correspondingly relaxed, even gracious upper body.

Jazz Calendar (1968)

In the social and stage dances of the 1920s and 30s, the fox trots, two-steps, lindy hops and tap dancing, there is complicated foot work, floor patterns full of twists and turns, and a flexible torso, all performed with the easy elegance of Fred Astaire. It is this influence from popular culture which is at the heart of *Jazz Calendar*. The ballet is loosely attached to the children's rhyme *Monday's Child is Fair of Face*, which is used as a stimulus to make seven different dances. The work created by Ashton and Jarman seems distinct from *Birthday Offering* but in the choreographic and dance movement styles, they have quite a bit in common. Clearly Ashton did not abandon his movement style just because he was choreographing to jazz and the composition of Richard Rodney Bennett also coloured the work. Not specifically composed for the ballet, the music had been made several years earlier and the dance owes its title to that of the music.

Gay activist, provocative film maker and gardener is how Derek Jarman is often described. It is thus surprising that this seemingly unconventional man collaborated on a ballet with a choreographer sometimes thought of as establishment, conservative and lacking in audacity. Their collaboration was caused by the cancellation of a new production of *Aida* at the Royal Opera House. In early November 1967, Ashton was asked if he could quickly rustle-up a new work to be premiered in January. He chose a jazz score by Rodney Bennett, also structured around the seven sections of the children's rhyme *Monday's Child is Fair of Face*, and sought advice on a designer from Nigel Gosling the art critic of *The Observer.* Jarman had just finished at the Slade, and Gosling, who had seen the Slade's graduation exhibition, recommended him. Ashton was taking a risk, using a new, untried art student but after listening to the music, Jarman produced some designs which Ashton liked. Not all found their way into the ballet but there were enough interesting ones to make both the partnership, and ballet, successful. Ashton had already worked with Rex Whistler, John Armstrong, John Piper and Graham Sutherland; so collaborating with artists considered avant-garde was a practice with which he was already familiar.

At the Slade, Jarman had specialised in set design, taking the course taught by Nicholas Georgiadas, who worked on several ballets with McMillan, and Peter Snow, a distinguished designer for theatre who had collaborated with Ashton on the ballet *Variations on a Theme by Purcell* (1955). Started in the 1930s by Diaghilev's scene painter Vladimir Polunin, the department has been midwife to a number of painters and theatre designers including Yolanda Sonnabend and Philip Prowse. In his two years there, Jarman designed miniature sets for ballet, theatre and opera and had been chosen to represent Britain at the 1967 Paris Biennale in theatre décor.[67] Guy Brett, art critic of *The Times*, considered Jarman's the best thing in the section. Jarman's contribution to film is well documented and highly regarded but his work in the theatre has not been given as much prominence and that for dance even less.

Despite a trend during the 1950s to reduce scenery and costumes to a minimum, influenced by the works of Balanchine, Ashton rarely used that aesthetic, though when he did the works were often supreme. *Symphonic Variations* and *Monotones* are two examples of minimalist costume and set. And he was well aware that the effect of highly original costumes on a dance work can be central to its perception. This is certainly the case with *Jazz Calendar*. Vaughan remarked that 'the best thing about [the work] was certainly Derek Jarman's designs, which were truly original and effortlessly typified the spirit of 'swinging London'.[68]

Is it Swinging London or Art Deco? *Jazz Calendar* was described as Ashton's attempt at cool by several critics but I agree with others who felt it owed more to the 1930s. Equally, its stage décor and costumes have links with that era. In 1974 Jarman worked again with Ashton on a piece entitled *Fashion Show*, which Vaughan records as having had a similar movement style to that of *Jazz Calendar*.

Jarman's Designs: 'A Packet of Liquorice Allsorts'

Of the critics, Vaughan is alone in identifying the ballet's links with the designs of Joan Miro for *Jeux d'enfants*, a work, choreographed by Massine in 1932 for Colonel de Basil's Ballets Russes. Cyril Beaumont described the ballet, about toys coming to life at night, as 'a kind of miniature review' with short dances for groups or soloists.[69] Miro used vibrant primary colours in the design. Many of the dancers wore unitards, unusual attire for dancers in the 1930s, and he used cut-outs on stage, brightly painted geometric freestanding shapes. Similarly in *Jazz Calendar*, Jarman created on-stage shapes and dressed all his dancers in unitards, except for the women in 'Thursday's Child', they had short skirts attached, and the man wore a multi-coloured two-piece (track) suit. It is not known whether Jarman knew of Miro's designs, though he enjoyed doing extensive research for his creations and just might have come across them. There are few photographs of *Jeux d'enfants* but the ballet was not performed in Europe after the 1930s. Like Ashton's ballet, there is no narrative but beyond that, and of course the décor, there cannot be much similarity between the two.

The designs are linked to the 30s by the varied skull caps worn in every number except Saturday's Child. The sparkles on the art-deco cap for Monday's Child are picked up in the hooped- shaped, sparkling mirror, placed just behind and to the right of the dancer, Vergie Derman, in the original cast. Dressed in a glowing, virginal white unitard which mutated into hot pink from the knees down, she was first seen framed by a huge scarlet circle, hanging centre stage. On several occasions in the dance, she circled her face with her hand, ballet mime for beauty, though she never actually looked into the mirror, standing near by.

Tuesday's set surprised with its sunshine yellow lighting and backcloth and a translucent pyramid of perspex bubbles, hiding the woman and acting as a prop for the legs of the two supine men in the opening pose. All three dancers, Anthony Dowell, Robert Mead and Merle Park were dressed in brilliant white. The woman's outfit had, what one critic described as a

> fantastic fringed costume that turns the classical leotard and tights into a kind of Platonic idea of the Charleston dress, while the men have silver stripes spiralling up one leg. [70]

Wednesday's set was dark, full of woe as the rhyme suggests, and the cutout was a raised Jean Arp-like hand with green splodges, hanging stage left. The woman, Svetlana Beriosova, sombrely dressed in black, was supported throughout by four men in black unitards, covered in lime green splodges.

Thursday's Child was Alexander Grant, dressed in a pink bowler hat and multi-coloured suit. He was accompanied on his journey by six women in varying shades of blue. The women's costumes range from indigo through royal blue and sapphire to a pale sky blue and they wear yellow and orange helmets. These are not skull caps, like the others but tight caps with yellow and orange balls all over. They were light as thistle down and easy to wear. On stage, the only object is a deep blue triangle, which, as one critic put it looks like a 'blue highway at the back of the stage, tapering into infinity'.[71] Lighting is used to emphasise travelling. At one point the dancers are fragmented by a flashing strobe, giving the effect of slow motion and from time to time their shadows are enlarged on the backcloth.

Friday is supposed to be loving and giving but Nureyev initially objected to his costume, mainly the tight skull cap in red and blue, and threatened not to perform. He later relented. In this duet he and Sibley wore unitards split vertically into vermilion and cobalt blue. Accompanied by blues' styled music, they were framed by a vibrant lovers' knot, matching the costumes.

Dancers, Ashton said, work harder than anyone else, so of course Saturday's Child comprised a male ballet class with chrome bars, a tall silver tower and a bright sunlit background. Colour was introduced by the towels and dressing gowns worn by the men as they entered. Sunday brought the cast together, led by a small female dancer, Ann Jenner, in a multicoloured fringed unitard. This is probably the number that led Jarman to describe the work as looking like a 'packet of liquorice allsorts dancing'.[72]

This was Jarman's first work in the theatre and his most successful.[73] As he put it, 'The beginning of my career was to resemble the end of anyone else's.'[74] For it catapulted him into the Royal Opera House and a gala performance. His designs, singled out for their contemporaneity and vivacity, were hailed as a triumph and Jarman as a 'discovery and a brilliant one'. One critic commented that Jarman caught 'clever parallels to Ashton's allusions yet preserve[ed] a simplicity that ought to wear well.'[75] Another critic agreed:

> credit... must go to the young designer Derek Jarman whose costumes and settings were not only bang up to the minute in style but more importantly they made their own valid comments in the context of this light-hearted look at the youth of today.[76]

What Jarman brought to Ashton's ballet was colour; hardly surprising, given his profound understanding of its power. It was this that gave the ballet its sixties appearance, while the colourful unitards made the dancers sleekly elegant. Colour was not only important to Jarman but fundamental to his approach to art. In his book *Chroma*, written not long before he died, he observes that the research he had done for *Blue* (1993) 'threw him deep into the spectrum' and into a search through his books to find out who had written on colour.[77] This turned out to be a mixture of writers from philosophy to art and from psychiatry to medicine. *Chroma* is a meditation on colour and on those who have written about it. He gives no examples of the colours he writes about because as he puts it 'context changes the way we perceive [colours].'[78] Red is a 'scarlet woman' or vermilion is 'The Queen of reds' and 'white is dead mid-winter, pure and chaste', while black can be sexy underwear or it can also be forbidden as in the 'black monk who gabbles black magic as he conducts a black mass.'[79] Blue, grey, yellow, green, rose, purple and translucence are all richly and opulently presented, with a discussion on each. The result is an eloquent treatise on colour and all the possible ways in which colour is used, perceived, enjoyed.

Jarman's use of contemporary materials for the geometric cut-outs supplied them with an up-to-date modernity. The glittering mirror, translucent pyramid and intricate love knot not to mention the aluminium barre and huge triangle all looked as though they had just been purchased at Habitat, the recently opened cool, Mediterranean-inspired household store. And Ashton used these geometric shapes to amplify his choreography.

Like all good stage backcloths, the plain cloth drew attention to the dancers, never competing with them for attention. Using cut-outs meant that for much of the piece, the backdrop could be pattern-less because their shapes cast giant shadows on it. Lit to compliment the dances, it had: smoky, seductive red for Monday, bright canary yellow for Tuesday, sombre and dark for Wednesday and blue for Thursday. Friday has a more sultry red. Saturday and Sunday were bright and shiny and the latter had all the days' shapes painted across the backdrop. Colour, light, shadow can transform the stage and affect our perception of a dance. In *Jazz Calendar*, these are a key feature of the work. But what caused the initial excitement amongst the press was the presence of a jazz band in the hallowed pit of the Royal Opera House.

Jazz Age References

The music had been commissioned by the BBC in 1964 but Richard Rodney Bennett adapted it for Ashton's dance. The score, hardly avant garde, sounded more like big-band jazz but it suited the choreography and helped Jarman to create the designs. Divided into seven parts, the music is rhythmically interesting and has a variety of instrumental solos. The *Sunday Times* critic found that

> the music is not... a coy kind of half-jazz... It is a very good jazz score-tailored to an occasion of course, but swinging all the way in very forthright jazz rhythms, allowing ample room for improvisation, and most rich in sumptuous tone colours of the kind to which Gil Evans and Marty Paich, among others, have accustomed us. It is also marvellously married with the choreography and excitingly played by the pit band which includes half the London jazz establishment: Ronnie Ross, Jackie Dougan, Tony Coe, Kenny Wheeler et al.[80]

Ashton came of age in the Jazz era of the late 1920s and 1930s and this score recalls that era. In an interview, given just before he died in 1988, Ashton mentioned his need for rhythm, commenting that his devotion to pulse probably stems from the period in which he was young 'Jazz or whatever, there was more sense of rhythm and pulse [then]'.[81] And when the choreography is analysed, the flavour is of the Jazz Age rather than the popular dances of the 1960s.

Vaughan notes that the dances probably owed much to show business and the revues of the 1930s. The numbers in musicals like *The Cat and the Fiddle* (1932), with music by Jerome Kern, in which Ashton worked alongside Buddy Bradley, and *After Dark*, again with Bradley, owe much, not only to the stage dancing of that era but also to the social dances: tangos and rumbas. The two also collaborated on *High Yellow* (1932) a ballet for the Camargo Society, with music by Spike Hughes, a young composer of jazz. Ashton loved the vitality of jazz and Bradley's polyrhythmic use of the body. Bradley's movement

> brought together the dynamic body movements of African-American vernacular dance with the tap-dance steps and rhythms of jazz improvisation to create a bold and inventive style.[82]

Throughout the 1930s, Ashton choreographed for at least twelve revues and musicals, so it is unsurprising that when it came to popular culture, Ashton was instinctively drawn to that era. Tellingly several of the older critics reviewing *Jazz Calendar* made the link with the 1930s. Writing in the *Daily Telegraph*, the dance critic A.V. Coton commented that:

Alexander Grant as Thursday's Child did a marvellous travelling dance modelled on Hollywood eccentric dancing of the 1930s; in fact much of the choreography was a take-off of dance patterns and ideas from that halcyon period.[83]

While in *The Stage*, Eric Johns alluded to that era, seeing the ballet as

sophisticated and satiric, not unlike the miniature ballets Cochran used to commission for Nikitina and Lifar in those glossy revues at the Pavilion when Delysia was the toast of the town and the Bright Young Things dictated the latest vogue.[84]

For those who remembered the 1920s and 1930s the link between the Bright Young Things and Swinging London was palpable. And if Ashton was tapping into his youth, the 1930s was the most obvious place to go. Although Jarman was not of that era, he captured both its elegance and its sophistication, marrying it to the psychedelic hedonism of the 1960s. Jarman was not enamoured of 1960s culture as evident from his reference to it as the 'swinging decayed'.[85] In spite of this, some aspects of the era crept in but were dispersed into the 1930s flavour of the work.

Choreographed Jazz

Much of the work's flavour and choreographic style can be gleaned from examining three dances: Monday's Child, Tuesday's Child and Thursday's Child, a solo, a trio and group dance respectively. This is not a dance with tutus, verticality, or, with an emphasis on turnout, so Ashton was not attempting to make it a conventional ballet. Despite the body-revealing costumes, the choreography is not primarily concerned with shapes in space but with motion. The dancers are not presented as ideals of either men or women but as people who enjoy dancing.

The solo in Monday's Child is particularly interesting, as some of it may well have been inspired by a number in the 1934 film *Evergreen*, choreographed by Bradley, in which, Jessie Matthews, dressed in a satin robe, dances around an elegant sitting room.[86] Her high kicks, slinky walks, spinning turns and thrusting hips remind me very much of Monday's Child.

Monday's Child

The curtain opens on a huge calendar with some dates picked out in bright luminescent colours. After a short overture, the frontpiece lifts on a darkened stage lit by the dancer's scull-cap and shiny cape. She stands in the centre of a giant red circle and begins with a mimetic action, circling the face with her fingers. This is ballet mime for beautiful, but Ashton makes it a more seductive gesture involving the shoulders and most of the hand. It is repeated in the middle of the dance and at the end, lest the audience forget the subject matter. All these circular movements make us more aware of the circle in which the dancer is framed, and the other circles and hooped mirror, adorning the stage. Shrugging off her cape, the dancer moves lazily around the stage like someone in a small, smoky, jazz cellar. Much of the emphasis is on the torso, which the dancer draws attention to by sliding her hands down both her sides and at times her legs. Un-balletic hips are thrust forward and shoulders operate in opposition to each other. In its conscious sexuality, the dance is unlike other Ashton movement. He does not often choreograph blatant sexuality, though sensuality is evident in many of his works. Here the woman draws attention to her self and her obvious physicality and the sexuality is strikingly stylised.

This dance also has a considerable element of floorwork. The performer sits on the floor, legs either curled on one side of her body or seductively stretching in a high extension, drawing attention to her leg by sliding her hands down to a pointed foot. The movement has been borrowed from the sexy stage dancing of the 1930s and 1940s. Perhaps here Ashton was also thinking of Cyd Charisse, whose dancing was described by Tony Parsons as having 'supreme erotic elegance'.[87] Derman, the dancer Ashton chose for this number, was strikingly beautiful with long legs, not unlike those of Charisse.

Derman also had a languid quality in her dancing that Ashton emphasised here with exaggerated use of weight. Rather than light, gravity-defying actions, he used heavily weighted movements giving the solo a feeling of endless time. Nothing is hurried, though there are little rhythmic moments that surprise. Ashton introduces a turning sequence, a reference to Summer in *Cinderella*, where the dancer performs four turns on two feet alternating between *en dehors* and *en dedans*, each ending with the arms stretched out to the side. These are followed by a fast series of *chaîné* turns, with the arms sliding down the body as she moves.

This is a brilliantly crafted dance, tightly knit, which reflects the stage cutouts. It has a recurring circular motif that is seen in the body shapes and in the leg work, for instance, when the dancer performs the Ashton signature step of *rond de jambe à terre*, accompanied by alternating shrugging shoulders. And the shoulder shrug is also a motif in the dance. At one point, the upper torso twists in opposition to the leg, softening the appearance of a series of low leg extensions with the supporting leg on pointe. It is like an exaggerated slow run made sophisticated by the shoulder shrugs: as she steps the arm and shoulder move in opposition to the extended leg. And, it is also used to parody Balanchine's *Agon*. As the dance ends, Derman slowly sinks, shrugging her shoulders one after the other. So do the women in *Agon's* trio, but that is a serious work to Stravinsky music.

There are no other dances quite like this in the extant Ashton work, though he may have choreographed similar ones in the revues. Not that it is devoid of Ashton's dance style. The sudden quick turns interjected after a series of languid phrases; the fluid use of the torso and arms, and arm moves that create circular and intricate lines around the body, are all Ashton traits.

Tuesday's Child

If Monday's Child owed something to the smoky jazz clubs of the 1930s then Tuesday's Child had more in common with the cool, spirited dances of Fred Astaire and Ginger Rogers. Tuesday's Child is full of grace; what could be more graceful than Astaire and Rogers? It is not the movement of Tuesday's Child that is similar, rather the fluidly joined phrases, the easy style of the dancers and the air of sophistication and effortlessness. Suffused in brilliant lemon yellow, the dance comprises a trio dressed in white and all three have tight white skull caps. The white unitards and skull caps remind us of Ashton's *Monotones* (1965), which has a similarly dressed trio, in white, with glittering belts and white skull caps but the dance has quite a different aura. Where *Monotones* is icy and intense, Tuesday's Child is sunny and stylish. It gleams, glitters and amuses. Dowell and Mead were chosen for both works but in *Jazz Calendar*, the bubbly Park replaced *Monotones's* stately Vyvyan Lorraine. As with Astaire and Rogers, the original cast has never been surpassed. Nobody has been able to make this dance seem so fluid or so easy. Ashton did not copy Astaire's choreography or even take movements from his dances but he created something that is just as good. It has the flavour of Astaire but without his steps.

The dance is divided into chunks, each with a dominating motif and the trio twists and turns and runs about the stage in a breathtaking sequence that lasts over three minutes, a sprint really. From the start, we know that the woman is going to be something of a plaything because she is the smallest and lightest of the trio. Although she is thrown from one man to the other, she also performs much the same movement as the men when all three dance together. Dominating the dance are turns, turns moving in one direction and then immediately the other way. Turns which end in a high kick or, for the woman, in an arabesque on pointe, supported by the two men. We are in familiar Ashton territory here. The winding and unwinding turns have links with those in the Fifield and Grey variations and with those he made for Dowell in *The Dream* or in Troyte's dance in *Enigma Variations*.

The dance sparkles because it is dominated by spatial projections. In other words, the movement extends beyond the limbs and there are few trace pat-

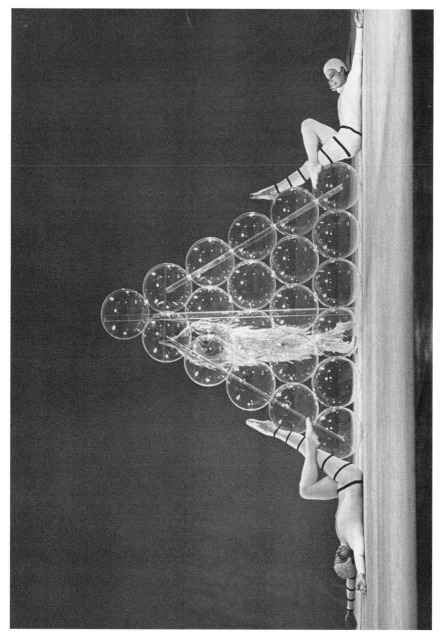

Jazz Calendar, Robert Mead, Marle Park and Anthony Dowell in Tuesday's Child. © Donald Southern. Courtesy of the Royal Opera House.

terns left by the limbs in the space. Ashton did this elsewhere, particularly in
Scènes de ballet where it creates sharp, cut-glass movement and in Nerina's
solo in *Birthday Offering*. In this piece, because of the fluidity of the phrasing,
the movement seems less spiky. And, there are impactive moments too, adding to the sharpness of the spatial projections, for instance, when all three
dancers, placed in a triangular shape, perform a heavy jump in second and
then into *arabesque,* or when the woman, on pointe, stabs the floor with one
foot.

Ashton loved dancers who could run fluidly like Isadora Duncan. He remembered that she could cover the stage in a remarkable way. While not
quite Isadora-like runs, those in Tuesday's Child cover the stage, seamlessly
punctuated by *jeté*-like jumps, making the run look fluent and effortless.[88]
Three times the dancers make big circular runs and the woman does other
smaller circles. The runs unify the piece, joining patterns of turns with sudden stops and a central section where the woman is thrown between the
men.

The central section is rather like the Lindy hop dances of the 1930s, where
the woman leapt onto her partner and was thrown to another on the dance
floor. In Tuesday's Child, the woman performs a turning jump into a *pirouette* with one man and then steps across to do another turning jump with the
other man who throws her back to the first. The acrobatic movement has
been anticipated by the opening somersault of the dance, in which the two
men turn the woman upside down after she emerges from the translucent
bubble-like pyramid. As in Monday's Child, Ashton uses the stage furniture,
the pyramid, in the choreography. The woman hides behind it at the beginning and the end and, during the dance, all three run behind it.

Recognisable elements of Ashton's style are present in this piece. The constant weight changes and changes in direction are one feature. Another is
the use of complex phrase patterns and elaborate use of stage space. Sometimes the dancers move up and down vertically, then across the stage, or they
form a triangle or move in wide sweeping circles. The floor patterns are very
different from the majority of those in *Birthday Offering.* They are perhaps
closest to those in Jackson's variation, though there the dance is much
shorter and denser and so seems more complex.

Alhough Ashton felt that choreography was a serious art form, he frequently made jokes and commented on his own choreography and that of
others. At one point in Tuesday's Child he parodies Balanchine's *Apollo,*
which the Royal Ballet acquired in November 1966. In the opening section
of *Apollo* (1928) all three muses pose in a vertical line going upstage with
arms rounded over the head. Then each bends, alternating from side to side.
The three dancers in Tuesday's Child do the same but with a jaunty jump to
one side and then the other. They hint too at *Monotones,* when each takes a

low *arabesque*. In *Monotones* the woman performs a supported, slow adagio movement, while the second man has a turning phrase but here, during the swirling lifts, one man swings the woman in a circle, while the other man has a continuous turning phrase.

Thursday's Child

The final section that I examine is Thursday's Child, for two reasons, because it is a group dance and because Alexander Grant, the soloist, was one of male dancers for whom Ashton most frequently choreographed. He was almost a muse for Ashton and his very distinctive dance style permeates the number, affecting the dancing of the six women. It is not totally unlike the movement Ashton made for Grant in *Daphnis and Chloe* but comedy is at its heart. I was one of the six women but the experience of dancing, though useful, is differ- ent from observing.[89] Even though it gives a privileged access to some of the movement, it can obscure other aspects.

The theme is travel, Thursday's Child has far to go, and it is the only dance in which Ashton uses the title literally.

Percival saw it as 'a zany jog-trot journey for Alexander Grant and a rag- time band of young women indefatigably indicating the discomfort of travel by train, ship, plane or foot'.[90] It is a fast moving dance with a relentless pace to a fast jazz waltz, which owes something to Nijinska. For instance, the arms generally remain beside the body, forcing the dancers to use the torso to generate the movement.

Grant, like Astaire, showed the dancing rather than the dancer. He re- mained blank-faced throughout the dance but is in constant motion. Starting with a succession of different walks and trots, he goes round in a series of concentric circles until he brings on the first trio of women. They enter travelling with a reverse *glissé* movement in which the working foot shoots forward and almost immediately draws back to fifth position on pointe. The hips are pushed backwards and the torso bends forward, giving the strides an air of nonchalance. These truncated, choppy walks take them across the front of the stage to meet the second female trio who enter with an *arabesque relevé* interspersed with a trot. All, including Grant, proceed to stage right, performing the same series of jerky *arabesques*.

Throughout this dance Ashton plays with the rhythm and the group. For the most part, the six women move to the regular, if jazzy, waltz rhythm, either doing one step to the bar or one to two bars. But, more often than not, Grant works against this. And, from time to time, he interrupts their sym- metrical patterning. The section following the opening is good example of this:

Phrase 1: The six women: in two lines of three, one behind the other, perform a series of *chaînés* turns into an *arabesque*, each alternating between upstage and downstage. The arms are pinned close to the torso.

Grant: simultaneously, between the two rows, does four jumped *fouettés* turns, each ending in fourth position with the front leg bent.

Phrase 2: The women split into two groups and perform different phrases: the stage-left group has a step into fourth position on pointe and then two steps crossing each other on pointe, led by the shoulders, and the upper torso is twisted at right angles to the lower body. The stage-right group does turns into a high kick backwards followed by a second high kick.

Grant, moving between and in front of the women, performs stepping turns: the first two are preceded by a lilting gallop and the following four are continuous. As he does so, he raises his hat.

The dance's genesis is in the music hall. Yet the actual steps come from the classroom, significantly altered, emphasising twisting and turning shoulders and jutting hips, to fit the jazzy style of the music. This pattern of ensemble work, split trios and Grant's interruptions are typical of the dance. Sometimes he performs the same movement, though in his own way; at other times, his phrases are quite different from the women's, as when he executes a series of stag leaps, ten in a row. Apart from the fact that the women are on pointe, the dance movement is not specifically gendered. The movement of both Grant and the women is relaxed and the feet almost parallel.

The short central section of the dance literally shows travel. All seven dancers mimic the race-walker, after which, the women become mannequins on the catwalk, before all regroup to descend in a lift. Together, they 'strap-hang' on a bus and form a boat around Grant who takes the oars. Raising and lowering their legs in *arabesque*, they mimic the actions of the rocking boat. An aeroplane materialises before they disperse to all corners of the stage. In a dance lasting almost five minutes, this literal section lasts only 40 seconds. At the end, we are reminded again of travel, as the women exit in twos, they slide forward then abruptly retract the advancing foot, a rocking repetitive movement that feels, and looks, like a train chugging along the tracks.

Grant leaves them exiting, and repeats his opening circles, only this time he continues till he is almost horizontal, supported only by his hand placed on the floor. As he progresses, his movement becomes heavier, more weighted, a characteristic of the whole dance. Both Grant's movement and that of the women is rooted firmly on the floor. These are not sylphs, rather, they are human women. They have no aerial movement and Grant's jumps are performed to emphasise the landing not the air.

Despite its carefree overtone, contributed by the jazziness and hippy movement, this dance is defined by its footwork and speedy changes of weight and direction. This is a fast dance speeding its way back and forth across the stage. The floor patterns are intricate and the movement is at times jerky. There are few sustained moments, though Grant's continuous phrases give the impression of smoother patterns. Neither the ensemble nor Grant pay much attention to each other. They are too busy travelling in all directions but what gives it excitement is the sheer irrepressible energy. Ballet steps, drawn only from a small pool, form the basis of the movement material.

Conclusion

Ashton's use of the popular stage dances is very unlike that of Balanchine, who had also worked with Bradley and imported American stage dancing and African American movement into his dances.[91] Characteristically Balanchine uses 'the arms held akimbo and "jazz hands"– palms presented with the wrists flexed'.[92] Like Balanchine, Ashton uses the hip thrusts and syncopated rhythms in 'Monday's Child' but the difference is essentially between their approach to the movement. Where Balanchine incorporated the style into strongly balletic pieces like *Rubies* (1967) or *Four Temperaments* (1946), Ashton drew on the atmosphere of the era, the relaxed nonchalance and, in 'Monday's Child', the laid-back, liquid cool of the era's singers, like Al Bowley or Leslie 'Hutch' Hutchinson.

Brenda Dixon Gottschild discusses the African American elements in Balanchine's choreography and finds that he integrated them seamlessly into his dance movement. She considers these to be:

> the displacement of hips or other parts of the torso, instead of vertical alignment; leg kicks, attacking the beat, instead of well-placed extensions; angular arms and flexed wrists, rather than the traditional, rounded *ports de bras* – all of these touches usher the viewer into the discovery of the Africanist presence in Balanchine.[93]

Ashton's use of jazz is not like that. He was more concerned to emphasise the spectacular footwork and body motion in movement that is generated from the torso. His dances stress an easy, relaxed, cool style with elegance and sophistication. It seems that he was more interested in behaviour than in bodily display. Balanchine drew the 'phrasing, counting and timing' from the Africanist elements in American culture but his dance movement is modernist and spare. Ashton's movement patterns in contrast emerged from his own dance background, his Cecchetti training and the de Valois training of the dancers and from that other iconic figure, Nijinska. He drew on her work as well as the jazz dancing of Bradley.

These three numbers in *Jazz Calendar* show Ashton in quite a different

Finale (rehearsal). © Derek Jarman, Keith Collins.

mood from most of his extant ballets. He had made other works that were inspired by popular culture, the 1931 *Façade*, for example, drew on the social dances of the era but he seems to have done little else that links so closely with the films and stage dancing of the 1930s, apart from his choreography for the revues and musicals. Yet, his style is, nevertheless, very much present.

Ashton described *Jazz Calendar* as a little ballet but for Jarman, the opening night was like Christmas day.[94] With its jazz band and vibrant costumes, it was not what Covent Garden audiences were used to and in later years several critics dismissed it as merely revue dancing.[95] Revues were considered to be mere show-business, entertainment rather than art. Yet this is misreading the ballet if we thought Ashton was only making a revue. The ballet is about dance itself and the fun of dancing. His collaboration with Jarman was significant and the costumes and sets innovative and it has major characteristics of Ashton's style.

These are dances about dancing and dance itself but Ashton also made narrative dances. The next chapter deals with two of these narrative works, and despite the stories, it still seems that Ashton chose the literary works more because he believed they would generate interesting dancing than because he could say something profound about contemporary life.

1. Balanchine, George (1992) 'Marginal Notes on Dance', in Sorell, Walter ed. *The Dance Has Many Faces*, Chicago: Capella Books, 41.

2. In Kavanagh, (1996) 596.

3. Vaughan, (1977) 355.

4. Vaughan, 284.

5. Vaughan, 355.

6. Cotton, A.V. eds. Sorley Walker, Kathrine and Lilian Haddakin(1975) *Writings on Dance*, London: Dance Books, 79 and 75.

7. Rambert, Marie (1972/1983) *Quicksilver*, London: Papermac, 121-122.

8. Ashton quoted in Vaughan, 1977, 231.

9. The formula is not exactly the same in *Beauty*.

10. Burt, Ramsay (1995) *The Male Dancer: Bodies, Spectacle, Sexualities*, London: Routledge, 163.

11. I examine this in Chapter V.

12. Irving, Robert (1991) 'The Conductor Speaks', *Dance and Dancers*, November, 20-21

13. Hilda Zinkin, interview with the author, 3rd June 2010.

14. Meinertz, Alexander (2005) *Vera Volkova: A Biography*, trans. Meinertz, Alexander and Paula Hostrup-Jessen, Alton: Dance Books.

15. Works by Léonide Massine, John Cranko and Andrée Howard were commissioned and there were two revivals of works by Michael Fokine.

16. Fifield, Elaine (1967) *In My Shoes: the Autobiography of Elaine Fifield*, London: W.H. Allen, 23. The Solo Seal is the highest examination of the RAD and Ashton contributed two variations to it during the 1950s.

17. Alexander Bland suggests that she entered the Sadler's Wells ballet in October 1946 but as this is based on the first time a name appears in a programme, she may have been dancing with the company while still a student. See Bland, Alexander (1981) *The Royal Ballet: The First 50 Years*, London: Threshold Books, 266.

18. My earliest training was also with RAD teachers and I can confirm that this was the case.

19. Woodcock, Sarah (1991) *The History of Sadler's Wells Royal Ballet, Now the Birmingham Royal Ballet*, London: Sinclair-Stevenson.

20. Clarke, Mary (1956) 'Elaine Fifield: Ballerina', *Dancing Times*, October, no. 553, 20.

21. Clarke, Mary (1955) *The Sadler's Wells Ballet*, London: A & C Black, 297.

22. Meisner, Nadine (1999) 'Obituary', *The Independent*, 25th May. (no page numbers available).

23. Lawson, Joan (1955) 'Madame Chrysanthème', *Dancing Times*, May, no. 536, 485

24. Holmes, Olive ed. (1982) *Motion Arrested: Dance Reviews of H.T. Parker*, Connecticut: Wesleyan University Press, 32.

25. Vaughan 1976, 321.

26. Kavanagh, 1996, 421.

27. Sitter out (1953) *Dancing Times*, February, no. 509, 276.

28. Richardson, P.J.S.(1952) 'Sitter Out', *Dancing Times*, July, no. 502, 589.

29. Clarke, Mary (1955) *The Sadler's Wells Ballet: A History and Appreciation*, London: A & C Black, 278.

30. Sorley Walker, Kathrine (1998) 'Svetlana Beriosova', *Dance Now*, summer, 7, no. 2, 39-49.

31. Anon (1952) 'Svetlana Beriosova', *Ballet*, July, 12, no. 7, 10-13

32. Ibid.

33. This is the closed, angular position that was common at the time and not the open Russian inspired attitude of today.

34. This is characterised by the shrugged shoulders and enquiring expression of both the Blue Skater and Puck in Ashton's *Les patineurs* and *The Dream*. It occurs in other works too and at the end of Fifield's variation in *Birthday Offering*.

35. Jordan, Stephanie (2000) *Moving Music: Dialogues with Music in Twentieth Century Ballet*, London: Dance Books, 231.

36. Quoted in Newman, Barbara (1982) 'Nadia Nerina', *Striking a Balance*, London: Elm Books, 133.

37. Clarke, Mary (1961) 'The Brink of Greatness', *Dancing Times*, March, no. 606, 345-6.

38. Ibid.

39. Nerina, Nadia (1960) 'Some Aspects of the Classical Technique', ed. Haskell, Arnold, *The Ballet Annual*, 79-83.

40. Anon (2008) quoted from *Daily Telegraph*, 'Obituary', 8th October, online.

41. Quoted in Kavanagh (1996), 367.

42. This *rond de jambe* is missing from later versions of the dance.

43. Plisetskaya, Maya (2001) *I Maya Plisetskaya*, trans. Antonia, W. Bouis, New Haven and London: Yale University Press, 30.

44. Ibid, 64.

45. Percival, (1992), 8.

46. Vaughan, 271.

47. Percival, (1992), 8.

48. Percival, John (1992) 'The Ballerina From Moscow', *Dance and Dancers*, November, 8.

49. Richardson, P.J.S. (1953) 'Homage to the Queen', *Dancing Times*, no. 514, July, 598.

50. Franks, Arthur (1957) 'Beryl Grey', *Dancing Times*, April, XLVII, no. 559, 306-7.

51. Interview with Hylda Zinkin 3rd June 2010.

52. Meinertz, (2007), 65.

53. Ibid, 65.

54. Volkova, Vera (1961) 'Frederick Ashton in Denmark', *Ballet Annual*, ed. Haskell, Arnold and Mary Clarke, no. 15, London: Adam and Charles Black, 56 and 59.

55. Meinertz, (2007), 53.

56. Ibid, 53.

57. Ibid, 53.

58. There exists a description of her classes written from memory by Audrey Harman, these remain unpublished.

59. Quoted in Meinertz, 87.

60. Linden, Tommy, quoted in Meinertz, 71.

61. May in Meinertz, 63.

62. Chappell, William (1951) *Fonteyn: Impressions of a Ballerina*, London: Spring Books, 57.

63. Quoted in Kavanagh, Julie (1996) 423.

64. See Preston-Dunlop, Valerie (2002) *Dance and the Performative: A Choreological Perspective – Laban and Beyond*, London: Verve publishing, 93.

65. Denby, Edwin (1986) *Dance Writings*, London: Dance Books, 59

66. Croce, Arlene (1978) 'The Royal Ballet in New York', *Afterimages*, London: Adam and Charles Black, 375.

67. Peake, Tony (1999) *Derek Jarman*, London: Little Brown, 128.

68. Vaughan, 355.

69. Beaumont, Cyril (1937, revised 1949) *Complete Book of Ballets*, London: C.W. Beaumont, 913.

70. Percival, John (10th January 1968) 'Good Joke and Good Ballet', *The Times*, no page numbers available.

71. Jarman, Derek (1984) *Dancing Ledge*, London: Quartet, 84.

72. In Royal Opera House press cuttings (Archives) Ian Woodward. No references and no newspaper mentioned.

73. Jarman's next commission came from Marie Rambert and was for the choreographer Stere Popescu, a Romanian who had defected to the West. It was doomed to failure. This was partly because Popescu spoke little English and partly because Jarman's designs were too extreme for the angst-ridden, though, conservative choreographer. Although the designs were generally praised, the choreography was not and on the second night Popescu took a fatal overdose. Jarman did one more ballet design for Festival Ballet but because of their highly conservative director, Beryl Grey, the ballet was cancelled after the opening night. Later, his designs were for contemporary dance. He did, though, work again in an opera house with John Gielgud. This was on Mozart's *Don Giovanni* for the Sadler's Wells Opera; a collaboration that had multiple problems, not least because both the director and designer were indecisive. It was to be *Jazz Calendar* that was the most successful of his stage designs. The marriage of a conventional choreographer and funky designer had worked surprisingly well at, of all places, Britain's bastion of respectability, the Royal Opera House.

74. Jarman, Derek (1984), 75.

75. Percival, John (10th January 1968) 'Good Joke and Good Ballet', *The Times*, no page numbers available.

76. Anon (10th January 1968) *Liverpool Daily Post*, 'Sick Nureyev Dances On' no page numbers available.

77. Jarman, Derek (1994) *Chroma*, London: Random House.

78. Ibid, 42.

79. Ibid, pages, 36, 10, 140.

80. Jewell, Derek (1968) 'Modern Varieties', *Sunday Times*, 21st January, no page numbers available.

81. Wohlfahrt, Hans-Theodor (1996) 'Ashton's last interview', *Dance Now*, 5, no.1, Spring, 25-30.

82. Berg, Shelley and Jill Beck (1996) 'Approaches to the Revival of Les Masques' in eds, Jordan, Stephanie and Andrée Grau *Following Sir Fred's Steps*, London : Dance Books, 41.

83. Coton, A.V. (10-1-68) 'Brilliant and Banal 'Jazz Calendar', *Daily Telegraph*, no page numbers available.

84. Johns, Eric (11-1-69) 'Royal Ballet's Jazz Romp' *The Stage*, no page numbers available

85. Peake, (1999), 126

86. The choreography is by Buddy Bradley.

87. Parsons, Tony (2010) 'My Hero' *The Guardian*, Saturday 22nd May Review section, no page numbers available.

88. Quoted in Vaughan (1977) 5.

89. The six women were, Lesley Collier, Carole Hill, Patricia Linton, Geraldine Morris, Susanna Raymond and Diana Vere.

90. Percival, John (1968) 'Good Joke and Good Ballet', *The Times*, 10th January, no page numbers available.

91. Banes, Sally (1994) 'Balanchine and Black Dance', *Writing Dance in the Age of Postmodernism*, New England, Hanover and London: Wesleyan University Press, 53-69

92. Ibid, 63.

93. Dixon Gottschild, Brenda (2001) 'Stripping the Emperor: The Africanist Presence in American Concert Dance', in Dils, Ann and Ann Cooper Albright eds. *Moving History/Dancing Cultures: A Dance History Reader*, Middletown USA: Wesleyan University Press, 336.

94. Jarman, (1984) 87.

95. Bland, Alexander (1981) *The Royal Ballet: The First 50 Years*, London: Threshold Books, 160.

Chapter 5
Narrative Dances:
An Abundance of Real Dancing

Ashton has always been regarded as a masterly story teller, yet he often reduces his narratives to a simple thread, halting them, here and there, to add an expressive variation or duet.[1] Early in his career, he admitted adjusting the story to suit his choreographic needs, adding that a realistic treatment was not his aim.[2] In both *Daphnis and Chloe* (1951) and *A Month in the Country* (1976), the narratives have been significantly reduced. Despite starting from the original sources, Longus' story of *Daphnis and Chloe*, and Turgenev's play for *A Month in the Country*, he adopted Maurice Ravel's version of the story for the first and focused only on Natalia Petrovna and her relationships with others in the household for the second. Ashton's ballets do not tell complex stories but they do present expressive and very human characters.

He felt that a ballet should deal with 'that which is spiritual and eternal rather than that which is material and temporal'.[3] And in an earlier article he argued that ballet was not a suitable medium for telling stories:

> The danger is that one comes upon situations that are purely literary and unballetic and are thus impossible to convey clearly to an audience without the use of words; for I personally do not like a ballet in which the audience has to spend three-quarters of the time with their noses in the programme to try and find out what is happening on the stage... In my balletic ideology, it is the dancing that must be the foremost factor, for ballet is an expression of emotions and ideas through dancing, and not through words or gesture.[4]

In other words, he did not believe that dance could handle the everyday. Art is not life and his narrative dances bear this out; they come from Greek mythology, plays, fairy tales, and earlier nineteenth century ballets. The subjects are timeless, not constrained by logic or reason, suffused in imagery and chosen as stimuli for creativity. They both limited and liberated his choreography but also generated the style. He chose the subject because it suited his dance style and to 'develop [him] as an artist and extend the idiom of the dance'.[5] Ballet, Ashton believed, 'must deal with serious matters' and what could be more serious than the timeless?[6] As Karen Armstrong points out in her book on myth,

> Mythology is an art form that points beyond history to what is timeless in human existence, helping us to get beyond the chaotic flux of random events, and glimpse the core of reality.[7]

Only some of his ballets use myth as a stimulus, yet all deal with serious subject matter. They are about dance itself and the narrative is subordinate to the choreography.

Where *Daphnis* is more concerned with movement style, *Month* is about characters and relationships. *Daphnis* has a complex story, *Month* does not. Between *Daphnis* and *Month*, Ashton made forty-four dance pieces, including the dances for three films and three operas, of these, only eleven have a narrative thread. In these earlier narrative pieces, there is little evidence that his purpose was to develop character, yet when he does, as in *Enigma Variations*, his characters are real flesh and blood. They are flawed, sad, happy, angry, contemplative, jealous and, sometimes, just plain difficult. These characteristics are only partially conveyed through silent acting and it is the dance movement which is central to the portrayal of character and this is what dancers need to interpret. Accessing Ashton's original source for the narrative is useful if it helps dancers to understand the movement but the essential features of the characters are present in the choreography.

In both works the other collaborators played a significant role. In *Daphnis and Chloe*, John Craxton, who designed the sets and costumes, also introduced Ashton to the Greek Islands and their traditional dances. In *A Month in the Country*, Julia Trevelyan Oman's set dictated the spatial paths of the dances. The music had been written earlier, Ravel for *Daphnis* and Frédéric Chopin for *Month*, the latter arranged by John Lanchbery.

Daphnis and Chloe: Sexuality and Ashton's Greek Ballets

Ashton used ancient Greek subject matter for several of his works. Beginning in 1928 with *Leda*, followed by *Pomona* in 1930, he made another seven dances based on ancient Greek themes. Between 1951 and 1953 he made three 'Greek' works, *Daphnis and Chloe*, *Tiresias* (1951) and *Sylvia* (1952) and he choreographed and directed Gluck's opera *Orpheus* for the Royal Opera House. His penultimate Greek dance, *Persephone*, made in 1961 had a Stravinsky score and speaking dancer.[8]

First choreographed in 1912 by Michel Fokine for Diaghilev's Ballets Russes, *Daphnis and Chloe* had few performances, though the score has been used by a range of choreographers since. Vaughan considers it to be Ashton's first fully mature work, 'and the first of a series of great ballets about love that he was to make in the next two decades – that recognise that sexuality and innocence are not mutually exclusive'.[9] Later he added that it is one of Ashton's greatest ballets. His genius shows in the spareness of much of the choreography, like an armature within the lushness of the score. The finale never fails to reduce me to tears by the sheer perfection and simplicity of its form.[10]

For the dance movement in *Daphnis*, Ashton drew on Maurice Emmanuel's book *The Antique Greek Dance*, written in 1896.[11] Emmanuel, a French composer, had first written the book as part of a thesis. His knowledge was based on an extensive study of the figures on Greek vases. We now know that his account is probably not accurate, but it provided Ashton with a substantial source, as I discovered when analysing the choreography, and helped him create a highly distinctive style.[12] Few of his earlier 'Greek' dances used parallel movement. Of his later works, the choreography of *Persephone* is closest in its use of Ancient Greek dance movement to that of *Daphnis and Chloe*. In *Persephone* the dance movement has parallel feet, and flattened, angular body shapes and the dancers generally move in lines horizontally across the stage. *Daphnis* has the added layer of quoting contemporary Greek folk dance. Ashton was not trying to reproduce Greek dance but he did use it to generate new dance movement and as a way of looking again at Greece and its ancient stories.

The ballet's story may seem trivial and inconsequential; the original tale was more complicated and sexually explicit. The ambiance is an idyllic, Ancient Greek island and Ashton was well read in Greek mythology: his library has several different well-thumbed copies of stories from Ancient Greece, as well as a copy of Longus' tale.[13] The story concerns two young lovers, who, after various adventures, including the abduction of Chloe and rescue by Pan, develop sexual awakening during the course of the novel. Ashton must also have appreciated the sexual significance of the God Pan, since, unlike Fokine's version, he presents him on stage. Pan, a man-beast with cloven hooves, was linked with sex and the countryside. He was particularly associated with lasciviousness and his pursuit of nymphs, two of whom had themselves transformed, rather than submit to his advances: Syrinx into reeds and Echo into a disembodied voice. Pan's potentially dangerous eroticism looms over a work which is seemingly about two innocent lovers. In Ashton's version, a front cloth, lowered in the interlude between Scenes I and II, depicts a monumental Pan, perhaps a reminder of the lustfulness of the original tale and of Daphnis' wanton response to Lykanion or a portent of the Pirate Bryaxis' attempted rape? As Simon Schama points out, Arcadia was associated with fecundity and sensuality, even sexuality, and it was this aspect that Ravel was coy about. He eliminated the earthiness of the story and replaced it with a much more sanitised Poussin-like idyll. The earlier ballet in 1912 reflected this, though Ashton strove to eliminate some of that innocence in his version.

The dancing, particularly in the duets, verges on the provocative. Daphnis' and Lykanion's duet is not only sensual but also sexually charged. Chloe's restricted dance in her white underwear, after her dress has been brutally torn off, if not displaying eroticism, is tantalising and tempts Bryaxis and his male Pirates. And the duet, after Daphnis and Chloe are reunited, is both uninhibited and sensual. This choreography anticipates another erotic moment in *Marguerite and Armand* (1963). In both these works, the woman throws her arms around the man's neck and abandons herself, as she is swung round in ecstatic circles.

Updating these ancient stories and themes seems to have been a twentieth century preoccupation.[14] Jean Cocteau's film *Orphée*, which set the Orpheus story in contemporary France, had premiered in November 1950 and it is probable that Ashton had seen it. He had too been to Greece on holiday and felt that the tradition of the old gods still infused Greek culture, though in a contemporary way.[15]

Adapting the Text

Despite a belief that Ashton was lazy, he was an assiduous reader, when it came to researching his ballets.[16] Nestling in the shelves of his working library was the biography of Ravel by Alexis Roland-Manuel, published in English in 1948. Ravel had a specific perception of Ancient Greece and as Roland-Manuel explains, he approached the score of *Daphnis and Chloe* from the perspective of eighteenth century France. In his diary, Ravel wrote that his aim was

> to compose a vast musical fresco, less concerned with archaism than with faithfulness to the Greece of my dreams, which is similar to that imagined and painted by French artists at the end of the 18th century.[17]

So even before Ashton updated it to the twentieth century, the work was shaped by eighteenth century France. And, he was also very aware of the earlier work, which he had not seen but had discussed with Karsavina, the original Chloe.

Despite annotating his own copy of Longus, Ashton eventually returned to Fokine's and Ravel's scenario. In the England of 1951, it would have been difficult for him to use the whole of the original story, which deals fairly overtly with sexuality and with Chloe's desires rather than those of Daphnis. Ravel was not interested in the erotic, however, and ignored Longus' account of the sexual desires of the two protagonists. He even eliminated Daphnis' sexual initiation by Lykanion in his score. Ashton paid no attention to this and restored the more lascivious elements of the duet, even if the music did not lend itself to such explicit passion.

Ashton used the six main characters from the original tale Daphnis, Chloe, Lykanion, Dorkon, Bryaxis and Pan as well as three Nymphs. Though the character of Pan was omitted from the 1912 version, depicted instead by a large shadow thrown on the backcloth, he is very much present in Ashton's ballet. Ashton's ensembles comprised Shepherds and Shepherdesses and Pirates, both men and women. Originally, he included Fauns and Dryads as walk-on parts but these were removed early on.[18]

The tale concerns two youngsters, Daphnis and Chloe, who are attracted to each other but still sexually innocent. Ashton's Scene I opens with a group of shepherds and shepherdesses bringing offerings to the Nymphs who reside in the grotto. Daphnis and Chloe join them and, after leaving offerings for the Nymphs, take part in the dancing. They are challenged by Dorkon and Lykanion, an older, more mature couple from the village. Dorkon, attracted by Chloe, attempts to pursue her, while Lykanion, a married woman, tries to seduce Daphnis. To settle the dispute over Chloe, Dorkon and Daphnis participate in a dance competition, which Daphnis wins. Yet, later, when Daphnis is left alone he is tempted by Lykanion and yields to her provocative embraces. As she exits, a group of Pirates enter and, in the ensuing chaos, Chloe is abducted. That night a distraught Daphnis is woken by the Nymphs who promise to alert Pan to Chloe's fate. Scene II shows the pirates den. Bryaxis, the pirate chief, enters with Chloe, tossed over his shoulder, and attempts to rape her. As she pleads for help, Pan enters, frightening the Pirates and rescuing her. In the final scene, Chloe is restored to Daphnis and they are joined by the ensemble in a joyous finale.

Although this is a pastoral tale, Schama reminds us of the presence of the sacred and profane in Arcadia and the musicologist, Deborah Mawer, notes the dichotomous elements in both the music and story of the ballet: between the living world and that of dreams (Daphnis does not know whether he has seen the Nymphs in reality or in a dream) and between the human world and that of the Gods.[19] There are other contrasting pairings between day and night, meadow and sea shore and between promiscuity and chastity. Ashton's telling of the tale was not purely a poetic vision, instead he forced us to confront its modernity and the sexual reality inherent in the tale as well as its idyllic moments.

John Craxton: A Sense of Place

Distancing the ballet from its 1912 version, Ashton decided not to clothe his dancers in ancient attire. To design the work, he chose John Craxton, a neo-romantic painter and friend, who by then was living in Greece and familiar with the contemporary culture there.[20] Ashton had worked with other neo-romantic artists during the Second World War, in particular Sutherland and Piper.[21] Craxton was influenced by both but, after his move to the Greek island of Poros, his work became infiltrated by the Arcadian, sun-drenched landscape and by cubism. Writing about Craxton's contribution in 1992, Jill Anne Bowden noted that the designs captured

> that most elusive of qualities – a sense of place; something we find in ballet when the dancers seem to move within the climate of a setting, in physical surroundings which emanate their own atmosphere.[22]

The bright, hot colours, rock and mountain shapes and Mediterranean olives, figs and grapes of this landscape form the backcloth for Scene I. Its sky has the dense blue of the Mediterranean and there are streaks of terracotta, green and cream often edged with black which make this a harsh, clearly defined landscape, typical of the south eastern Mediterranean. Craxton explained that the backdrop

> shows the forms of a mountain range opposite Poros and called the 'Kimomeni' or sleeping woman. It looks very like a sleeping woman. I rather based the whole ballet on my actual experience of the Greece I knew and loved.[23]

The designs for the other scenes also have this intensity of colour and the patterns are angular. Bowden points out that Craxton's landscape is

> a thing of hard scissored edges, with between these geometric lines, a flow of shaped, varied colour, sometimes so ochreous in tone that it is small wonder that those [in the audience] who had anticipated lush sylvan glades were astonished, though the more perceptive among them acknowledged its veracity.[24]

The costumes of the women too were suffused with colour: pink, yellow, turquoise and sky blue, while the men had pastel shirts and darker trousers. No distinction was made between principal dancers and the group. In scene II, the Pirate scene, the dancers had different costumes. The male pirates wore short boots with knee length breeches and open shirts and the women had a pale coat with Grecian geometric patterns on the back and down the front, covering dark, knee-length dresses. Both the men and women had headscarves. According to Craxton, these outfits were loosely based on Cretan costumes, though he claims that it was Fonteyn who designed all the sheperdess's costumes.[25] 'She turned the skirts round underneath and pleated them outside and got this material that hung well and moved well.'[26]

Interestingly when Dowell, as the director of the Royal Ballet had the sets and costumes redesigned in 1994, they were neither appropriate nor admired and seemed to violate the style, which shows the importance of the original costumes. They are a necessary part of the choreographic style and not just an addendum. Craxton's costumes and sets were restored in 2004 for Ashton's centenary, with slight alterations to some of the Pirate costumes.

Schama observes that 'There have always been two kinds of arcadia: shaggy and smooth; dark and light; a place of bucolic leisure and a place of primitive panic.'[27] Craxton and Ashton acknowledged both. The smooth scenes of the first and third scenes recreate the pastoral landscape of Greek mythology, while primitive panic is pervasive in scene II, the Pirate scene. In that scene, the dark rising cliffs on either side are menacing and the choreography is spatially confined, a reflection of Chloe's imprisonment and imminent danger.

Ravel's Music and Fokine's Ballet

Ravel particularly enjoyed working for dance and he composed more than ten scores between 1909 and 1929. Deriving much of his aesthetic from Diaghilev and the Ballets Russes, he believed in the union of the arts, remarking that a

> holistic view strongly supports audio-visual and literary combination: Poets, musicians and painters must all come together to restore to us the grandeur and completeness of theatrical emotion.[28]

This meant that the score was closely tied to the narrative and, perhaps too, to the original choreography.

Mawer notes that Ravel and Fokine worked together on the story and because of Ravel's aversion to the more sexual aspects of the story, the sexuality was significantly reduced, resulting in a pair of lovers who are altogether more naïve than in Longus.[29] Yet, this marriage of score and Ravel's narrative does not seem to have affected other choreographers because several subsequent productions have been more sexually explicit. Ashton introduced unequivocal sexuality into the duet between Daphnis and Lykanion and Chloe lies across Daphnis' knees at the end of their final duet, submitting openly to his embraces. Graham Murphy's production for the Sydney Dance Company in 1982 was even more explicit, restoring the notion of sexual awakening and desire from the original story by Longus. Clearly the music could survive different interpretations.

Yet English critics found the music overwhelming, better played in the concert hall than the theatre and this affected their approach to Ashton's ballet. Haskell considered the choreography 'bold', but because of the music there were 'brilliant flashes of illumination, leaving the inevitable blanks and *longueurs*.[30]

Both Mawer and Simon Morrison have written extensively on the first collaboration between Fokine and Ravel for the Ballets Russes. Morrison, disagreeing with Mawer, suggests that the ballet was anything but a collaboration. The only record of the meeting of Fokine and Ravel is in 1909 and Morrison notes that there is little to suggest that they met again before 1912. Fokine had not heard the orchestral version until the opening night and so choreographed to the piano. As a result, Morrison argues, Fokine emphasised the metre and rhythm but not the music's texture, something Ashton rectified in his later version of the work.[31]

Morrison charts the different ways in which the two creators, three if Bakst the designer is included, approached the work. Fokine's derived from a more 'literal archaism', based on the poses and shapes of the ancient Greek vases.[32] Léon Bakst's Greece is imaginary, his background showing a grove of Cyprus trees, a miniature Greek temple and three large nymphs at the entrance to the Grotto, while his costumes were taken from ancient Greece but, apart from those for the two principal dancers, were vividly coloured and patterned with bold geometric shapes.[33] Ravel's music is invested with a more dreamlike quality, described by Morrison as 'an amorphous score [fabricated] from a shape-shifting, assemblage of tonal, modal and whole-tone syntax'.[34] The dichotomy between the different interpretations resulted in a ballet layered with diverse approaches to the neoclassic. Morrison notes that its 'visual layer [was] composed of flowing lines and bright colours, its aural layer of floating motives and blended timbres'.[35]

As Mawer argues, none of the approaches to Ancient Greece can be considered authentic. Fokine's Greece was shaped by attitudes forged in St Petersburg and subsequently Paris, while Ravel's came from eighteenth century France. Added to this was the Paris of 1912 which viewed ancient Greece as an arcadia, a long lost 'golden age'.[36] Nevertheless, Mawer concludes the three were to some extent unified by their Russianness. This includes Ravel who was heavily affected by the music of Nicolai Rimsky-Korsakov and Alexander Borodin.[37] Wisely, Ashton did not attempt to recapture the 1912 version, discarding the Ancient Greek costumes and, despite its parallelism, putting the dancers on pointe. His perspective adds yet another layer to the classicism of Ancient Greece, giving it an up-to-date interpretation for the 1950s and, even today, it still appears current.

The Choreography: A Masterpiece of Eloquence and Poetry

With three scenes and an interlude, the ballet lasts approximately fifty three minutes. In it Ashton explores both ancient and contemporary Greek dance, coloured always by the *danse d'école*, and the whole is shaped by Ashton's style. The dance features mix the past with the present and some of those, from contemporary Greece, were inspired by Craxton. Apparently, Craxton had demonstrated some of the dances he had encountered there to Ashton. It is a studied mix of Ancient, traditional and classical dance and the choreography must signify as an early example of fusion in ballet.

Dancing in Greece, whether in ancient times or today, is an integral part of both social and religious life but not all the dances are similar.[38] Writing about dance in Greek culture, Yvonne Hunt explains that dances can be grouped into those of the mountains, of the islands and of the towns. Hunt also argues that because so little is known about the dances of Ancient Greece, no similarity between them and the contemporary folk dances can be assumed.[39] A characteristic of most Greek dances is the open-circle and counter-clockwise paths and, in the past, the separation of men from women in the lines. In some dances, arms placed on each other's shoulders link the participants, in others they are joined by handkerchiefs. Dances of the islands capture the wave-like undulations of the sea and are lighter in feeling and more flowing.[40] It is probably this element that was conveyed to Ashton by Craxton who had witnessed these dances on Poros.

The dance movement is a careful melding of flattened bodies, from ancient Greek vases, and Ashton's own use of the *danse d'école*; the choreography reflects the patterns of the traditional dances, though he also emulated some of their movement. For example, the deep knee bends and hand slapping of the feet is reminiscent of those traditional dances. From the *danse d'école* there are *ronds de jambes à terre*, made lush by deep bends of the upper back, *attitudes* both forward and back, and, in the quicker moments, a range of *sissonnes*, and several variations of the 'Fred step'. These step motifs are peppered throughout this beautifully crafted work, picked up by the soloists and used in a range of inventive ways. They do not stray far from the Grecian flavour of the whole and the *rond de jambes à terre* in Chloe's dance in Scene III are defined by a tap of the hand on the raised foot and accompanied by arms which snake upwards and out to end in flattened palms. It is a pose from a Greek statue or vase and adds to our sense of place. Although there are five major roles in the ballet, it is in many ways an ensemble work in which, like Nijinska's *Les noces*, the group shines. As one reviewer noted 'Rarely is a corps de ballet so well served by a choreographer and rarely has a choreographer been so gratifyingly rewarded by a corps de ballet.'[41]

Apart from the Pirate scene and the joyous, insistent finale, reminiscent of *Les noces*, the other scenes in the ballet have a peaceful, more tranquil, atmosphere.

Group Dances in Scene I
The ballet opens with an ensemble dance for six shepherds and six shepherdesses, lasting about six minutes. It is early morning, outside a grotto to Pan,

surrounded by olive trees and cypresses. The swelling sound of the music also gives the impression of day breaking. Arriving in ones and twos, the men and women place offerings at the entrance to the cave, paying tribute to the God. It is a leisurely start and redolent of the early morning feel of the Mediterranean.

The twelve dancers line up, in two groups, hands on each other's shoulders, as in a Greek folk dance, and languidly sweep from side to side, the two groups moving in opposite directions. Facing each other, the men start with a weaving, walking step before they make a sudden reversal with a lilting jump to the knee; as they rise the women begin, using the same sequence. The parallel movement, flattened bodies and frieze-like procession, evoke their origins in antiquity but are also suggestive of contemporary Greek dance: the shoulder-height arms, the slow deliberate motion, the sudden jump to the knee and the separation of men and women. Moving back and forth, the dancers end the short sequence together, posing momentarily with one pointed foot crossed over the ankle, resting on the floor. This call and answer continues, alternating between the men and women but they are always joined at shoulder height within their group. Swapping places with each other, they playfully run back and forth, in and out of each other's lines. A sustained *rond de jambe à terre* is accompanied by a leisurely rotation of the head. We are in the south eastern Mediterranean and there is no sense of urgency in the dance movement.

The choreography uses these few motifs, walking, running, dropping to the knee, *rond de jambe à terre* and the leisurely head rolls, in different ways. Sometimes, the leg is raised in a sideways attitude recalling the kneeling position and sometimes the jumps to the knee are accompanied by a dragging movement of the working leg, and the languid head movement, leaning back or sideways, persuades us that we are in a hot, sunny climate. The call and response motif, which is tossed back and forth from men to women, testifies to the youthfulness of the characters in its playfulness. The dance subsides into two diagonals facing upstage to greet Daphnis and then Chloe, who arrive from different sides of the stage but almost immediately exit. As the music swells with the wordless voices of the chorus, the dancers continue their linear patterned movement but the leisurely steps of the dancers are now punctuated by sudden toe taps, a more urgent step to pointe or a swooping jump. Ashton never allows the movement to become dull and this playful change of dynamic, not motivated by the music, is typical of Ashton's dance and choreographic style. Dropping to a few notes the music subsides and with the reappearance of Daphnis and Chloe, all together pay homage to Pan. This dance is elegantly crafted and coherent. The economy of movement and the references to both ancient and modern Greece are woven, tapestry-like, into a stylish stage picture.

When discussing the work, the critics tended to focus on the leading couples but what emerges, when examining the ballet in more detail, is the significance of the ensemble work. Not only does the group of men and women convey the spirit of the work, they are also a dominant aspect of it. Ashton is perhaps reminding us of the role of the Greek chorus in the plays of Ancient Greece. Certainly the group does seem to act as a commentary on the main characters. The ensemble dominates each scene and generates the atmosphere. It is a significant force: serene in the opening; more frenetic during the confusion between the couples; ruthless in the Pirate scene and celebratory in the finale. During the calmer scenes, the fusion between folk and ancient Greek dance is more dominant, though the finale in Scene III returns to contemporary Greek dance. Although ensemble work is not what Ashton is generally known for, in this and works such as *Scènes de ballet* (1948), the choreography for the group is paramount.

Quartet and Group dances in Scene I

The tranquillity is suddenly disrupted as Lykanion and Dorkon enter. The music changes to a brisker, slightly threatening sound and the ordered friezes and flattened shapes are thrown into disarray, replaced by a more chaotic stage picture. In a group, prefiguring a similar one in *La fille mal gardée* (1960), the women pull Chloe downstage as they perform a travelling series of sharp, quick *relevés* into *arabesque*.[42] She escapes and they continue the *arabesque* phrases across the front of the stage. The men catch Chloe and, forming a circle around her, hold her aloft. As the women join the circle, moving counter-clockwise, we are again reminded of the final moments of *La fille mal gardée*. Now they perform variations of the 'Fred step' getting quicker, all making them struggle to fit in all the movements to the music.

To Chloe's horror, she is claimed by Dorkon and Lykanion begins her seduction of Daphnis. The two women are passed back and forth between the male protagonists until Daphnis threatens Dorkon and a momentary fight ensues. The choreography appears to disintegrate into confusion but is in fact tightly controlled. The shepherds and shepherdesses continue to perform quick footwork and variations of the 'Fred step' forming circles and straight lines behind the two couples. Each of the two women turns into arabesque and then Chloe is lifted out of the way by Dorkon, high above his head and then replaced between the two men. At this moment the two couples form a group with Chloe placed between the two men, holding one hand of each. Lykanion places her hand on Daphnis' shoulder, taking a deep *arabesque*. Chloe appears trapped, which Mawer interprets as representing Chloe's restraint and repulsive feelings towards Dorkon. She observes that:

Chloe's uncomfortable, confused demeanour is conveyed by her crossed arms, pulled in opposite directions by her competing suitors.[43]

The pace quickens and the two couples join with the ensemble, all performing a cut off version of the 'Fred step', moving to stage left and then right. The tussle ends in a dispute, which can only be settled by a dance competition between Dorkon and Daphnis.

Daphnis's Solo in Scene I

Few films of the original Daphnis, Micheal Somes, exist, most recordings were made when he was over forty, past his prime, and when he had lost much of his early agility. By examining his solo in the dance competition with Dorkon, however, his skill and artistry can be determined. Besides, the dance is proof of his superiority over his rival Dorkon and is there to demonstrate his dance talent. Clarke described Somes as a lyrical dancer with exceptional musicality, who also possessed 'effortless elevation'.[44] Lasting over two minutes, his competition dance demands all of these abilities and more: elevation, a facility for turning and a lyrical, legato quality which emphasises line. In style, the dance could not be more different from that of Dorkon, where the movement is heavy, even clumsy, with clenched fists and strong, angular arms, further emphasised by the louder music of his dance.

Ashton knew how to celebrate a dancer's best features and in this dance, one of the few still in the repertory that he made for Somes, he pays tribute to Somes' line. For the first minute and twenty seconds, the performer dances with a crook, initially supported on his shoulders, fastened by his arms hooked over the top. It straightens and elongates the whole of the upper back and shoulder area of the body but this would be incidental if the movement did not emphasise the extended line. This posture flattens the body and helps to sustain the antique style. As a result, the movement has to be generated from the torso, bringing a weighted element to the dance, although, paradoxically, the dancer seems light.

Daphnis's dance is formed by a series of phrases each of which stops in a flattened, elongated pose, promoting a serene, elegant quality, a *Danse légère et gracieuse* as its music is titled. The opening section comprises a series of extended phrases. Starting centre stage, facing the audience, the dancer rises to a low, open *arabesque* with the arms flattened, in parallel with the raised leg; he ends in a fourth position *croisé*; the arms change, moving upwards but remaining in parallel with the legs. The line is stretched to face stage right, with the front arm extending upwards to a line way beyond the body. This phrase is repeated before the dancer makes two steps to a further *arabesque*, this time ending on a bent supporting leg with the other foot pointed, crossed in front of the body, and the torso bending forward. The line of the body is now reversed and stretches down into the floor. Following on, the dancer performs slow, controlled *pirouettes*, not the fast furious turns of Dorkon, with each ending in a stretched fourth position. For the turns, the crook is held horizontally in front of the body at chest height. Then comes a change in the movement's dynamic with a flurry of *sissonnes*: two over and one forward repeated with the crook once more on the shoulders and the line is taught and elongated. We would not notice this line if it was not for the tension between the end of the crook and the pointed foot, either raised in *arabesque* or pointed on the floor. Our eye is drawn to the link between the two as if an invisible thread pulls them together and consequently emphasises the position.

This apparently tranquil dance is active spatially. Lines project into the space; tension is created between the bodily extensions; linear patterns form around the body and our eyes see the flattened poses because the dancer focuses our attention on them through a sustained pause. When there is a flurry of jumping, approximately a minute into the dance, the dancer bounces rhythmically and without stopping, the ending of each jump forms the preparation for the next. The final minute of the dance is performed without the crook but the poses remained flattened, with parallel feet, sideways to the audience.

In this short dance, Ashton demonstrates craft, heritage and a masterly lyricism. If he was trying to pay homage to Somes, then this dance alone would be sufficient. It appears to have slow adagio-like movement because the music is dominated by strings, woodwind and harps, sounding gentler and less aggressive than in Dorcon's dance. As ever, Ashton fools us into believing that we are witnessing a quiet, slow lyrical dance, when actually it is full of jumps and turns, celebrating Somes' buoyant jumps. Because of the crook across the shoulders, the *sissonnes fermés* look like slow elongated steps and not the quick, abrupt jump usually associated with the step. That we believe this is a slow, lyrical dance happens for two reasons: the way in which the crook extends the upper body to complement the low arabesques and the emphasis on *épaulement*. Both draw our attention to the dancer's elegant linearity and make us believe we are watching adage.

It is a solo with sudden stops in flattened shapes, either with the crook or, with angular arms in a sideways pose, as if on a Greek vase. Finishing in a flattened position on the floor, the dance retains its Grecian motif. Yet, despite the flattened shapes, this dance is pure Ashton style. There are the minor steps, used as major motifs, continuous phrases without pauses and an extensive use of the spatial paths around the body, all shaped by what we perceive to be Antique.

Daphnis and Chloe. Margot Fonteyn as Chloe. © Roger Wood. Courtesy of the Royal Opera House.

Chloe's Dances in Scenes II and III and Finale

Of all the dances Ashton made for Fonteyn, the movement in *Daphnis*, particularly the variation in scene III, is perhaps the most appropriate: subtle, unpretentious, measured and requiring restraint. There are no flashy turns or balances, instead, there are little steps onto pointe, swift *ronds de jambes à terre*, little taps of the foot and hops on pointe and a quick twist of the pelvis, on pointe, with the arms clasped above the head. Dominated by a solo flute, the dance has all the allure and decorum associated with Fonteyn.

In this scene, Chloe is surrounded by a semi-circle of shepherds, moving from one foot to the other tapping out the pulse, echoing Chloe's quick taps; the women sit in a flattened position on the ground. This stage picture evokes a similar moment in the earlier, Pirate scene, where Chloe is taunted and threatened by the Pirates who form a close semi-circle around her. In her solo in Scene II, she performs innumerable *arabesques*, jumped, stepped and turned all with her hands bound by a rope. The dance moves between strongly held poses and sudden, desperate moments of collapse. The contrast is between her desire to flee and her awareness of being both trapped and in danger. Bryaxis hovers, at times attempting to molest her.

In Scene III, Chloe is once again enclosed by a group but this time in quiet celebration. Although the dance is confined, she now moves without restraint, travelling from side to side and in short diagonal bursts. Just before the end, she has a quick joyous circle of small *balancé*-like waltz steps and a turning jump. The flattened spatial pattern and curling arm movements give the dance a strong definition, contrasting with the haunting, though lyrical, sound of the flute.

A phrase that distils the essence of the work and perhaps of Fonteyn too, is the short complex section near the beginning of the dance, repeated later. Ashton draws our attention to Chloe's arms, her head, and her sharply articulated feet. The arms counterpoint the legs with twirling wrists and movement that snakes up the side of the body: as she makes a quick step into a low attitude behind, she taps the sole of her working foot ending in a, low, over-crossed *arabesque*.

She then makes a quick *rond de jambe à terre* as far as the side position, then the leg shoots across the supporting leg into a second quick *rond de jambe à terre* from front to back, and ends with a final tap of the foot.

This whole phrase is accompanied by circling arms. The right arm moves in a curved path upwards in front of the face before ending at the side of the body while the left, beginning up, travels down the side of the body and then up in front of the face.

It ends, level with the head, to make a design in which the wrists are flexed and the palms of both hands face upwards.

This is a swift smooth phrase with the accent on the final position. Curling patterns are formed around both the upper and lower body disturbing the space and making us aware of the shapes which form in the body. It is a highly complex phrase in which Ashton emphasises Fonteyn's ability to create moments of contrast, throughout a short, complex phrase of movement. The whole dance has rich variety, slow fluid passages are followed by little hops on pointe, sudden quick jumps and euphoric waltzing. As Fonteyn performs the dance, it is light, sensual and rapid. She joyously taps her foot, and as she snakes her arms above her head, throws it back with a laugh. Just as in Daphnis's dance, the space around the body is disturbed but in more intricate ways than it is in that of Daphnis. But as in his dance, Chloe's movement, for the most part, comprises minor steps. And, it is very different from the earlier more confined dance in Scene II. In Scene III, the dance has flat shapes, a less restrained use of space and the movement seems to be spontaneous.

Choreographically Chloe's two dances are tightly knit. The first has a recurring *arabesque* motif while the second uses the quirky little foot taps and *rond de jambe* to punctuate the dance and form the dominant motif. The tapping motif is picked up again by the whole group during the finale.

Many of the critics commented on the lack of homogeneity in the work. Coton described the dances for the soloists as academic, classical style and, for the groups, as a mingling of 'Greek, Cretan and what appears to be Balkan folk-dance elements' that created a startling effect.[45] It is a strange comment because it is not clear what he means by 'academic classical' dance, neither did he notice how Ashton modified the *danse d'école*, flattening it and generally adapting it to suit the particular work.

The final celebration section in Scene III has a similar sort of excitement to Scene IV of Nijinska's *Noces*, without the sombre atmosphere of that work. Ashton uses the group, swollen by the dancers who were Pirates, now shepherds and shepherdesses, to create a celebratory end. All perform the same movements, though, sometimes, in staggered groups, including Daphnis and Chloe when they join part way through. Here, each member of the group holds a handkerchief, in Grecian traditional dance style, and the dancers form into straight lines, enlivening the stage with a profusion of colour. Exhilaration and elation is created through the movement as well as through the music. As the latter builds to a climax, Ashton empties the stage bringing back Daphnis and Chloe alone. Vaughan describes it as a master-stroke: 'he turns in the centre and she circles him in a *chassé coupé jeté*'.[46] When discussing the music Ashton remarked that he

Daphnis and Chloe. Margot Fonteyn as Chloe, Michael Somes as Daphnis. © Roger Wood. Courtesy of the Royal Opera House.

found the music so wonderful and so beautiful and so overwhelming sometimes that I felt that it was like waves that were going to submerge me, and I had great difficulty in keeping my head above it, especially in the last scene, where there's a great surge of music – I found it difficult to match it with movement, because it seemed to me that perhaps it was almost better to stand still.[47]

The ensemble's movement is made up of jumps, hops, skips and leaps. They enter the stage attached by the scarves they are holding but even after separating, the scarves are used throughout. This is such an exciting finale because the movement is continuous and the steps follow each other without breaks. These are simple, hopping steps which do not detract from the music and the unbroken movement adds to the excitement. It is not bacchanalian but nevertheless conveys the revelry and festive nature of the moment. Fokine's finale was apparently more orgiastic. He gave each of his lines of dancers contrasting movement and different pulse patterns.[48] But if Fokine's dancers seemed to express a kind of 'collective abandon', Ashton's do not. They are more controlled yet no less exhilarated.[49]

Craxton's scenery and costumes are apposite, contributing to the fluency of the movement and the Mediterranean atmosphere. And the group dances, which are so finely arranged and designed, are central to the choreography. Group work is frequently ignored when critics discuss the work, but the choreography reflects Ashton's skill in handling groups and of his continuous dialogue with the early works of Nijinska.

The negative comments from the 1951 critics have proved to be unjustified. A few isolated voices praised the choreography and décor but as with *Illuminations*, these were mainly the American critics in New York. Yet many today regard it as a masterpiece. A comment made by the critic Elsa Brunelleschi that 'the ballet lacked the Ashton touch, even that he had made it 'tongue in cheek', that Ravel's music 'was never intended to be used as a skit and [that] the ballet is not a charade to play naughty pranks with' demonstrates the inflexibility and reluctance to accept difference of some of these critics.[50] Others suggested that the ballet showed 'an uncertainty not only of period but of idiom.[51] Analysis has indicated otherwise. As an example of Ashton's dance movement and choreographic style, it demonstrates the solidity of his choreographic craft and his skill in moulding motifs to suit his subject matter and how the dancers and set designer, also prompted and shaped his choice of movement and choreographic motifs.

A Month in the Country

Interviewed before the opening night Ashton explained that the work ' "… is a small ballet for eight people. Don't expect big ballets from me". "I'm at what you'd call Beethoven's quartet period. I'm not interested in massive things anymore"'.[52] Premiered on 12 February 1976, near the end of his career, *A Month in the Country* is an intense exploration of love, infatuation and relationships with all their messy human aspects, based on the 1855 play by Turgenev. As Ashton put it 'I like to portray human emotions and situations... I'm very interested in the human heart and all its complexities';[53] and in this work, he follows the effect of illicit passion on three individuals.

The ballet deals more fully with character than most of his other narrative works, so it is not at all like *Daphnis and Chloe*. Sorley Walker regarded it as a companion to *Enigma Variations* (1968):

> Both are rewarding period pieces concerned with subtle studies of character and relationships within an intimate circle of people. Both have romantic and nostalgic elements, and a delicate theatrical touch.[54]

Yet *Month* has much more. Each character develops differently. Natalia Petrovna who starts out as the indulged, bored wife becomes a passionate, if despairing, lover; her ward Vera, whose immaturity is palpable, develops into the dreamy adolescent before becoming both a disappointed and angry woman as she confronts reality. Beliaev, the tutor, changes from a carefree, shy, even gauche, student to a sophisticated and ardent suitor. No other works of Ashton have this subtle character development, not even *Marguerite and Armand* (1963), which is more a study of ardour than of character, made as a vehicle for Fonteyn and Nureyev. *The Observer's* Alexander Bland noted that Ashton referred to *Month* as a kind of Phèdre story adding that 'we may be sure that he [Turgenev] has special sensitivity to the nuances of age and class, national character, period, environment and, above all, the convulsions of the human heart.'[55] In his choreography for Natalia and Vera, Ashton captured these subtle differences of age and the class differences between Rakitin and Beliaev are revealed through Ashton's use of the stage. Beliaev does not have command of the furniture or gesture in the same way as Rakitin.

Isaiah Berlin notes that personal relationships meant everything to Turgenev and as both Kavanagh and Vaughan make clear, personal relationships were also vitally important to Ashton.[56] The in-depth study of relationships in Ashton's ballet may not be biographical but it is fuelled by Ashton's own experiences. In the last two decades of his life, Ashton had fallen passionately in love with a much younger man, who had both an 'intoxicating and rejuvenating' effect on his late years.[57]

The criticism that Ashton could only make works that were conservative, nostalgic and sentimental does not take his ingenuity into account nor his acute understanding of people.[58] Few could hear William Wordsworth's 'still sad music of humanity' like Ashton and it is perhaps in this work most of all that he gets to the heart of human relationships.[59] We know too that Ashton admired Wordsworth. He had spent the summer, before making *La fille mal gardée*, reading Dorothy Wordsworth's Journals, enjoying her quiet reflections on the countryside.[60] Unlike MacMillan, Ashton did not make gut-wrenching material. He was more concerned to understand temperament and sensibility.

Ashton had decided to make a ballet based on Turgenev's play in 1968 but it took eight years before he found suitable music. His choice of Chopin was the result of a conversation with Berlin, a friend and expert on Turgenev, who had translated the play. It is probable that the two men communicated about the play, although Ashton's copy was translated by Emlyn Williams. The stage directions in that version suggest that Vera is playing Chopin when the curtain rises, so perhaps Berlin's proposal was a happy coincidence. The score was formed jointly between Ashton, Martyn Thomas and the conductor Lanchbery, who made the final arrangement.[61] Jordan has written a detailed analysis of this and points out that the choreography and approach to the music is typical of Ashton's music style. He often formed dance rhythms independent from the music, creating a conversation between the two.[62] She also pays tribute to Lanchbery's adaptation of the music, concluding that '*Month* has established itself as one of the richest integrations of music and narrative choreography in the repertoire'.[63]

Trevelyan Oman had already been asked by Ashton to do the decor in 1968 after she had produced a realistic setting and detailed period costumes for *Enigma Variations*. She took a similar approach to this work, which is considered her finest design for theatre.[64] The ballet is set in the drawing room of a rather grand country house, with a pale palette of cream and faded gold.

> This is a ballet in which every object in Julia Trevelyan Oman's country house setting looks not only real, but literally functional. It is a ballet in which people fan themselves in the heat, work at writing desks and carry walking sticks.[65]

At the rear of the stage, large French windows open on a view of a bridge leading off into the garden. A piano stands at the back on the audience's right and on stage are a chaise longue and a comfortable chair. There is just enough room to dance. The set suggests wealth and class and looks more like one for a play by Noël Coward or Terence Rattigan than for a ballet. The set conveys a grand household though not an aristocratic one. But in order to communicate the family's class, Trevelyan Oman needed to create an opulent ambiance even if it is a little grandiose for a mid-nineteenth century Russian country estate.

The atmosphere is one of comfort and tranquillity; surely anyone could be happy here. Despite its security, the setting refutes the reality of the characters' situation. Though, because the set is cluttered, it creates the claustrophobic atmosphere of the play and that of the family. Trevelyan Oman establishes an idyllic ambiance but, as in all idyllic places, despair also lurks. The chaise longue is used by Ashton throughout, becoming Natalia's prop or solace when things begin to go wrong.

The women's costumes are mainly blue and white. Natalia, dressed in a calf-length white bell shaped dress, has a blue ribbon at the waist, while both Vera and Katia, the maid, have cream tops with blue skirts. The men are in pale grey or beige suits, except for Beliaev who wears a Russian peasant shirt with check trousers instead of the peasant breeches. None of this attire would look amiss in a mid-nineteenth century Russian household. It all looks quite authentic, almost realistic which is possibly why critics linked the ballet with *Enigma Variations*.

Vaughan found the design to be the weakest element of the work, criticising the grand residence and symmetry of the set and the decision to decorate the walls of the salon with paintings from contemporary etchings of *Don Giovanni*, although the opening music is informed by variations on a theme from that opera.[66] Strangely few critics are in agreement with Vaughan or at least do not mention the setting at all. The décor works and the costumes do not distract from the dancing or impair movement and more than adequately set the scene and atmosphere of the era.

Ashton's Adaptation of the Play

With an extensive range of characters and a detailed scenario, the play takes place over five acts and lasts well over two hours. Ashton's distillation of the text is around thirty-five minutes long and it seems that he worked out the scenario himself. Set deep in the Russian countryside, the story centres on the family. Only the main protagonists are included: Natalia Petrovna, Vera, Kolia, Yslaev, Katia, Beliaev and Rakitin and there is also a walk-on footman. Natalia Petrovna is a bored upper-class woman, admired by Rakitin, a friend of her husband Yslaev. She has a son Kolia and a ward Vera. Into this melange comes Beliaev, a tutor engaged for Kolia for the summer. Like the Sylph in *La Sylphide*, he creates chaos, though unintentionally. All of the women fall under his spell and he readily responds to Natalia's advances. But Vera too falls in love with him and happening upon Beliaev and Natalia in an embrace, jealously calls the members of the household to witness the scene. The ballet ends with a devastated Natalia, a puzzled Yslaev and the departure of Beliaev and Rakitin. By focusing on Natalia's relationships with Rakitin, Yslaev, Beliaev and Vera, Ashton makes her the centre of the ballet. Beliaev is at the root of the household's upset but Rakitin's disappointment, Vera's venom and Yslaev's confusion are caused by and directed at Natalia.

Michael Redgrave's introduction to the Williams translation is the most heavily underlined section of Ashton's copy of the play and, apart from some of the stage directions, only a few comments from the characters are highlighted in the body of the play. Ashton was clearly guided by Redgrave's description of the characters. Natalia should be both romantic and comic, 'capable of being not only entrancing but exasperating and the balance has to be kept with flair and virtuosity'.[67] Rakitin is 'intelligent, but over-subtle, and his subtleties make him seem a plodder', though Redgrave insists that he is also a man of passion, as the final act makes clear.[68] Vera is more problematic because of the dramatic change that has to take place near the end. At the outset, she is young, almost child-like, but becomes an adult during the course of the play (and ballet). Redgrave sees her as serious and at times cold with an element of self-dramatisation. She is certainly a less attractive character than Natalia. Yslaev, Natalia's husband, should be depicted as a gentleman and Katia, the maid, as the temptress. She should, Redgrave believes, exude sex. 'When she offered Beliaev raspberries they became the apple in the garden of Eden.'[69]

The essential thing about Beliaev, Redgrave notes, is that he must be beautiful:

> If Rakitin is the mirror to Natalia's heart... the young tutor is the bright morning sun. To his rays all the young women respond like flower petals – the budding Vera, the dewy Katia and Natalia the rose in bloom – and he is unconscious of all this...[70]

Redgrave remembered that in the first performance he saw, Beliaev was played by a young Robert Donat. 'There was just that look in the eye, direct and lively, piercing, a sort of clumsy peasant grace.'[71] Ashton outlined this section and Dowell, of all the men in the Royal Ballet at the time, fitted this description. Beliaev is not clearly depicted in the play, which centres on the family, and we learn more about him from Vera than from his own conversations with others. (Ashton highlighted Vera's comment in the play that 'the whole household loves him'.) Beliaev's shyness is marked in the play and he is presented as very young, eight years younger than Natalia. Although he has already appeared on stage, Vera's excited description of him gives the audience a real glimpse of his high spirits and attractive manner:

> He was chasing a squirrel and climbed up and up , till he could shake the top – we felt quite frightened – then he made a bow-and arrow for Kolia, then he betted me that I couldn't play a mazurka, and I won, then we ran out again and then...[72]

Vera's lines feed the ballet and generate Ashton's narrative, which makes Beliaev a more pivotal figure than he is in the play.[73] Ashton gives him more definition and a slightly older more reticent personality, especially as interpreted by Dowell. Beliaev's first variation is slow, dependent on wide expressive *port de bras* and controlled, deep, indulgent movements. And this was partly to suit Dowell's talents and because Ashton put his own stamp on the ballet. In the quartet with Natalia, Kolia and Vera, however, Beliaev is exuberant and playful as in Vera's description.

In Ashton's copy of the play, the work is divided into two sections and Ashton underscored several stage directions and some lines of dialogue for inclusion in the ballet.[74] Natalia's indifference to Rakitin's attentions, the appearance of Beliaev at the open widow, and the references to Vera's piano playing all come from the early part of the play as are Vera's lines quoted above.[75] Natalia is not only eight years older than Beliaev but also his social superior; the costumes display this but so too do the performances of the two characters. Beliaev is also less patrician than Rakitin and the ways in which the two men interact with Natalia are illuminative. Where Rakitin is formal, distanced even, though he would like not to be, Beliaev is more exuberant, Ashton had to hint at what is spoken in the play. Little exchanges between the characters have been marked and these are condensed into the duets that make up the emotional core. To shape his narrative, he selected the more introspective dialogues: those in which the characters hint at their feelings or their emotional state. For example, the moment when Natalia realises she is in love with Beliaev has been highlighted in Ashton's text. Having access to the text Ashton used could benefit future performers, as it is clear that this version of the play is fundamental to his interpretation. He was not concerned with merely telling the story, as the omission of several characters testifies. Before making the ballet, Ashton had also immersed himself in Turgenev's novels and letters and, as with Rimbaud, books about Turgenev, so, the atmosphere of the ballet was also derived from Ashton's reading.[76]

The Dancers

As ever, Ashton made the most of his dancers' talents. He focused on what they were best at, adding his own specific touches, challenging them to their limits. Prior to *Month*, he had only made one substantial dance for Lynn Seymour (Natalia): *Les deux pigeons/The Two Pigeons* (1961) and the first of the Isadora Duncan waltzes: *Brahms-Waltz* (1975). There were some who complained that Seymour lacked understanding of strict academic form but Ashton ignored that for, when she was still a student in 1956, he made the 'Classical Variation' for the RAD's Solo Seal examination, using Seymour as his model.[77] Pamela May, who owned the variations, pointed out that the dance demonstrated the 'elegance and softness of Seymour's style of dancing'.[78] She had a mixed training in Canada, which included tap dancing, and ballet from an ex-Russian dancer, Nicolai Svetlanoff. According to Seymour, he taught her about flow, the plasticity of movement and how to convey emotion with a hand gesture or a half-turn of the head and eyes.[79] In 1954 she joined the Sadler's Wells School and worked there with Winifred Edwards, whose teaching was entirely based on de Valois's syllabus. Clearly strict academic form was not central to Ashton's needs. Yet, in *Month*, her variation comprises detailed expressive footwork with fluid, though often gestural, arm movements. Her much praised fluidity was reserved for the duet.

Dowell's variation has little trace of traditional male dancing, such as an expansive use of space and conspicuous show of strength. Shape, line and expressive arm movement were not associated with male ballet dancing, at least not in the 1970s. Ashton made eleven major roles for Dowell and the most significant variations are found in *The Dream* (1964), *Enigma Variations* (1968), *The Sleeping Beauty* (1968), *Month*, *Orpheus* (1978) and *Le Rossignol* (1981). Phrases threaded through these variations demonstrate Dowell's restraint and control. Dowell, famed for his agility, could turn and jump easily and Ashton made use of this too, occasionally giving him demanding turns and frenetic bursts of fast jumps. Most of the choreography in *Month* takes advantage of Dowell's qualities emphasising his fluidity, line and exquisite use of arms. But perhaps the most telling aspects are the sudden contrasts in dynamic: a slow, long, drawn-out phrase is followed by a quick burst of vitality. It is typical of Ashton's dance movement style and occurs at several moments in the work, not only in Beliaev's entrance variation but also when performing alone during the quartet.

Dowell was trained at the Royal Ballet School, first at White Lodge and subsequently at the Upper school at Barons Court. There he was taught by Claude Newman, who had been a pupil of both Astafieva and Bedells. Newman was a disciplinarian and Dowell appreciated that.[80] Later he had Harold Turner and Errol Addison. Turner had spent some time with Rambert and so had a background in Cecchetti work, while Addison had studied with the Maestro himself. Dowell remembers the latter as treating him well and helping to give him confidence. Like Seymour, he had joined the School when de Valois syllabus was first introduced, which honed his ability to move at speed and make quick directional changes easily, as well as providing core strength.

For Vera, Ashton chose Denise Nunn a young Australian dancer who had joined the Royal Ballet in 1974. Trained in the RAD style, Nunn had some experience of dancing Ashton work from taking part in the Solo Seal examination. Reviews from her performances in the Royal Ballet School's annual performance in 1974 in which she danced Friday's Child from *Jazz Calendar* and the slow second section of MacMillan's *Concerto* (1967), suggest she was more of a legato dancer. Yet in *Month* he made the most of her strong feet, speed and fluid arms. She responded well to his dance style and her variation includes off-balance turns, quick challenging footwork and an abundance of signature steps.

The role of Kolia is less clearly defined though his dance gives a rare example of highly spectacular movement in an Ashton ballet. It was given to Wayne Sleep, a short virtuoso dancer, trained at the Royal Ballet School. The dances for Katja (Marguerite Porter) are limited, yet typically use a variety of quick runs and *pas de bourrée* on pointe, which suited Porter's highly arched feet and shy manner. Porter, although considered a beauty, did not have the voluptuous quality that Redgrave suggested was central to Katja's character but her role in the ballet is limited, so perhaps an emphasis on eroticism was unnecessary. The other characters have little dancing, their roles confined, mainly, to silent acting.

The Choreography

Ashton relates the story through silent acting, solos, duets and an elated quartet. Four duets dominate the second half of the work, while the opening scenes comprise solos. There are no set-pieces because the solos and duets emerge from the action, fusing with the subsequent scene. Vaughan points out that Ashton had used an operatic structure for the ballet with arias (dance) alternating with recitative (acting).[81] And while several of Ashton's narrative works include some silent acting, *Month* is perhaps the only one that is quite so close to a Mozart opera. There is silent acting in *The Dream* (1964) but it does not have the aria/recitative aspect of *Month*. *Marguerite and Armand* (1963) is a chamber piece but dominated by the two main protagonists. It has some short sections of silent acting but mainly comprises duets. Vaughan observes that all three were condensed from much larger works but have little else in common.

Shortly after the curtain lifts, Natalia rises from the chaise longue, instructing Vera to play for her and sweeps across the stage to begin her dance. This is followed by Vera's dance, which leads into a short comic section, involving everyone on stage in a search for Yslaev's mislaid keys. Kolya performs next in an exuberant dance with a ball. Beliaev enters and Ashton stops the action, just enough for us to realise the significance of the moment. A short silence and a lawn curtain ruffled by the breeze add to the magic of the moment before he, unaware that he has caused a sensation, mundanely hands a kite to Kolya. With only Natalia and Rakitin remaining on stage, Beliaev performs a slow, spellbinding variation which results in Rakitin's exit. Throughout the dance Rakitin observes Beliaev and seems to have been disturbed by Beliaev's presence. The spell is broken and the section comes to an end with a high-spirited dance for Natalia and Beliaev who are presently joined by Kolya and Vera.

This lively moment makes us conscious of Beliaev's significance in the household; it stimulates the women, pushing them into elated and expansive movement. The tempo speeds up and we witness Natalia's fast turns and high extensions while Vera is lifted high by Beliaev, both have been emboldened by the tutor and it shows in their uncharacteristic movement. This quartet makes us uncomfortably aware that Beliaev's presence threatens to disrupt the apparent stability of the household, particularly as Natalia is left both animated and disturbed.

The second section begins with a brief duet between Rakitin and Natalia, which is followed by Vera and Beliaev. When Natalia discovers them, the scene blows up into a major upset. Rakitin arrives just as it has ended. Pacifying Natalia, he guides her through the French windows and they exit together, performing the 'Fred step'. The subsequent brief duet between Katja and Beliaev serves to lessen the tension, before the emotional heart of the work occurs: the duet between Natalia and Beliaev. It is a real moment of ecstasy which ends brutally with a venomous attack by Vera and the ballet gradually draws to its inevitable conclusion.

Three Variations

Natalia is a sophisticated woman, trapped in the countryside and confined by a dull marriage. We recognise this from the moment she leaves the chaise longue and travels upstage to the piano where Vera is playing. Beginning with two lilting walks, she continues striding with bent knees on pointe, making rhythmic skips in between the walks; the arms gesture in the air, as though she is conversing. The walk is reminiscent of Marguerite's backward walks in the duet, after Armand's father leaves her in *Marguerite and Armand*. In both cases, these swift striding walks have to be performed with an effortless elegance, effectively hinting at the character's maturity.

Spatially this dance has much in common with the dances of August Bournonville, whose work Ashton admired. There are no long travelling phrases, no real progressions. And it links with several of the dances in *Birthday Offering*, particularly those of Fifield and Jackson with their intricate, speedy footwork and restless floor patterns. Choreographically it comprises a series of phrase clusters, I counted five, linked to those of the music, each repeated on both sides, though not always identically. So in the repetition of the opening phrases, there is a turn, omitted when the phrase is repeated and later when the dancer performs *a grand pas de basque sauté* twice, the cluster is only performed once.

Natalia's dance has complex floor patterns. From upstage right, she travels in two oblique diagonals, followed by a longer diagonal from approximately centre stage to downstage right. The patterns then become highly capricious moving in little oblique bursts from stage right to stage left and just before the dance ends, there is a small circle, performed just off-centre. It is one of Ashton's more complex stage patterns, evoking those of the Bride's variation in *Le baiser de la fée* but made more intricate because each phrase cluster starts facing one way and finishes facing the other. These multi-faceted clusters continue almost without pause throughout the dance.[82] That Natalia is bored and somewhat unreliable emerges from this solo, particularly through the edgy floor paths. This restless zig-zaging floor pattern is also noted by Jordan who argues that the 'musical and rhythmic means contribute further to this', giving the dance a feeling of edginess.[83] Although the steps used encompass Ashton's range, there is something else which makes them distinctive and particular to this work; the complex use of the upper body. Was Ashton driven by the music, the dancer or the character for his choice of steps? I think perhaps all three.

The music for this dance comprises Chopin's variations on a theme from Mozart's *Don Giovanni* and Jordan points out the musical complexity in the opening phrase, noting that the movement 'hold[s] its pulse but meet[s] and part[s] with its accent structure,' adding that 'her little hiccup rhythm cheekily anticipates and then echoes the same rhythm in Mozart'.[84] Arlene Croce also notes that Ashton's 'skill as a dramatist is invested mainly in his dances... his steps... give us more story than any official scenario could'.[85] And Natalia's opening dance bears this out, not just in the floor patterns and musical style but also in the steps.

This opening phrase cluster epitomises the dance as a whole. Seymour's movement qualities and Ashton's dance movement style, which contains both signature steps and typical stylistic phrases, combine to make this phrase cluster characteristic of Ashton's style.

A step into a small *saut de basque*[86] is followed by a *chassé pas de bourrée* travelling diagonally; a second quick turn on two feet is followed by a *dégagé* of the right foot and bend of the torso over the working leg; a step into fourth position on pointe and short pause.

A quick *petit battement* follows into a rapid *rond de jambe à terre* and a turning *pas de bourrée* on pointe with picked up feet; then a second quick *petit battement* into a bend towards the working leg and second quick *rond de jambe à terre* with a further abrupt bend towards the foot.

The whole phrase is then repeated to the other side, moving diagonally to stage left.

It is an odd choice of steps because most of them come from small, insig-

A Month in the Country, Lynn Seymour. © Antony Crickmay. Courtesy of the Victoria and Albert Museum.

The upper back curves backwards, the head is tilted looking over the front shoulder and the arms are stretched in a long line. Natalia's pose is the embodiment of sophistication.

nificant, classroom exercises and do not seem to be there to highlight the ballerina's virtuosity. The *saut de basque*, which should be a large virtuoso turning jump on one leg, is low, quick and barely discernible, more like a turning walk. The first *pas de bourrée* is a forward travelling step, continuing into a second turn before being abruptly stopped by the emphasis placed on the *dégagé*. Yet, what we notice most is the movement into fourth position, the body design. It is a typical Ashton moment. The upper back curves backwards, the head is tilted looking over the front shoulder and the arms are stretched in a long line. It demands great flexibility in the upper body, which Seymour had wonderfully. But the end of the phrase, with its repeated *rond de jambe à terre* and picked up *pas de bourrée*, provides even more action and complexity because each step finishes with a deep bend over the working leg. Paradoxically, the phrase appears fluid because the arms are drawn upwards in two circular *port de bras* and, each time the dancer pauses, we see her curved body shape, making the whole cluster seem flowing and understated. Ashton pushes the dancer to make full use of the upper body but the nature of the movement also encourages precise footwork. This combination creates polyrhythmic body actions, so that different rhythms and dynamics occur in upper and lower body.[87]

This is an extraordinary opening to any dance. So much is crammed into the phrase but none of the steps fall within the academic demands of the classroom. The opening *pas de bourrée* does not need flat turnout nor closure in fifth position; in the *rond de jambe à terre*, the upper body is more important than the footwork and none in themselves are spectacular or even, apparently, difficult movements. A major motif is the *petit battement battu*, present in almost every group of phrases. In the classroom, the *petit battement battu* is mainly regarded as a training step but it is a signature Ashton step, used to create a slight hiccup in a phrase. Competing for importance is the *pas de bourrée* used in a myriad of ways. The *pas de bourrée*, also considered to be a linking step, becomes a major movement, particularly when used more for travel than for its rhythmic interest.

As observers, we are drawn to the curved shapes that punctuate the flow of the phrase. These are almost more important than the intricate footwork and, if it gives the appearance of ease, this is because the swirling arms complicate the space around the body and make the phrases seem fluent. The curving arms and clear body designs in the upper body continue throughout this short variation accompanied by the quick intricate footwork: lilting *bourrées courus*, short sharp *sissonnes*, quick, stuttering *petits battements* and sophisticated walks on pointe. But what increases the apparent sophistication of the character are the held shapes. It is as though Natalia is carrying on a conversation, pausing just to catch her breath.

A Month in the Country, Denise Nunn. © Antony Crickmay. Courtesy of the Victoria and Albert Museum.

Vera's wide spread arms suggest youth and exuberance in complete contrast to Natalia's on page 200.

Seymour makes the *port de bras* appear mimetically gestural. They do not seem incongruous in the realistic surroundings; she could just be chatting to Rakitin. In addition, her changing *épaulement*, while bringing out her sophistication, also reveals a slightly erratic quality.

Of all the dances I have examined in this book, this dance, and, its opening phrase cluster in particular, has a wealth of stylistic details, contained in little over a minute. No other choreographer could have made this short dance section, none would have packed the phrase cluster with so much movement nor would they have given up the chance to display the dancer's virtuoso talents.

Not only are the steps Ashton uses transformed from their classroom originals but they are also used for different purposes. The *saut de basque* travels horizontally rather than vertically, the *petits battements* create a stutter and arrest the flow and the *rond de jambe à terre* is used to emphasise the curved shape of the upper body. The space around the torso is highly active and there are dynamic changes in each phrase, created by the sudden stops and contrasting dynamic between the filigree *pas de bourrée* and sweeping *rond de jambe à terre*.

In fact the dancer controls our perception. She communicates through the upper body but then encourages us to look at her feet. It is apparently what Pavlova did and Seymour had Pavlovian feet. The steps have probably been chosen as much for their dynamic range as for their elaborate footwork but they are also there to focus our attention on Seymour's feet. Seymour remembered that Ashton had originally fallen in love with her feet: 'I love glorious insteps. You have them.'[88] When Seymour performs the dance, she moves effortlessly through it concealing the difficulties. Later dancers have inevitably slowed the music, spending more time on getting the steps right. But this brief examination of the phrases suggests that is not what Ashton's dance is about. He would have chosen other movement if he had wanted to flaunt the ballet steps or make them appear academic.

Yet Seymour always found his work difficult:

> Fred's very demanding and his things are always puffy. What with extra bending and flinging and backbending and moving your head, there's no chance to relax, none at all. You can't really compare his style to Kenneth's, but they're both into doing these intricate, footsy solos for me all the time, all sort of knitting downstairs and not able to drop a stitch.[89]

Vera's solo, which follows immediately has a similar range of steps: *pas de bourrée* and *bourrée couru*, *petits battements battus* and several, different, small jumps. Despite this, Vera's dance is quite unlike Natalia's. It does not have the sophisticated poses and the arms are not used in the same way. The floor paths too are more expansive, as befits a young woman, and she has less bending and twisting. The dance is characterised by her swinging arms, which adds to an impression of youthful exuberance.

The floor patterns travel in longer, more continuous phrases, although there are typical Ashton stutters, interrupting the long diagonals and circles. Vera begins upstage left and travels diagonally to downstage right and then across the front of the stage, before moving in a big circle back to where she began. The next set of phrases takes her to centre stage and then back to the piano before she hastens down a diagonal, to end flopped in a conveniently placed chair.

The phrase clusters are less dense than those of Natalia, with much more breathing space, which makes Vera seem younger, less sophisticated. Her circular path around the stage has a repeated run on pointe, punctuated by little jumps, which end with a sliding *arabesque à terre*. Her swinging arms make the phrases appear both childlike and playful. And later, in a backward travelling phrase, the awkwardness of the movement makes the character appear gauche, though captivating.

The opening phrases of Vera's dance are lively and high spirited. Not only does Ashton use small clipped steps but he also has the dancer perform swift, circular, arm movements. The motif of small unassuming steps is continued from Natalia's dance, which gives the ballet coherence but is changed to present a wholly different character. Starting upstage left, the phrase cluster comprises:

> *Chassé, coupé, ballonné*[90] followed by a *piqué*, with straight working leg, moving forward and back to *arabesque*. The phrase is repeated before the dancer performs a parallel run on pointe to the corner stage right, This is followed by three jumped *retirés*, on the same leg, closing in front, behind in front. The phrase cluster is then performed to the other side.

In this cluster, Ashton uses the *ballonné* to create texture. In other words, he disrupts the continuity by altering the dynamics of the step and this affects the flow of the phrase, cutting off the end of the step rather abruptly. To complicate things, the *ballonné* and the *coupé* have to be performed in one beat, so that the jump becomes little more than a hop. The speed of the three steps, combined with the bend of the upper body towards the working leg, prevents the supporting foot in the *ballonné* from stretching fully. This makes the *ballonné* almost unrecognizable and the *coupé* is transformed from a sharp abrupt movement to a shuffle from one foot to the other. By the same token, the *chassé* is almost imperceptible but as it is recorded as a *chassé* in the Benesh score, it should have that sliding quality.[91] Because the arms are moving too, and the torso bends sideways, Vera's opening section is energetic and full of life. The activity is more conspicuous since the limbs move along different paths, adding to the complexity of the phrase: the arms progress in a circular path while the path of the legs is straight.

The circle which follows involves parallel runs on pointe and, from the previous phrase, repeats the *piqué* forward and back. The swinging arms which accompany it make Vera appear nonchalant. Ashton wanted to give an impression of youthfulness and had picked the dancer Denise Nunn not only for her youth but also because she looked right. Once again Ashton uses a simple motif, the parallel runs on pointe, as the structuring element of the dance but they also add to the character's liveliness. Each time she repeats them, they are slightly changed and coupled with different steps: arms are sometimes out at the side at shoulder level or raised above the head. The runs happen in three out of the five phrase clusters and typify the unsophisticated nature of the character.

Apart from *Enigma Variations*, in many of Ashton's narrative ballets, the variations are more about dance itself, yet here the two variations are not only about dance but also create the characters. Ashton's masterly crafts-manship comes to the fore in these dances. Both are structured around motifs of small unassuming steps and the second dance picks up on aspects of the first, so there is a consistent style throughout, at least as far as the solo dances are concerned.

Beliaev's appearance brings a dark note into the seemingly relaxed atmos-phere of the first section. He enters just after Kolia has performed a lively virtuoso dance with a bouncing ball. The air is light but when Beliaev enters through the French windows there is a moment of stillness. Everyone on stage is motionless. Then Vera runs towards him. Her swift, parallel runs on pointe are like that moment in *Daphnis* when as Pan is heard, one of the Pirate Women breaks away from the crowd and runs across the stage. It breaks the tension. As Vera and Kolia are packed off by Natalia, Beliaev moves to follow but is stopped by Natalia. His dance which follows takes us unaware. There is no preparation no opening pose, as in the earlier varia-tions; he just goes straight into it. Starting, dreamily, with two smooth *rond de jambe à terre*, Beliaev gathers pace in a controlled multiple turn ending in an *attitude* on *demi-pointe* followed by a deep *arabesque penchée*. It is as though he is thinking or dreaming about something else and appears to be completely oblivious of Natalia and Rakitin, standing downstage and upstage respec-tively.

We perceive his solo as slow and languid because of the restrained lei-surely pace of the music and the way in which the notes trickle slowly out. But, like many Ashton dances, this is deceptive. In fact, the dancer has to move much more rapidly than the music suggests. There are no pauses; end-ings and preparations become one, so that the movement phrases are continuous. Once again, Ashton uses a simple phrase, *chassé, coupé, assemblé,* as the main motif, but the way Dowell performs it is both luxurious and indulgent. The dance needs this kind of quality to succeed.

This striking passage occurs just after a flurry of scissor-like *changements*. There are five *chassé, coupé, assemblé* phrases in a row with wide-sweeping gestural arms, opening out from the centre of the body, spreading almost to the side. In balletic mime, the gesture is one of giving and generosity but here it is part of the phrase giving the actions a kind of extravagance. At the heart of the dance, and this section in particular, is *épaulement*. The five phrases show the body in various ways to the audience, using the corners of the stage: we see an open position, crossed position, a second crossed position moving backwards, then in a turning motion and finally directly forward. Ashton revels in Dowell's luscious arms and pliant upper back, quite an embarrassment of riches. But these directional changes are all controlled within the dominating motif of the *chassé, coupé, assemblé* phrase. The *assemblé* is developed in the next set of phrases into an extended fourth position on a bent supporting leg and an abrupt step, on the other leg, into *arabesque*. There follows a series of smooth runs, with similar opening arms to the earlier five phrases.

It is a quite remarkable variation not just in its choice of movement but musically too. As Jordan points out, the independent dance rhythms and accents create a 'lively conversation with the music', as when the sharp *arabesques* cross the pulse, it looks 'doubly wild against Chopin's continuing legato'.[92]

The dance has the kind of movement Ashton typically made for Dowell, which is deceptively simple but never gives the dancer a moment to draw a breath, though it seems to ebb and flow. But despite these fluent, gliding phrase clusters, the flow is sometimes interrupted. Initially it is the flurry of *changements*, later there are a series of fast *chaînés* turns. The flowing runs, the extravagant arms and the sudden contrasts also appear in Ashton's *Eurydice: Dance in the Elysian Fields* made for Dowell two years later, to Gluck's flute solo from *Orpheus*. As with Beliaev's dance, the music is stately and tranquil with a haunting melody, not the kind of music usually chosen for male balletic movement.

Ashton made the most of Dowell's easy dance style to present Beliaev as a gracious, slightly diffident young man and he conveys his beauty through his movement. Vaughan described the *Orpheus* variation as 'profoundly beautiful' and so too is this solo, leading us to associate the performer with the movement; both are profoundly beautiful.[93] It matches Redgrave's description of Beliaev in the play's introduction as 'the bright morning sun'.

These three variations have typical Ashtonian features: linking steps transformed into dominant features; steps used to create texture in a phrase; phrases with complex floor patterns; phrases dominated by the upper body;

phrases with multiple spatial patterns creating filigree lines around the body and continuous phrase clusters. By this stage of his career Ashton's style was supremely confident, so it is no surprise to find him using very basic steps as major motifs. The *rond de jambe à terre*, for example, infiltrates most of the solo variations in this ballet but is it also used elsewhere, either reflectively as in Beliaev's dance or the beginning of Jaeger's dance (Nimrod) in *Enigma Variations* (1968) or to make us suddenly aware of the upper body as in Natalia's dance or Dora Penny's in *Enigma*. It is not part of the Fred Step, one of the few signature steps absent from that phrase, but its importance lies in its powers of communication. An equally important aspect of all three dances is Ashton's focus on the upper body. In each dance, upper body movement helps to convey the character. As Joan Acocella has noted, 'Ashton favoured small precise steps... [and] was concerned with the body's social parts – head, arms, hands – the parts we uncover and use in dealing with one another.'[94]

The Duets

It can be argued that Ashton's pas de deux divide into two: those influenced by Petipa and those which are not. For example, the duets in ballets like *A Wedding Bouquet* (burlesqued), *Cinderella*, *Scènes de ballet* (quintet) and the Pigs in *The Tales of Beatrix Potter* are all in conversation with Petipa. The non-Petipa duets tend to come in narrative ballets or works abstracted from a narrative. In *Month* the two major duets have connections with other Ashton love duets that go back as far as the White Skaters in *Les Patineurs* (1937). Duets from *The Wanderer* (1941), *The Two Pigeons* (1961), *Marguerite and Armand* (1963), *The Dream* (1964), two in *Enigma Variations* (1968) and *Meditation from Thaïs* (1971) have themes and motifs that are similar, though not identical. In most we find the *bourrée couru*, low skimming lifts, long phrase threads and moments when the woman slips down into a semi-splits, but is held by her partner. They also have solo sections when the two dancers split, sometimes performing separately and sometimes as individuals, performing the same movements. In the latter, the dancers frequently travel in a semi-circle both performing little hops and small *grands jetés*. The significance of these sections lies in the togetherness: their actions are designed to occur simultaneously. Just as in the solo dances, unimportant steps are given intensity and significance, making them potent and extracting them from their function and role within academic dance. Phrases of animated upper body movement abound, and even when the couple are depicting fairies, as in, for example, *The Dream*, it contributes to the human qualities of both the dancer and character.

Much of the choreography in the duets is deceptively simple and is characterised by a lack of athleticism, few technical feats, few spectacular lifts and no multiple turns or 180 degree extensions. But the dances are not boring. Ashton makes us see these simple movements anew. A running *bourrée couru* appears at unexpected moments, precisely controlled to expose a moment of ecstasy, as in the brief duet in *Symphonic Variations*, when it seems like breaths in between the flowing, low *jeté* lifts or at the end of Natalia's duet with Beliaev when it seems to express hopelessness.

The choreography for many of these duets makes the dancing appear to flow effortlessly. Phrases move seamlessly from one to another and we are unaware of the density of movement, the dancers appear to glide through the dance. But Ashton also uses stillness. Frozen moments, such as a curved pose with one arm raised or a moment on the floor when the dancers curl their arms around each other's heads, create stillness, giving brief pictures amidst the continuous flow. This carefully organised relationship between stillness and flow communicates both vivaciousness and tranquillity.

Absent from the duets are the complex floor patterns of the solo dances, although the couples travel, covering relatively extensive space. In contrast, in a typical nineteenth-century duet, the couple do not move far off centre; the aim is to display the dancers' adage. But Ashton's aims are different, for his duets rarely contain the quiet controlled adage of the nineteenth century, just the reverse actually, and, stylistically, they have much in common with his dances for the single dancer.

Beliaev's duet with Vera and Beliaev's then with Natalia are at the heart of *A Month in the Country*, but it is also worth looking at the three brief duets between Natalia and Rakitin because they help to build the story and, with deft economy, convey much about Natalia and their relationship. To begin with, they perform a short light-hearted back to back dance, occurring immediately after Vera flops into a chair at the end of her dance. It is a friendly but distant encounter and sets the tone for the rest of their movement. In the other duets, Natalia either has her back to Rakitin or is struggling to escape from his embraces. Their second encounter initiates the duets section and takes place just after the joyous quartet, which has affected all four participants.

In this second duet, Rakitin enters and embraces Natalia from behind. She mistakenly supposes it to be Beliaev and tries to hide her confusion when realising her mistake. After a few moments struggle on the chaise-longue, she rushes away from him but he follows. Raising her just above the floor, one arm around her waist, the other holding her hand, he swirls her round twice. Her legs are in a low semi-split position and these split-legged lifts usually herald a special moment in a couple's relationship, a trance-like effect in Vera's duet, ecstasy in *Symphonic* and reunion in *The Two Pigeons* but not here. Having just become aware of her feelings for Beliaev, Natalia is not pleased to encounter Rakitin. In this duet the low spinning lift is accompanied by Natalia's slightly desperate gestures as she draws her hand across her brow. It is a prelude to her struggles to escape Rakitin's embraces. Interestingly, though there is much gesture and silent acting in the scene, these encounters are danced.

At one moment, Rakitin draws her arm across her body, while she rests in a low *arabesque*. The gesture happens again in her duet with Beliaev but there it lasts longer; they pause. It is a very close encounter as Beliaev envelops her with the arms. The same moment in the Rakitin duet is brief and she immediately wrenches away from him. Two similar positions but so differently employed. This is typical Ashton; the same pose or movement occurs but we perceive it so differently each time. Natalia's final duet with Rakitin consists only of the Fred Step. Each time this phrase is used it is performed with slight alterations and here it becomes a travelling step: linking arms, the two move upstage to leave by the French windows. In many of Ashton's works, the Fred Step signifies pleasure but here it is an omen. From henceforth, the relationships will begin to unravel.

Vera's duet with Beliaev has quite a different flavour from those encounters. As in her earlier variation, the space is carefully organised, though the dancers cover much more of the stage. Indeed, extensive travelling is at the heart of this duet. It is quite breathtaking in its scope and speed. The pair literally rushes around the stage and much of the time, they are moving together. Ashton chooses walks of all sorts, backwards, forwards, sideways, rhythmically complicated, jumped and even running, as a main motif.

Another major motif is the *bourrée couru* danced by Vera to suggest floating; Vera is literally floating on air. She is in love with Beliaev and blissfully happy. The *bourrée couru* is threaded through: sometimes Vera is at arm's length sometimes Beliaev supports her around the waist and sometimes she moves away; her steps flow and glide smoothly, towards him or, at times, quite apart from him.

The duet begins with a lift, which Macaulay finds exceptionally sensual even erotic. Held under the arms, she is raised up by Beliaev and as he brings her down, one foot beats against the other in a frisson of little beats. Her eyes are closed; this is Vera's moment of ecstasy.[95] Producing an impression of bliss is only part of Ashton's purpose, he is also advancing the story. Beliaev has merely brotherly affection for Vera and so, in much of the dance, he holds her away from him by the wrists at arm's length, or high above his head. Their duet is more like a children's game, he twirls her this way and that and they even have a series of turns, travelling on the diagonal, back to back, grasping each other's hands at the end of each turn. The dance is thus saved from being just another love duet. This arm's length hold is a very Ashtonian device because it is also used to make the upper body more pliant, more flexible. Beliaev and Vera together bend to left and right, forwards, back and then in a circle together. Later, this phrase returns, though this time in a crossed fourth position, the arms point upward, first Vera's and then Beliaev's. At other moments, Vera slides gently into a semi-splits position and the moment recurs in Natalia's duet later, though there it is more fiercely passionate.

Ashton's most potent device, the low lift where the woman is held just above the ground away from the man's body, recurs several times in Vera's duet but none more spellbinding than when she is raised from a low ground skimming moment to right above the man's head. Schama describes Johannes Vermeer's painting *Girl with a Pearl Earring* (1665) as a work which probes the relationship between innocence and desire and it is just such a relationship that Ashton investigates here.[96] Time and again Ashton uses similar stylistic phrases. Their repetition gives coherence to his style and is an example of how, despite different subject matter, he has a tight control over the stylistic features. So his choreography is not just an amorphous collection of steps. Yet there are no dazzling moments, no spectacle, just seemingly effortless dancing.

Natalia's duet with Beliaev is quite different, though many of the same phrases and motifs recur. It too is fluid, continuous, with few pauses for breathing, but it seems more frenetic. Yet, it has some pauses, and phrases which have strong, contrasting elements and, like Ashton's other sensual duets, there are similar stylistic details, as well as a number of other Ashtonian qualities. From Nijinska there is both the flow and absence of breath pauses and, from Duncan, the fluidity and rapturous, expressive arms.

Here Ashton takes liberties with the play. Where Turgenev only hints at the passion, Ashton gives it an eroticism taking it beyond the sensual. If Vera's opening little *battements* are just a brief quiver, Natalia's, repeated three times, literally throb. As Beliaev carries her across the front of the stage with her front leg bent at the knee and her back leg stretched in *arabesque*, her front leg beats rapidly in and out. It reminds us of Vera's beats but is now more emphatic, charged with passion. The lifts are bigger than those in Vera's duet, more like the lifts in *Marguerite and Armand*. Natalia runs, jumps and is thrown high in the air before being caught in a kind of fish-dive position. As in the earlier work, it suggests the intense even violent feeling between the two.

The duet also contains many *arabesques*: deep in a *penchée*, upright with one arm curved above the head, on the floor and some which transfer into an *attitude* in front. There is a moment when Natalia drops to her knees and with Beliaev holding her hands, together they perform a quick tangling circle of the arms, which ends when Beliaev pulls her into a deep *penchée arabesque*. It is a moment of acute tenderness and profound intimacy. Ashton makes us see Seymour's beautifully supple *arabesque* but he also uses it to express the passion and intimacy of the couple.

The *bourrée couru* returns as a major step and is used initially by Natalia to accompany a moment when Beliaev walks alongside her, echoing a similar moment in Vera's duet where it is unashamedly light-hearted. It recurs in the final section when Natalia drifts from side to side, barely held under the arms by Beliaev but, this time, it heralds the end of the relationship.

This duet in *Month* is truly tragic. It registers the ecstatic moment but also its finality. When the orchestra enters near the end of the piano solo in the Andante spianato, Natalia becomes aware that her moment of intense bliss is ending. Vera bursts in and, observing the pair, alerts the whole household: a violent delight with a violent end. The ballet rushes to its conclusion with the hasty departure of both Beliaev and Rakitin, leaving Natalia with a bleak future.

Coming near the end of Ashton's career, this ballet is a summary of the dance movement he made for Seymour, drawing on her talents: her deep arabesque, fluent movement and liquid arms, her acting skills and promoting her highly arched feet, constructing phrases which twist, turn, curve, swoop and bend. The role of Beliaev also makes the most of those of Dowell. Ashton drew out qualities rarely seen then in a male dancer and so closely tied to the role. The solo movement focussing almost entirely on an extravagant use of the shoulders, upper back and arms makes us aware of Beliaev's expressive and communicative gifts and later, in the exuberant quartet, his high spirits. It demands technical and interpretative sophistication, showing Dowell at his peak.

Conclusion

The Royal Ballet generally performs *A Month in the Country* every couple of years, indicating that it is one of Ashton's most popular creations. While he allowed his dancers to influence the work, he has given future dancers enough space to enable them to interpret the dance movement successfully if they wish. Both of the works covered in this chapter were made with powerful creators and yet this has not placed restrictions on their interpretability. Where *Daphnis* is more concerned with dance movement and the ways in which academic ballet can be fused with other dance movement, *Month* uses it for narrative ends.

Ashton's aims differ, but throughout both works, his stylistic features recur. Linking steps used as major movements, academic steps cut short or used for purposes other than their original intention and steps chosen specifically for their ability to create texture within a smooth phrase. His characteristic phrase patterns too appear: phrases in which the arms so disturb the space around the body that they seem wholly made-up of arm movements, phrases with complex floor patterns and phrases with contrasting dynamic or energy elements. In others, upper and lower body have different patterns, creating polyrhythms in the body and there are some phrases in which the dynamic emphasis draws attention to a body design.

Jordan has described how inventive Ashton is with his music and how despite musical repeats, he confounds our expectations with a different phrase of dance movement, so a repeated phrase of music does not have a similar repetition of the dance movement. With his dance movement phrases, he does quite the opposite, using the same steps again and again, though in different contexts, and with a variety of altered dynamics. When these steps reappear, they are often given unusual companions, for instance, a *pas de bourrée* is followed by a non-travelling *rond de jambe à terre*, and some have altered dynamics, the emphasis is changed, so we no longer recognise them. He does the same with his phrases; the same movement pattern is performed in both these duets, but not only are we unaware of this, it seems to look quite different second time around. It is part of Ashton's choreographic intelligence to be so inventive with so little; he limits his choice of movement and, in so doing, develops a rich and complex dance vocabulary.

In their different ways, both *Daphnis and Chloe* and *A Month in the Country* are quintessentially Ashton and they demonstrate the potency of his art, intense, varied but, more than anything, possessing an apparent simplicity. Walking, running, stepping, swooping and a lack of breathing space are some of the most significant aspects of his choreography, seemingly easy yet fiendishly difficult to perform. This is really the essence of Ashton's style.

1. Neufeld, James (1996) 'The Expanded Moment: Narrative and Abstract Impulses in Ashton's Ballets', in eds. Jordan, Stephanie and Andrée Grau, *Following Sir Fred's Steps: Ashton's Legacy*, London: Dance Books, 22-28.

2. Ashton quoted in Vaughan (1977) 124.

3. Ashton, Frederick (1958) 'The Subject Matter of Ballet: A Symposium', in Haskell, Arnold, ed. *The Ballet Annual 1959*, London: Adam and Charles Black, 39.

4. Ashton, Frederick (1951, second ed. 1992) 'Notes on Choreography', in Sorrell, Walter ed. *The Dance has Many Faces*, Chicago: Capella Books, 31-33.

5. Ibid.

6 Ashton, (1958), 39.

7. Armstrong, Karen (2005) *A Short History of Myth*, Edinburgh: Cannongate, 7.

8. for information on this see Morris, Geraldine (2008) 'Visionary Dances: Ashton's Ballets of the Second World War', *Dance Research*, 26, no.2, 168-188.

9. Vaughan (1977) 249.

10. Vaughan, David (1995) *DanceView* , 12, no. 3 Spring, no page numbers available.

11. Emmanuel, Maurice, & Beauley, Harriet Jean, (1916) The Antique Greek Dance, after Sculptured and Painted Figures ... by Maurice Emmanuel .. with drawings by A. Collombar and the author, New York, London: John Lane company.

12. See too Vaughan, 1977, 248.

13. Church, Reverend Alfred (1880) *Stories from the Greek Tragedians*, London: Seeley, Jackson and Halliday; Longus (1947) *Daphnis and Chloe*, London: Richard Lesley; Gide, André (1948) *Theseus*, London: Horizon; Gide, André (1934) *Persephone*, Paris: Gallimard; Lowes Dickinson, G. (1920) *The Greek View of Life*, London: Methuen; Lang, Andrew (1924) *Tales of Troy*, London: Longmans, Green & Co.; Lang, Andrew (1924) *Tales of the Greek Seas*, London: Longmans, Green & Co.

14. Of course it was not just in the 1950s that the myths were updated. Picasso with his Minotaur drawings, made during he 1930s, had updated and confronted the myths as had James Joyce in both *Ulysses* (1922) and *Portrait of the Artist As a Young Man* (1916) amongst many others.

15. Vaughan, 1977, 246.

16. Both Marie Rambert and Ninette de Valois suggest this, though even Ashton himself admits it!

17. Quoted from Roland-Manuel's biography of Ravel in Hussey, Dyneley (1948) 'Ravel's "Daphnis and Chloe"', *Dancing Times*, no. 455, August, 581-582, though I have used the translation by Orenstein from Deborah Mawer 'Ballet and the Apotheosis of the Dance', in (2000) *Cambridge Companion to Ravel*, Cambridge: Cambridge University Press.

18. Early photographs of the production suggest they came on in Scene II with the arrival of Pan.

19. Mawer (2006) 80.

20. Jill Anne Bowden suggests it was Craxton who decided to put the dancers in contemporary dress. See my article (2008) 'Visionary Dances: Ashton's Ballets of the Second World War', *Dance Research*, 26, no.2, 168-188.

21. Morris (2008) *Dance Research*.

22. Bowden, Jill Anne (1992) 'John Craxton, Daphnis and Chloe and Greece', *The Dancing Times*, LXXXII, no. 981, 851-853.

23. Bowden (1992).

24. Bowden (1992).

25. Bowden (1992).

26. Daneman, Meridith (2004) *Margot Fonteyn*, London: Viking Books, 266.

27. Schama, Simon (1995, my edition 2004) *Landscape and Memory*, London: Harper Perennial, 517.

28. quoted in Mawer, Deborah (2006) *The Ballets of Maurice Ravel: Creation and Interpretation*, Hampshire and Vermont: Ashgate, 21.

29. Mawer, (2006) 84.

30. Haskell, Arnold (1952) *The Ballet Annual*, Adam and Charles Black, 26.

31. Morrison, Simon (2004) 'The Origins of *Daphnis and Chloe*', *Caliber: Nineteenth Century Music*, 28, Summer, 50-75.

32. Morrison, (2004) 58.

33. Morrison (2004) 56.

34. Morrison (2004) 58.

35. Morrison (2004) 57.

36. Mawer (2006) 93.

37. Mawer, (2006) 103.

38. Hunt, Yvonne (1996) *Traditional Dance in Greek Culture*, Athens: Centre for Asia Minor Studies: Music Folklore Archive.

39. Hunt, ibid, 21.

40. Hunt, ibid. 17.

41. Anon (1951) *The Stage*, 12th April, no page numbers available.

42. In *fille*, this occurs in the picnic scene with Colas and Lise and the arabesque sequence across the front of the stage reappears in Act II where the Friends perform during the finale.

43. Mawer, 120.

44. Clarke, Mary (1995) 'Obituary, Michael Somes', *Dancing Times*, LXXXV, no. 1012, 347.

45. Haddakin, Lilian and Kathrine Sorley Walker, eds. (1975) *Writings on Dance 1938-68 by A.V. Coton*, London: Dance Books, 78.

46. Vaughan 1977, 248.

47. Quoted in Vaughan, 248, from an interview with Walter Terry.

48. Morrison, (2004), 69.

49. Morrison, 2004.

50. Brunelleschi, Elsa (1951) 'Four Opinions on *Daphnis and Chloe*', *Ballet*, June, 11, no. 5, 11.

51. Bland, Alexander (1951) 'Four Opinions on *Daphnis and Chloe*', *Ballet*, June, 11, no. 5, 13.

52. Anon, (6/2.1976) 'Fred the Great', *Evening Standard*, no page numbers available.

53. Ibid.

54. Sorley Walker, Kathrine (19/02/1976) 'A Month in the Country', *The Stage*, no page numbers available.

55. Bland, Alexander (8/02/1976) 'Ashton's Month in the Country', *Observer*, no page numbers available.

56. Berlin, Isaiah (1979) *Russian Thinkers*, Middlesex UK: Penguin Books, 273.

57. Kavanagh, 488.

58. Buckle, Richard (1982) *In the Wake of Diaghilev*, London: Collins, 279.

59. Quote taken from Wordsworth, William (1798), *Lines Composed a few miles above Tintern Abbey, on re-visiting the banks of the Wye during a tour, July 13,1798*, in Harrison, G.B. (1950) *A Book of English Poetry*, London: Penguin Books, 245.

60. See Vaughan, 1977, 302.

61. Kavanagh, 1996, 547.

62. Jordan, Stephanie (2000) *Moving Music: Dialogues with Music in Twentieth Century Ballet*, London: Dance Books, 263.

63. Jordan, 264.

64. Strachan, Alan (2003) 'Julia Trevelyan Oman', *The Independent*. 13th October, no page numbers available.

65. Anderson, Jack (1976) 'Life Literature and The Royal Ballet: New York Spring Season', *Dance Magazine*, August, 47.

66. Vaughan, (1977) 403.

67. Redgrave Michael (1943) 'Introduction', in Williams, Emlyn (translator) *A Month in the Country*, London: William Heinemann, xi.

68. Ibid, xii.

69. Ibid, xiv.

70. Ibid, xiii.

71. Redgrave in Turgenev, xiii.

72. Turgenev, Ivan, Williams trans, 13.

73. Ashton's copy of the play in Ashton Library Royal Ballet School, 49.

74. In Ashton's copy of the play the work is divided into two acts only.

75. Turgenev, Ivan, trans. Emlyn Willians (1943) *A Month in the Country*, London: William Heinemann, 6-13.

76. Vaughan (1977) 394.

77. Lawson, Joan (1961) 'The New Generation of The Royal Ballet', in Haskell, Arnold, ed, *The Ballet Annual*, London: Adam and Charles Black, 94-103.

78. Anon (1996) 'The Solo Seal Variations', in Jordan, Stephanie and Andree Grau, eds. *Following Sir Fred's Steps*, London: Dance Books, 158-160.

79. Austin, Richard (1980) *Lynn Seymour: An Authorised Biography*, London: Angus Robertson Publishers, 20.

80. Dowell in Dromgoole, Nicholas and Leslie Spatt (1976) *Sibley and Dowell*, London: Collins, 22.

81. Vaughan (1977) 397.

82. For a longer discussion of the *Baiser* variation see Morris, Geraldine (2006) 'Ashton and MacMillan in Fairyland: Contrasting Styles in *Le Baiser de la Fée*', *Dance Chronicle*, 29, no.2, 133-160.

83. Jordan (2000) 264.

84. Jordan (2000) 263.

85. Croce, Arlene (1978) *Afterimages*, London: A & C Black, 222.

86. According to Rhonda Ryman (1998, *Classical Ballet Terms* Cecchetti, Toronto: Dance Collection Danse Press/es, 91) this is an RAD term and it is described as a *grand jeté en tournant en dedans*, though her description is slightly different from that of the RAD, see Ryman, Rhonda (1995) *Dictionary of Classical Ballet Terminology*,, London: Royal Academy of Dancing, 78.

87. Morris, Geraldine (2001) 'Dance Partnerships: Ashton and His Dancers', *Dance Research*, 19, no.1, 11-59.

88. Seymour, Lynn (1985) *Lynn*, London: Panther Books, 391.

89. quoted in Newman, Barbara (1982) *Striking a Balance: Dancers Talk About Dancing*, London: Elm Tree Books, 231.

90. This opening movement could also be described as a *coupé fouetté raccourci* but having the sliding movement before also alters this movement. That term does not appear in Beaumont's dictionary and Ryman (1998) indicates that the term does not

come into the Manuals, so was not used by Cecchetti. Whatever the terminology, Ashton did not tend to use it when working with dancers but demonstrated and asked for a quality rather than a step.

91. Strictly speaking chaser means to chase but as Glasstone points out, it has also come to be interpreted as a sliding step. See Glasstone (2001) *Classical Ballet Terms: An Illustrated Dictionary*, London: Dance Books, 15.

92. Jordan (2000) 263.

93. Vaughan, 1999.

94. Acocella, Joan (2007) *Twenty Eight Artists and Two Saints*, New York: Pantheon Books, 225-6.

95. Macaulay, Alastair (1987) *Some Views and Reviews of Ashton's Choreography*, Guildford: National Resource Centre for Dance, 36.

96. Schama, Simon (2004) *Hang Ups: Essays on Painting (Mostly)*, London: BBC Books, 67.

Where Now for Ashton Style?

Ashton would probably be surprised by the detailed attention I have given to these six ballets but each shows the variety of his work, in his choice of subject matter, his choreography and the consistency of his style. Although he is generally given the label of 'classical choreographer' I find this description limiting. It leads dancers to perform the choreography as though it was synonymous with classroom movement and, as a result, the vital elements of his style are removed or smoothed out. Using such a label can conceal rather than illuminate the richness of both his dance movement style and choreography. His choreography challenges the classroom movement, changed to accommodate his own personal idiom. Ashton left a rich heritage of dance movement and choreography for future dancers to interpret. But its survival depends on recognition that the *danse d'école* is not in itself the dance and so very different from choreographed dance.

While giving an inventory of steps and how they should be performed is neither appropriate nor desirable as a way of demonstrating stylistic traits, I can offer a brief summary of what I consider to be the major features of Ashton's dance style. He made small adjustments to the steps of the *danse d'école* and this created difference and, although he uses a broad range of steps, his stylistic traits are found in the smaller, less significant steps. So, linking steps and steps usually seen as little more than training exercises, such as the *rond de jambe à terre*, often become major motifs in his dances. He plays with all these steps, clipping them, amplifying them and altering the effort elements to create contrast. Sometimes he arrests the flow of the phrase by abbreviating one movement in order to enlarge another. So a key feature of his style is the emphasis on dynamic contrast. From stage dancing, he introduced polyrhythms in the body, so that different body parts move to different rhythms and, like Nijinska, he removed the 'breath pauses' from phrases, creating sustained continuous threads of movement. This pushes the dancer to move faster and diminishes the emphasis on shape. There are too distinctive body designs, many of which are characterised by a twist of the upper body and there are some phrases which appear razor-sharp, created by an emphasis on the body design. Virtual lines made by the limbs, particularly the arms, are complex in an Ashton dance. The space around the body is disturbed and intricate, created by these virtual lines. And Ashton's phrases are complex, restlessly moving back and forth across the stage requiring the dancer to twist, turn, curve and swoop. While there is little doubt that Ashton's dancers made a significant contribution to the style, they did not dominate it, so the style can be retained without their presence. Today's dancers would benefit from examining the performances of these earlier dancers; not in order to imitate but to understand which aspect of their talent is given priority.

It is now over twenty years since Ashton died, too long ago for most of today's dancers to remember how his work was performed during his lifetime and we need to give these dancers the opportunity to understand and value his work. In outlining my interpretation of his dance and choreographic style, I hope to have written something that could be useful to future dancers and rehearsal directors. Style is not fixed but there are aspects that need to remain. Speed is of the essence and keeping up the brisk tempi of the Ashton era prevents dancers from emphasising shape at the expense of motion. Alterations that simplify the movement by removing a complex action of the upper body damage the style too but when a dancer amplifies the dance and makes us look at other possibilities with the movement, it can be exciting.

Ashton's dances provide dancers with a fertile ground for exploration. They are also exhilarating and interesting for audiences and, as examples of superb craftsmanship, from which new choreographers can learn, they are supreme. He was a master of understatement, so there is not much spectacle in his work but there is poetry, fun, intensity and above all humanity.

Ashton's work is part of a particular era though not confined to the time in which it was first choreographed. Appreciating and understanding past works adds to our understanding of today's works and equally some of today's dances can enhance our knowledge of the past. Just as Ashton's dialogue with Petipa changes our appreciation of Petipa's ballets, so the references in David Bintley's work enhance our view of Ashton's. The present is always in dialogue with the past.

During his lifetime, Ashton was respected and honoured by the establishment but his dances were also loved by the public. An Ashton evening would always fill the House. His dancers venerated him too and as Fonteyn put it, 'he was, above all, a very *human* being, and for that, as much as for his extraordinary talents, he was beloved by all'.[1] His works are still valued but their movement style is very unlike that of today. With the establishment of the Ashton Foundation, steps are being taken to secure their future and, with the goodwill of both the Royal Ballet and its School, their future now should be more assured. It is my hope too that this book will have also contributed to their survival.

1 Quoted in Kavanagh (1996) 598

Bibliography

Acocella, Joan (2007) *Twenty Eight Artists and Two Saints*, New York: Pantheon Books

Adshead, Janet ed. (1989) *Dance Analysis: Theory and Practice*, London: Dance Books

Adshead-Lansdale, Janet (1999) *Dancing Texts: Intertextuality and Interpretation*, London: Dance Books

Adshead-Lansdale, Janet (2007) *The Struggle With the Angel: A Poetics of Lloyd Newson's Strange Fish*, Alton: Dance Books

Amory, Mark (1998) *Lord Berners: the Last Eccentric*, London: Chatto & Windus

Anderson, Jack (1976) 'Life Literature and The Royal Ballet: New York Spring Season', *Dance Magazine*, August, 47

Anon (1952) 'Svetlana Beriosova', *Ballet*, July, 12, no. 7, 10-13

Anon (1982) 'Retrospective', *Illustrated London News*, February, no page numbers available

Anon (2004) *100 Years of Dance: A History of the ISTD Dance Examinations Board*, London: ISTD

Armstrong, Karen (2005) *A Short History of Myth*, Edinburgh: Cannongate

Ashton, Frederick (1951/1992) 'Some Notes on Choreography', in Sorell, Walter, ed. *The Dance Has Many Faces*, Chicago: Capella Books, 31-34

Ashton, Frederick (1954) 'Marie Rambert: A Tribute from Frederick Ashton', *Dancing Times*, no. 412, January, 151

Ashton, Frederick (1958) 'The Subject Matter of Ballet: A Symposium', in Haskell, Arnold, ed. *The Ballet Annual 1959*, London: Adam and Charles Black, 38-39

Ashton, Frederick in Crisp, Clement in Cohen (1974) 'Frederick Ashton: A Conversation', in Cohen, Selma Jeanne, ed. *Dance as a Theatre Art*, London: Dance Books, 169-173

Ashton, Frederick (1976) 'From Sir Frederick Ashton', in Crisp, Clement, Anya Sainsbury and Peter Williams, eds. *Ballet Rambert: 50 Years and On*, London: Scolar Press, 34

Bachmann, Marie-Laure (1991, reprinted 1993) *Dalcroze Today: An Education Through and Into Music*, trans. Parlett, David, Oxford: Clarendon Press

Balanchine, George (1937) 'Ballet Goes Native', *Dance*, December, 13

Balanchine, George (1992) 'Marginal Notes on the Dance', in Sorell, Walter ed. *The Dance Has Many Faces*, Chicago: Cappella Books, 35-43

Banes, Sally (1994) 'Balanchine and Black Dance', *Writing Dance in the Age of Postmodernism*, New England, Hanover and London: Wesleyan University Press, 53-69

Bartenieff, Irmgaard, Martha Davis and Forrestine Paulay (1970) *Four Adaptations of Effort Theory in Research and Teaching*, New York: Dance Notation Bureau

Bay-Cheng, Sarah (2004) *Mama Dada: Gertrude Stein's Avant-Garde Theatre*, New York and London: Routledge

Beardsley, Monroe and William, Kurtz Wimsatt (1954) 'The Intentional Fallacy' in Wimsatt, William Kurtz *The Verbal Icon: Studies in the Meaning of Poetry*, Lexington: University of Kentucky Press, 3-18

Beaton, Cecil (1951) *Ballet*, London: Wingate

Beaton, Cecil (1950) *Vogue*, no title and no page numbers available

Beaumont, Cyril 'On examinations in the Cecchetti Syllabus', *The Dance Journal*, 1, 9, February (1927) 41, 43, 44

Beaumont, Cyril (1937, revised 1949) *Complete Book of Ballets*, London: C.W. Beaumont

Beaumont, Cyril (1945) *The Diaghilev Ballet in London*, London: C.W. Beaumont, 180

Beaumont, Cyril (1945) *Anna Pavlova*, London: C.W. Beaumont

Beaumont, Cyril (1955) 'In Memoriam - Lionel Bradley', in Haskell, Arnold, ed. *The Ballet Annual 1955*, London: Adam and Charles Black, 46 and 49

Bedells, Phyllis (1954) *My Dancing Days*, London: Phoenix House

Bennett, Toby (1997) 'Cecchetti and the British Tradition', *Dance Now*, 6, no.3, Autumn, 55-59

Bennett, Toby (1998) 'Cecchetti Movement and Repertoire in Performance', *Twenty First Annual Conference*, Oregon: Society of Dance History Scholars, 203-209

Berg, Shelley and Jill Beck (1996) 'Approaches to the Revival of Les Masques' in Jordan, Stephanie and Andrée Grau, eds. *Following Sir Fred's Steps*, London : Dance Books, 38-46

Berlin, Isaiah (1979) *Russian Thinkers*, Middlesex UK: Penguin Books

Blackmuir, R.P. (1958/1983) 'The Swan in Zurich', in Copeland, Roger and Marshall Cohen eds. *What is Dance?*, Oxford: Oxford University Press, 354-361

Bland, Alexander (1951) 'Four Opinions on *Daphnis and Chloe*', *Ballet*, June, 11, no. 5, 13

Bland, Alexander (1955) 'Marie Rambert', *The Ballet Annual*, no. 9, London: Adam and Charles Black

Bland, Alexander (8th February, 1976) 'Ashton's Month in the Country', *Observer*, no page numbers available

Bland, Alexander (1981) *The Royal Ballet: The First 50 Years*, London: Threshold Books

Blasis, Carlo (1968/1954) *An Elementary Treatise Upon the Theory and Prac-*

tice of the Art of Dancing, trans. Mary Stewart Evans, New York: Dover Books

Boos, Paul (1995) 'Teaching Balanchine Abroad', *Ballet Review*, 23, no. 2, Summer, 69-78

Bowden, Jill Anne (1992) 'John Craxton, Daphnis and Chloe and Greece', *Dancing Times*, June LXXXII, no. 981, 851-853

Bradley, Lionel (1937-1953) *Ballet Bulletin*, in the collection of the Theatre Museum, Victoria and Albert Museum, London

Brunelleschi, Elsa (1951) 'Four Opinions on *Daphnis and Chloe*', *Ballet*, June, 11, no. 5, 11

Buckland (2007) 'Crompton's Campaign: The Professionalisation of Dance Pedagogy in Late Victorian England', *Dance Research*, 25, no. 1, 22

Buckland Teresa (2011) *Society Dancing: Fashionable Bodies in England 1870-1920*, London: Palgrave

Buckle, Richard (25th July 1950) 'Ballet', *Observer*, no page numbers available

Buckle, Richard (1980) *Buckle at the Ballet*, London: Dance Books

Buckle, Richard (1947) '"Abstract" Ballet', *Ballet*, 4, no.5, November, 20-24

Buckle, Richard (1982) *In the Wake of Diaghilev*, London: Collins

Burgin, Victor (1986) *The End of Art Theory: Criticism and Postmodernity*, London: MacMillan

Burt, Ramsay (1995) *The Male Dancer: Bodies, Spectacle, Sexualities*, London: Routledge

Carter, Alexander (2004) 'Destabilising the Discipline: Critical Debates about History and Their Impact on the Study of Dance', in Carter, Alexander, ed. *Rethinking Dance History: A Reader*, London and New York: Routledge

Carter, Alexandra (2005) 'London 1908: A Synchronic View of Dance History', *Dance Research*, XXIII, no. 1, Summer, 36-50

Cavell, Stanley (1969/1976) *Must We Mean What We Say?*, Cambridge: Cambridge University Press

Clarke, Mary (1955) *The Sadler's Wells Ballet: A History and Appreciation*, London: A & C Black

Clarke, Mary (1956) 'Elaine Fifield: Ballerina', *Dancing Times*, October XLVII, no. 553, 20

Clarke, Mary (1961) 'The Brink of Greatness', *Dancing Times*, March LI, no. 606, 345-6

Clarke Mary (1969) 'The First Wedding Bouquet', *Dancing Times*, November LX, 69

Clarke, Mary (1995) 'Obituary, Michael Somes', *Dancing Times*, LXXXV, no. 1012, 347

Clarke, Mary (2004) 'Royal Ballet', *Dancing Times*, 95, no. 1132, December, 51, 53

Clarke, Simone (2007) 'Talking Point', *Dancing Times*, 97, no1157, January, 11

Challis, Chris (1999) 'Dancing Bodies: Can The Art Of Dance Be Restored To Dance Studies?', in McFee, Graham, ed. *Dance Education and Philosophy*, Oxford: Meyer & Meyer Sport (UK), 143-153

Chappell, William (1951) *Fonteyn: Impressions of a Ballerina*, London: Spring Books

Coton, A.V. (Edward Haddakin) (10th January 1968) 'Brilliant and Banal 'Jazz Calendar', *Daily Telegraph*, no page numbers available

Coton, A.V (1975) *Writings on Dance*, Sorley Walker, Kathrine and Lilian Haddakin, eds. London: Dance Books

Crisp, Clement (2007) 'Into the Labyrinth: Kenneth MacMillan and his Ballets', *Dance Research*, 25, no. 2, winter, 188-195

Croce, Arlene (1978) 'The Royal Ballet in New York', *Afterimages*, London: Adam and Charles Black, 375

Daneman, Meridith (2004) *Margot Fonteyn*, London: Viking Books

De Mille, Agnes (1958/1982) *Dance to the Piper* and *Promenade Home*, New York: Da Capo Press

Denby, Edwin (1986) 'A letter on New York City's Ballet', in *Dance Writings*, London: Dance Books, 415-430

De Valois, Ninette (1937) *Invitation to the Dance*, London: The Bodley Head

De Valois, Ninette (1957) *Come Dance With Me*, London: Hamish Hamilton

De Valois, Ninette (1977) *Step by Step*, London: W.H. Allen

De Zoete, Beryl (1950) 'The 1,000,000 Mile Journey: V with a reminiscence of Jaques-Dalcroze, *Ballet*, 10, no.2, 34-38

Dickinson, Peter (2008) *Lord Berners: Composer, Writer, Painter*, Woodbridge: The Boydell Press

Dixon Gottschild, Brenda (2001) 'Stripping the Emperor: The Africanist Presence in American Concert Dance', in Dils, Ann and Ann Cooper Albright eds. *Moving History/Dancing Cultures: A Dance History Reader*, Middletown USA: Wesleyan University Press, 332-341

Dodds, Sherril (2004) *Dance on Screen: Genres and Media from Hollywood to Experimental Dance*, Basingstoke, Hampshire and New York: Palgrave

Dominic, Zoë and John Selwyn Gilbert (1971) *Frederick Ashton: A Choreographer and his Ballets*, London: Harrap

Doob, Penelope (1978) 'A Conversation with Sir Frederick Ashton', *York Dance Review*, no.7, Spring, 16-25

Dowler, Gerald (2011) 'British Style RIP', in *Dancing Times*, June, 101, no. 1210, 27-29

Dromgoole, Nicholas and Leslie Spatt (1976) *Sibley and Dowell*, London: Collins

Dydo, Ulla (2003) *Gertrude Stein: The Language That Rises 1923-1934*, Evanston, Illinois: Northwestern University Press

Edwards, Leslie (2003) *In Good Company*, London: Dance Books

Emmanuel, Maurice (1916) *The Antique Greek Dance, after Sculptured and Painted Figures ... by Maurice Emmanuel ...* with drawings by A. Collombar and the author, trans. Harriet Jean Beauley, New York, London: John Lane Company

Espinosa, Edouard (1914) 'Attitudes and Arabesques', *Dancing Times*, no.51, December, 76-81

Espinosa, Edouard (1916) 'Some Errors in Tuition', *Dancing Times*, no. 73, October, 79-85

Espinosa, Edward (1946) *And Then He Danced: The Life of Espinosa By Himself*, London: Sampson Low and Marston

Fifield, Elaine (1967) *In My Shoes: the Autobiography of Elaine Fifield*, London: W.H. Allen

Fonteyn, Margot (1975) *Margot Fonteyn*, London: W.H. Allen

Franks, Arthur (1957) 'Beryl Grey', *Dancing Times*, April, XLVII, no. 559, 306-7

Garafola, Lynn (1989) *Diaghilev's Ballets Russes*, New York and Oxford: Oxford University Press

Genée, Adeline (1922) 'Correct Arms', *Dancing Times*, no.139, April, 595-599

Genné, Beth (1982) 'PJS Richardson and The Birth of British Ballet', *Dance History Scholars Proceedings*, Fifth Annual Conference, Harvard University, February.94-101

Genné, Beth (1996) *The Making of a Choreographer: Ninette de Valois and Bar aux Folies-Bergère*, Wisconsin: Society of Dance History Scholars

Gifford, Mary (2007) *Lord Berners: Aspects of a Biography*, Unpublished PhD Thesis, Kings College, University of London

Glasstone, Richard (1994) 'The Royal Ballet School: A Neglected Legacy', *Dance Now*, 3, no. 4, 50-53

Glasstone, Richard (2008) 'Talking Point', *Dancing Times*, 98, no. 1174, 11

Glasstone, Richard (2001) *Classical Ballet Terms: An Illustrated Dictionary*, London: Dance Books

Gottlieb, Robert (20th June 2004) 'Importing A Native Son: Honouring Balanchine in Russia', *The New York Observer*, no page numbers available

Guest, Ivor, (1992) *Ballet in Leicester Square*, London: Dance Books

Haskell, Arnold (1930) *The Marie Rambert Ballet*, London: British-Continental Press

Haskell, Arnold and P. J. S. Richardson (1932, facsimile reprint 2010) *Who's Who in Dancing 1932*, London: The Noverre Press

Haskell, Arnold (June 2, 1937) *The Bystander*, 460

Haskell, Arnold (1937) 'Balletomane's Log Book', *Dancing Times*, no. 321, June, 280, 281, 287

Haskell, Arnold (28th April, 1937) 'A New Choral Ballet', *The Daily Telegraph'*, Wednesday 12

Holmes, Olive ed. (1982) *Motion Arrested: Dance Reviews of H.T. Parker*, Connecticut: Wesleyan University Press

Hunt, Yvonne (1996) *Traditional Dance in Greek Culture*, Athens: Centre for Asia Minor Studies: Music Folklore Archive

Hussey, Dyneley (1948) 'Ravel's "Daphnis and Chloe"', *Dancing Times*, no. 455, August, 581-582,

Hutcheon, Linda (1989) *The Politics of Postmodernism*, London: Routledge,

Hutchinson-Guest, Ann (1989) *Choreo-Graphics: A Comparison of Dance Notaion Systems from the Fifteenth Century to the Present*, New York: Gordon and Breach

Irving, Robert (1991) 'The Conductor Speaks', *Dance and Dancers*, November, 20-21

Jarman, Derek (1984) *Dancing Ledge*, London: Quartet

Jarman, Derek (1994) *Chroma*, London: Random House

Jennings, Luke (2004/05) 'They Must Be Wedded', *Dance Now* 13, no. 4 Winter, 20-23

Jewell, Derek (21st January, 1968) 'Modern Varieties', *Sunday Times*, no page numbers available

Johns, Eric (11th January 68) 'Royal Ballet's Jazz Romp' *The Stage*, no page numbers available

Jones, Bryony (2003) *The Music of Lord Berners (1883-1950) 'The Versatile Peer'*, Aldershot, Hampshire: Ashgate

Jordan, Stephanie and Andrée Grau, (1996) *Following Sir Fred's Steps: Ashton's Legacy*, London: Dance Books

Jordan, Stephanie (2000) *Moving Music*, London: Dance Books

Jordan, Stephanie (2007) *Stravinsky Dances: Re-Visions Across A Century*, Alton: Dance Books

Karsavina, Tamara (1930) *Dancing Times*, quoted in *Dancing Times*, (1995) January LXXXV no. 1012, 419

Karsavina, Tamara (1953) 'Second Act of Giselle', *Dancing Times*, November no.518, 75

Kavanagh, Julie (1996) *Secret Muses: The Life of Frederick Ashton*, London: Faber and Faber

Kelly Brigitte (2009) *'Mim': A Personal Memoir of Marie Rambert*, Alton: Dance Books

Kersley, Leo and Janet Sinclair (1997) *A Dictionary of Ballet Terms*, London: A &C Black

Kersley, Leo (1993) 'Stanislas Idzikowski', in Bremser, Martha, ed. *Interna-*

tional Dictionary of Ballet, Detroit, London, Washington: Saint James Press, 687-690

Kavanagh, Julie (2007) *Rudolph Nureyev: The Life*, London: Penguin Books

Konecny, Mark (2004) 'Dance and Movement in the Cabaret', *A Journal of Russian Culture*, 10, 133-146

Kostrovitskaya, Vera and Alexei Pisarev (1995) *School of Classical Dance*, London: Dance Books

Lawson, Joan (1955) 'Madame Chrysanthème', *Dancing Times*, May, no. 536, 485

Lawson, Joan (1961) ''The New Generation of The Royal Ballet', in Haskell, Arnold, ed, *The Ballet Annual*, London: Adam and Charles Black, 94-103

Lieven, Peter (1936) *The Birth of Ballets-Russes*, London: George Allen and Unwin

Macaulay, Alastair (1983) 'Ashton our Contemporary: Trivia and Rhapsodies', *Dancing Times*, LXXII, no 874, 784-786

Macaulay, Alastair (1987) *Some Views and Reviews of Ashton's Choreography*, Guildford: National Resource Centre for Dance

Macaulay, Alastair (2003) "A Question of Balance", "Sur quel pied danser", *Conference on Dance and Literature*, Lincoln College, Oxford, April, unpublished paper

McFee, Graham (1992) *Understanding Dance,* London and New York: Routledge

McFee, Graham (2011) *The Philosophical Aesthetics of Dance: Identity, Performance and Understanding*, Alton: Dance Books

Mackrell, Judith (2004) 'Royal Ballet Triple Bill', *The Guardian*, 25th October, no page numbers available

Mara, Thalia (1966) *The Language of Ballet: A Dictionary*, New Jersey: Dance Horizons

Mawer, Deborah (2000) 'Ballet and the Apotheosis of the Dance', *Cambridge Companion to Ravel*, Cambridge: Cambridge University Press, Ebook: Digital Object Identifier: 10.1017/CCOL9780521640268.009

Mawer, Deborah (2006) *The Ballets of Maurice Ravel: Creation and Interpretation*, Hampshire and Vermont: Ashgate

Mears, Stephen (2007) 'Talking Point', *Dancing Times*, 97, no. 1159, March, 11

Meinertz, Alexander (2005) *Vera Volkova: A Biography*, trans. Alexander Meinertz and Paula Hostrup-Jessen, Alton: Dance Books

Meisner, Nadine (25th May 1999) 'Obituary', *The Independent*, no page numbers available

Mitchell, Donald (1981) *Britten & Auden in the Thirties: The Year 1936*, London: Faber and Faber

M. J. (James Monahan?) (29th April 1937) 'Ballet At Sadler's Wells', *The Manchester Guardian*, 12

Monahan, James (1965) 'Dividends of Nostalgia', *Dancing Times*, LV, no. 652, January, 177-179

Moore, Lilian (1950) 'Ashton's New Ballet', *Dancing Times*, no. 475, April, 410-411

Morley, Sheridan (1969) *A Talent to Amuse*, London: Heineman

Morris, Gay (2005) 'Balanchine's Bodies', *Body & Society*, 11, no. 4, 19- 44

Morris, Geraldine: (2000) 'The Role of Dance History in Performance Interpretation', *Dance History: The Teaching and Learning of Dance History: Proceedings of the Society of European Dance History Scholars Conference*, 92-102

Morris, Geraldine (2001) 'Dance Partnerships: Ashton and His Dancers', *Dance Research*, 19, no.1, 11-59

Morris, Geraldine (2003) 'Problems with Ballet: Steps, Style and Training', *Research in Dance Education*, 4, no.1, 17-30

Morris, Geraldine (2004) 'Ballet as Sport v Ballet as Theatre: Is the Qualitative at odds with the Mechanical', *All About Ballet, Proceedings of the Society of European Dance History Scholars Conference*, www.eadh.com,

Morris, Geraldine (2006) 'Ashton and MacMillan in Fairyland: Contrasting Styles in *Le Baiser de la Fée*', *Dance Chronicle*, 29, no.2, 133-160

Morris, Geraldine, (2008) 'Artistry or Mere Technique: The Value of the Ballet Competition', *Research in Dance Education*, 9, no 1, 39-54

Morris, Geraldine (2008) 'Visionary Dances: Ashton's Ballets of the Second World War', *Dance Research*, 26, no.2, 168-188

Morrison, Simon (2004) 'The Origins of *Daphnis and Chloe*', *Caliber: Nineteenth Century Music*, 28, Summer, 50-75

Nears, Colin and Bob Lockyer (1988) *Dance Masterclass: The Dream*, BBC Production

Nerina, Nadia (1960) 'Some Aspects of the Classical Technique', in Haskell, Arnold, ed. *The Ballet Annual*, 79-83

Neufeld, James (1996) 'The Expanded Moment: Narrative and Abstract Impulses in Ashton's Ballets', in Jordan, Stephanie and Andrée Grau, eds. *Following Sir Fred's Steps: Ashton's Legacy*, London: Dance Books, 22-28

Neuman, Shirley and Ira B. Nadel (1988) *Gertrude Stein and the Making of Literature*, Hampshire and London: MacMillan Press

Newman, Barbara (1982) *Striking a Balance*, London: Hamish Hamilton

Newman, Barbara (2004) 'Yuri Fateyev', *Grace Under Pressure*, Alton: Dance Books

Nicholas, Larraine (2007) *Dancing in Utopia: Dartington Hall and its Dancers*, Alton: Dance Books

Index

Acocella, Joan 207

Adshead-Lansdale, Janet 9, 10, 12, 13, 14, 16, 18, 21

Addison, Errol 196

Amory, Mark 30

Antique Greek Dance, The 175

Armelagos, Adina 14, 16

Armstrong, John 155

Armstrong, Karen 173

Arp, Jean 157

Ashton Foundation 218

Ashton, Frederick:

Ballets:

Apparitions 64, *Baiser de la fée, Le* 64, 199, *Birthday Offering* 1, 22, 24, 27, 63, 126, 128, 129-154, 164, 198, *Brahms-Waltz* 195, *Cinderella* 64, 129, 133, 142, 144, 147, 161, 207, *Dante Sonata* 51, 103, *Daphnis and Chloé* 1, 22, 25, 26, 28, 29, 30, 64, 113, 144, 151, 165, 173, 174-189, 191, 205, 211, 212, *Dream, The* 19, 135, 162, 196, 197, 207, *Enigma Variations* 25, 112, 113, 131, 162, 174, 191, 192, 193, 196, 205, 207, *Façade* 63, 64, 87, 92, 127, 131, 133, 168, *Fille mal gardée, La* 69, 135, 141, 142, 143, 183, *Five Brahms Waltzes in the Manner of Isadora Duncan* 69, *Foyer de danse* 77, *High Yellow* 64, 159, *Homage to the Queen* 93, 136, 144, 146, *Illuminations* 1, 22, 23, 28, 29, 30, 77, 99-120, 190, *Jazz Calendar* 1, 21, 22, 24, 27, 126, 127, 154-168, 197, *Leda and the Swan* 5, 174, *Madame Chrysanthème* 133, *Marguerite and Armand* 176, 191, 197, 198, 207, 210, *Masques, Les* 64, 67, *Meditation from Thaïs* 207, *Month in the Country, A* 1, 22, 25,

26, 28, 31, 69, 139, 173, 174, 190-212, *Monotones II* 69, 115, 116, 117, 126, 155, 162, 165, *Noctambules* 128, *Ondine* 116, 117, *Patineurs, Les* 112, 126, 135, 136, 207, *Persephone* 22, 62, 140, 174, 175, *Picnic at Tintagel* 128, *Pomona* 174, *Quest, The* 146, *Rendezvous, Les* 88, 126, 133, 135, 147, Rio Grande 77, *Romeo and Juliet* 150, *Scènes de ballet* 19, 62, 69, 79, 115, 126, 136, 152, 164, 183, 207, *Sirènes, Les* 146, *Sylvia* 62, 128, 143, 152, 174, *Symphonic Variations* 19, 20, 69, 103, 116, 117, 126, 155, 208, *Tales of Beatrix Potter* 10, 11, 87, 207, *Tiresias* 29, 174, *Tragedy of Fashion, A* 59, 128, *Two Pigeons, The* 29, 113, 195, 207, 208, *Valse, La* 64, 128, *Valse nobles et sentimentales* 115, 133, *Variations on a Theme by Purcell* 136, 155, *Wanderer, The* 112, 207, *Wedding Bouquet, A* 1, 11, 21, 22, 23, 24, 27, 30, 77-99, 110, 113, 115, 119, 120, 127, 207, *Wise Virgins, The,* 103

Operas:

Albert Herring 22, *Death in Venice* 22, *Fairy Queen, The* 22, 77, *Four Saints in Three Acts* 64, 77, 78, *Manon* 22, *Orpheus* 22, 174, 196, 206, *Rossignol, Le* 22, 92, 108, 196, *Traviata, La* 22,

Style: 13, 14, 19, 22, 24, 99
 choreographic style: 59, 70
 dance movement style: 38, 59, 70, 91
 stylistic actions: *arabesque,* 16, 44, 45, 46, 50, 56, 60, 91, 96, 108, 130, 134, 137, 140, 142, 145,

147, 148, 154, 164, 165, 166, 183, 184, 187, 188, 204, 205, 209, 210, 211, *assemblé*, 56, 94, 137, 205, 206 *attitude*, 44, 46, 56, 131, 135, 140, 142, 145, 181, 205, 210, *bourrée couru*, 61, 62, 65, 66, 90, 91, 93, 94, 103, 116, 130, 137, 144, 145, 201, 203, 207, 208, 209 211, *bourrée, pas de*, 20, 21, 61, 88, 90, 91, 96, 152, 153, 199, 201, 203, 212, *chaîné*, 137, 145, 161, 166, 206, *chassé*, 61, 90, 91 199, 204, 205, 206, *coupé*, 21, 205, 206, *coupé ballonné*, 204, *coupé-posé*, 45, *coupé-jeté*, 45, *coupé renversé*, 140, *entrechat*, 17, 86, 91, 94, 116, 137, 139, *épaulement*, 48, 49, 61, 91, 92, 94, 113, 119, 136, 140 142, 146, 150, 185, 206, *glissade*, 5, 58, 91, 93, 94, 137, *grand jeté*, 54, 87, 207, *jeté*, 116, 135, 208, *pas de chat*, 5, 21, 90, 91, 94, 110, 135, 143 *petit battement*, 110, 113, 115, 135, 199, 201, 203, 210, *petit jeté*, 91, 92, 116, 117, *port de bras*, 47, 49, 55, 65, 144, 195, 17, 130, *pirouette* 137 144, 147 148, 164, 185, *posé*, 21, 54, *posé retiré*, 135, 140, *relevé*, 135, 139, 154, 183, *retiré*, 50, 54, 137, 152, 154 *rond de jambe*, 17, 126, 188 *rond de jambe à terre*, 21, 110, 116, 139, 143, 161,181, 182, 187, 199, 201, 203, 205, 207, 212, 217 *rond de jambe en l'air*, 90, 137, 145, *saut de basque en tournant*, 88, 90, 93, 135, 199, 201, 203 *sissonne*, 94, 181, 185, 201
Association of Teachers of Operatic Dancing of Great Britain (AOD) 43, 44, 45, 47, 48, 51
Astafieva, Seraphina 44, 95, 196
Astaire, Fred 64, 95, 113, 162, 165
Auden, W. H. 102

Austen, Jane 153
Autobiography of Alice B. Toklas, The 30, 78

Bachmann, Marie-Laure 53
Baer, Van Norman, Nancy 59
Bakst, Léon 180
Balanchine, George 7,8, 63, 79, 105, 106, 107, 126, 153, 155, 162, 164, 167
Ballets: *Agon* 162, *Allegro Brillante* 128, *Apollo* 164, *Diamonds* 153, *Four Temperaments, The* 167, *Luna Park or the Freaks* 79, *Rubies* 167, *Triumph of Neptune, The* 78, 79
Ballet Club 63
Ballet Rambert 30
Ballets Russes 15, 25, 38, 42, 43, 44, 53, 60, 61, 78, 95, 139, 174, 179
Ballets Russes de Monte Carlo 15
Barnett, Robert 107
Bartenieff, Imgard 18
Beaton, Cecil 22, 23, 30, 77, 103, 104, 105, 115
Beaumont, Cyril 29, 38, 44, 45, 47, 48, 65, 156
Beethoven, Ludwig van 191
Bedells, Phyllis 39, 95, 196
Bennett, Richard Rodney 22, 127, 155, 159
Bennett, Toby 49
Beriosova, Svetlana 128, 129, 138-141, 157
Berlin, Isaiah 191, 192
Berners, Gerald (Lord) 22, 23, 30, 77, 78, 79, 84, 85, 86, 87, 94, 96, 97, 99, 146
Bewicke, Hilda 40
Bey-Cheng, Sarah 78
Biches, Les 59, 60, 61, 62, 87, 88, 90, 94, 95, 113, 137, 139
Bilingin 83
Bintley, David 218
Blackmur, R.P 106
Bland, Alexander 52, 54, 191

Blasis, Carlo 16, 17
Blue 158
Bolm, Adolph 38, 39
Boos, Paul 7
Borlin, Jean 63
Borodin, Alexander 180
Bournonville, August 7, 198
Bowden, Jill Anne 178
Bowley, Al 167
Brae, June 96
Bradley, Buddy 37, 63-65, 95, 159, 160, 167
Bradley, Lionel 29, 97
Brett, Guy 155
Britten, Benjamin 22, 23, 30, 77, 99, 100, 101, 103, 107, 118, 119
British ballet 77
Brunelleschi, Elsa 190
Buckland, Theresa 39
Buckle, Richard 29, 119
Burgin, Victor 15
Butsova, Hilda 40

Cat and the Fiddle, The 159
Cavallazi, Malvina 39
Cavell, Stanley 10, 11, 15,
Cecchetti, Enrico 5, 13, 39, 43, 45, 47, 49, 50, 53, 54, 55, 56, 61, 70, 96, 107, 132, 141, 167, 196
Cecchetti Society 47, 51
Cecil Sharp House 56
Chaconne 17
Challis, Chris 8,
Chanel, Coco 128
Chappell, William 151
Charisse, Cyd 161
Chester, J. W. 79
Chopin, Frederick 22, 174, 192, 199
choreographic style 12, 14, 22,
Choreutic strand 18
Chroma 158
Clarke, Mary 97, 98, 136, 141, 184
Claudel, Paul 101
classicism 16
Cloustine, Ivan 43

Cochran, C.B. 63, 79, 160
Cocteau, Jean 176
Collins, Keith 31
Colonel de Basil's Ballets Russes 156
Concerto 197
Coppée, François 112
Coppélia 134, 141
Cormani, Lucia 44
Corot, Jean-Baptiste 79
Coton, A. V. 127, 160, 188
Coward, Noël 192
Craske, Margaret 47, 48, 50, 95
Craxton, John 22, 30, 31, 174, 177, 178, 179, 181, 190
Crisp, Clement 98
Croce, Arlene 29, 154, 199
Crompton, Robert 40
Cygne, Le 66

Dalcroze see Jaques-Dalcroze
dance analysis 9,
Dance Journal, The 47
dancers' style 14, 41
Dancing Times 29, 41, 44, 47, 48
Danse d'école 1, 2, 4, 5, 8, 16, 19, 20, 21, 24, 29, 38, 39, 42, 43, 56, 60, 70, 88, 91, 99, 120, 126, 127, 130, 131, 132, 143, 180, 181, 188, 217
Davies, Siobhan 12,
decipherability 14, 15, 16
Delahaye, Ernest 101, 110
Delibes, Léo 128
Delysia, Alice 160
Denby, Edwin 29, 106, 107, 154
Derman, Vergie 156, 161, 162
Diaghilev, Serge 25, 40, 43, 69, 77, 139, 155, 174, 179
Dickinson, Peter 30, 79
Dior, Christian 128
Dixon Gottschild, Brenda 167
Dodds, Sherril 28
Dolin, Anton 40, 44
Donat, Robert 194
Don Giovanni 193, 199

Doone, Rupert 102
Dowell, Anthony 19, 26, 131, 156,
    162, 178, 194, 195, 196, 206,
    211
Duncan, Isadora 15, 18, 37, 52, 54,
    64, 69-70, 164, 210
Duncan, Raymond 52
Dydo, Ulla 23, 78, 83, 93

Eco, Umberto 9,
Edwards, Leslie 40
Edwards, Winifred 196 (see too
    Fredova)
Effort/ Shape 18, 19
Egorova, Lubov 150
Elgar, Edward 79
Elvin, Violetta 128, 131, 144-146,
    147, 148, 154
Emmanuel, Maurice 175
enchaînement 21, 47, 48, 56
English School 39, 56, 57, 91
Espinosa, Edouard 42, 43, 45, 55, 56,
    95
Etude 62
Evergreen 63, 64, 160
Everybody's Autobiography 31

Fairy Doll, The 134
fancy dancing 39, 40
Farrell, Suzanne 153
Fashion Show 156
Fateyev, Yuri 7,
Field, Lila, Academy 42, 54
Fifield, Elaine 30, 128, 131, 132-
    136, 154, 198
Fokine, Michel 18, 51, 68, 69, 139,
    174, 175, 176, 179, 180, 190
Fonteyn, Margot 26, 30, 51, 64, 68,
    86, 128, 129, 130, 131, 132,
    141, 148-153, 154, 178, 187,
    188, 218
Foster, Susan 10
Franks, Arthur 146
'Fred Step' 21, 90, 181, 183, 184,
    198

Fredova, Vera (Winifred Edwards) 40

Garafola, Lynn 18
Gavotte Pavlova 67
Genée Adeline 38, 45, 136
Genée Alexander 39
Genné, Beth 57
Georgiadas, Nicholas 155
Gerdt, Elizaveta 144
Gide, André 22
Gilmer, Theodore 39
Girl with a Pearl Earring 210
Giselle 10, 68, 86, 141
Glazunov, Alexander 22, 128, 129
Glasstone, Richard 6
Gluck, Cristoph, Willibald, von 22
Gosling, Nigel 155
Gottlieb, Robert 7
Gore, Walter 64
Grace of Monaco, Princess 128
Graham, Martha, technique 15
Grant Alexander 23, 26, 157, 160,
    165, 166, 167
Grigoriev, Serge 69
Grey, Beryl 128, 131, 146-148, 154
Guest, Ivor 39,

Haskell, Arnold 52, 97, 98, 179
Hayden, Melissa 106
Hazlewood, Charles 102, 107
Helpmann, Robert 96
Hepworth Taylor, Mrs 40
Honor, Mary 96
Howard, Andrée 54
Hughes, Spike 64
Hunt, Yvonne 181
Hutcheon, Linda 27
Hutchinson-Guest, Ann 18,
Hutchinson, Leslie 167

Idzikowsky, Stanislav 48, 50, 95
Illuminations, Les (poems) 100, 101,
    102
Imperial Russian Ballet 50, 60, 139

Imperial Society for Dance Teachers (ISDT) 40, 47
Imperial Society for Teachers of Dancing (ISTD) 47, 49, 51
intentionality 11, 12, 13
Intentional Fallacy, The 11
Irving, Robert 128
Isherwood, Christopher 102
Italian Renaissance 17
Izambard, Georges 100

Jackson, Rowena 128, 131, 132, 136-138, 153, 154, 164, 198
Jarman, Derek 22, 24, 30, 31, 127, 155, 157, 158, 159, 160, 168
Jaques-Dalcroze, Émile 52, 53, 54, 56
Jenner, Ann 157
Jennings, Luke 91, 98
Jeux 67, 139
Jeux d'enfants 156
Joffrey Ballet 28
Johns, Eric 160
Jones, Bryony 85, 86
Jordan, Stephanie 20, 25, 92, 126, 140, 192, 199, 206, 212
Joyce, James 81
Jude, Robert 27

Kavanagh, Julie 2, 103, 136, 191
Karsavina, Tamara 15, 18, 37, 38, 69, 120, 176
Karina, Madame (Karen Lindahl) 44
Kellaway, Leon 132
Kelly, Brigitte 53
Kern, Jerome 159
Kirkland, Gelsey 105
Kirstein, Lincoln 104, 118
Kosloff, Theodore 43
Kostrovitskaya, Vera 6, 7
Kschessinska, Mathilde 96
Kyaksht, Giorgi 38

Laban, Rudolf 5, 18, 19, 20
Lake, Molly 49
Lambert, Constant 77, 84, 87, 102

Lanchbery, John 174, 192
Lane, Philip 79
Lawson, Joan 134
Le Clerq, Tanaquil 106, 107, 119
Legat, Nicholas 43, 55, 56
Lepri, Giovanni 17
Levasseur, André 22, 128, 146
Lifar, Serge 160
Linden, Tommy 150
Lieven, Peter 67
Lloyd, Maude 53
Longus 25, 173, 175, 176, 179

Macaulay, Alastair 2, 28, 126, 209
McBride, Pat 112
McFee, Graham 14, 15, 16
Mackrell, Judith 98
MacMillan, Kenneth 128, 155, 192
Magallanes, Nicholas 107, 119
Makarova, Natalia 65
Manchester, P.W. 96
Markova, Alicia 40, 44,
Massine, Léonide 42, 55, 63, 156
Matthews, Jessie 160
Mawer, Deborah 177, 179, 183
May, Pamela 48, 50, 56, 151, 195
Mead, Robert 157, 162
Meinert, Alexander 150
Metropolitan Ballet 139
Mille de, Agnes 52
Miro, Joan 156
Monahan, James 97, 98
Moore, Lilian 106
Mordkin, Mikhail 38, 43,
Moreton, Ursula 44, 132
Moroda, de, Derra 47, 56
Morris, Gay 106
Morrison, Simon 180
Murphy, Graham 179

Nerina, Nadia 128, 131, 132, 141-143, 145, 154, 164
Newman, Claude 196
Newson, Lloyd 14
New York City Ballet 23, 77, 99, 105

New York Times 117
Nicholas, Larraine 27
Nijinska, Bronislava 15, 18, 22, 37, 55, 59-63, 64, 70, 87, 88, 92, 94, 95, 107, 128, 139, 165, 167, 188, 190, 210, 217
Nijinska, Irena 107
Nijinsky, Vaslav 53, 67, 139
Nikitina, Alice 160
Noces, Les 22, 59, 60, 61, 77, 93, 94, 181, 188
Nugent, Ann 118
Nunn, Denise 196
Nureyev, Rudolf 31, 141, 142, 157
Nutcracker, The 50

Oman, Julia Trevelyan 22, 174, 192, 193
Orphée 176

Palmer, Christopher 102
Page, Ashley 118
Paris Biennale 155
Park, Merle 157, 162
Parker, H. T. 134, 136
Parkinson, Georgina 60
Parsons, Tony 161
Pavlova, Anna 14, 37, 38, 39, 41, 43, 64, 65-67, 68, 69, 70, 94, 120, 134, 135, 136, 203
Pears, Peter 102
Percival, John 23. 118, 145, 146, 165
performance style 12,
Petipa, Marius 24, 26, 37, 50,59, 60, 62, 63, 120, 126, 129, 130, 153, 218
Phillips, Ailne 132
Picasso, Pablo 78
Piper, John 155, 178
Plisetskaya, Maya 66, 144
Polunin, Elizabeth and Vladimir 56, 155
Porter, Marguerite 30, 197
Porter, Peter 102

postmodernism 14
Poussin, Nicolas 71, 175
Preobrajenska, Olga 55, 132, 139, 150
Preston-Dunlop, Valerie 5, 18, 19
Prowse, Philip 155
Pruzina, Anna 50, 95
Purcell, Henry 22, 77

Rake's Progress, The 57
Rambert, Marie 13, 42, 51, 52, 54, 58, 61, 102, 128, 141, 196
Rambert school 49
Rattigan, Terence 192
Ravel, Maurice 22, 25, 173, 174, 175, 176, 179, 180, 190
Redgrave, Michael 194, 206
Richardson, Philip John Sampey (PJS) 29, 38, 40, 42, 43, 44, 45, 46, 51, 98, 118, 136, 146
Rimbaud, Arthur 22, 30, 31, 77, 99, 100, 101, 103, 110, 112, 115, 118, 119, 195
Rimsky-Korsakov, Nikolai 180
Ripman, Olive 39, 40
Robinson, Marc 81
Rogers, Ginger 162
Roland-Manuel, Alexis 176
Romanova, Maria 150
Rosa, Madame, 54
Roslavleva, Natalia, 7
Rowell, Bonnie, 10, 11, 15, 16,
Royal Academy of Dancing (RAD), 43, 51, 132, 136, 196
Royal Ballet, 6, 23, 24, 27, 28, 59, 127, 139, 141, 150, 178, 194, 211, 218
Royal Ballet School, 196, 218
Rubinstein, Ida, 18, 22, 59, 102
Ruses d'Amour, 129, 152

Sacre du printemps, Le, 53
Sadler's Wells Ballet, 24, 54, 105, 120, 127, 128, 131, 139, 144, 153

Sadler's Wells Theatre Ballet, 132, 139, 141
Sadler's Wells School, 44, 49, 50, 55, 56, 132, 136, 146, 150, 196
Satie, Erik, 79
Scènes de ballet (Glazunov), 129, 135
Schama, Simon, 175, 177, 179, 210
Schollar, Ludmilla, 139
School for Choregraphic Art, 55
Scully, Frances, School 132
Seasons, The 128
Second World War 79, 84, 102
Semyonova, Marina 144
Sergeyev, Nicholas 50, 95
Seymour, Lynn 26, 30, 69, 195, 196, 199, 203, 211
Shaw, Brian 136
Shiraiev, Alexander 43
Sibley, Antoinette 19, 136, 157
Sibthorpe, H.S 95
Sirridge, Mary 14, 16
Sitwell, Sacheverell 77
Sklar, Deirdre 18
Sleep, Wayne 197
Sleeping Beauty, The 10, 24, 50, 62, 63, 79, 87, 116, 129, 130, 136, 138, 146, 152, 196
Snow, Peter 155
Sokolova, Lydia (Hilda Munnings) 41, 43
Somes, Michael 21, 26, 184, 185
Sonnabend, Yolanda 155
Sorley Walker, Kathrine 55, 96, 191
Stacey, Edna 39
Starkie, Edith 31, 99, 100, 101, 102, 110, 112
Steadman, Alison, Academy 42, 43
Stein, Gertrude 22, 23, 30, 31, 77, 78, 79, 81, 83, 84, 85, 86, 87, 90, 93, 94, 97, 98, 99, 115, 119
steps (non stylistic): *adage*, 48, *arabesque temps levé*, 61, *balancé*, 187, *ballonné*, 21, 204, *ballon*, 48, 68, *bourrée*, 17, *brisé vole*, 113, *changement*, 206, *contretemps, demi*,

94, 137, *dégagé*, 199, 201, *développé à la seconde*, 21, *elancé*, 146, *fouetté jump*, 143, *fouettés*, 136, 166, *grande allegro*, 47, *grand battement*, 145, *grand jeté en tournant*, 65, *grand pas de basque sauté*, 198, *jeté en avant*, 94 *jeté en tournant*, 56, *petit batterie*, 56, 133, *petit jeté en tournant*, 143, *piqué*, 204, 205, *plié*, 58, 65, 154, *posé turn*, 148, *relevé envellopé*, 140, *renversé* 6, *rond de jambe en l'air, grand* 110, *saut de chat* 142, *sissonne en tournant*, 56, *temps de poisson*, 19, *temps levé*, 144, *tour en l'air*, 108, 115
Steps of the Ballet 134
Stravinsky, Igor 22, 53, 79, 162
Stuart, Charles 22
style 4, 5, 6, 7, 8, 9,10, 13, 14
Sutherland, Graham 155, 178
Svetlanoff, Nicholas, 196
Swan Lake 50, 141, 146
Sylphide, La 193
Sylphides, Les 50, 51, 68

Tallchief, Maria 62
Tchaikovsky, Pyotr Ilyich 79
Tchernicheva, Liubov 69
terre à terre 47, 48, 56, 90
Terry, Walter 29
They Must. Be Wedded. To Their Wife 23, 81, 84, 97
Thomas, Martyn 192
Thornley, George 25
Toklas, Alice B, 78, 84, 94, 119
Train Bleu, Le 128
training 4,5,7,8, 11, 16, 17, 31, 37, 38, 41, 47, 51, 56
Tudor, Antony 54
Turgenev, Ivan 30, 173, 191, 192, 195, 210
Turner, Harold 196

Ulanova, Galina 65

Vaganova, Agrippina 4, 6, 7, 144, 150
Valis Hill, Constance 63
Valois, Ninette de 38, 39, 40, 42, 43, 48, 49, 50, 51, 54, 56, 57, 58, 65, 88, 96, 132, 139, 151, 167, 196
Van Praagh, Peggy 132
Vaughan, David 2, 62, 64, 105, 112, 115, 126, 127, 144, 156, 159, 174, 188, 191, 193, 197, 206
Vaughan Williams, Ralph 79
Verlaine, Paul 31, 100, 102, 110, 112, 115, 117
Vic-Wells Ballet 50, 54, 77, 78, 95, 97
Vilzak, Anatole 139
Volkova, Vera 132, 139, 144, 150, 151
Vorhaus, John 94

Walczak, Barbara 106
Whatley, Sarah 12, 13, 16
Whistler, Rex 155
Williams, Emlyn 192, 194
Wills, Abigail 118
Wilson, Laura 49
Wollheim, Richard 14
Wood, Edmée 27
Wood, Michael 27
Woolf, Virginia 81
Wordsworth, Dorothy 192
Wordsworth, Mrs 39, 40, 54
Wordsworth, William 191, 192

Zanfretta, Francesca 44, 56
Zeffirelli, Franco 22
Zinkin, Hylda 131
Zoete, Beryl de 53